Branching Out,
Digging In

American Governance and Public Policy Series

Series Editors: Gerard W. Boychuk, Karen Mossberger, and Mark C. Rom

Branching Out, Digging In

Environmental Advocacy and Agenda Setting

SARAH PRALLE

Georgetown University Press / Washington, D.C.

As of January 1, 2007, 13-digit ISBN numbers will replace the current 10-digit system.
Paperback: 978-1-58901-123-6

Georgetown University Press, Washington, D.C.

Library of Congress Cataloging-in-Publication Data

Pralle, Sarah Beth.
    Branching out, digging in : environmental advocacy and agenda setting / Sarah
Pralle.
        p. cm. — (American governance and public policy series)
    Includes bibliographical references and index.
    ISBN 1-58901-123-6 (alk. paper)
    1. Forest policy—British Columbia—Clayoquot Sound Region. 2. Forest policy—
California, Northern. 3. Forest management—British Columbia—Clayoquot Sound
Region. 4. Forest management—California, Northern. 5. Environmental policy—
British Columbia—Clayoquot Sound Region. 6. Environmental policy—California,
Northern. I. Title. II. American governance and public policy.
    SD568.B7P73 2006
    333.7509711—dc22

                                                                      2006006684

This book is printed on acid-free paper meeting the requirements of the American
National Standard for Permanence in Paper for Printed Library Materials.

13   12   11   10   09   08   07   06   9   8   7   6   5   4   3   2
First printing

Printed in the United States of America

For Carole and Robert Pralle, with love and thanks

Contents

Illustrations

Tables

Figures

Acknowledgments

I owe a great deal of thanks to many people whose participation in this project and support during my research and writing made this book possible. My greatest debt is to Peter May at the University of Washington, whose encouragement, guidance, and intellectual advice was unequaled. He was a sounding board for my ideas, helped me clarify my thinking, and read early versions of the manuscript, always returning drafts in record time with helpful comments. I am deeply grateful for his unending support; this book would not exist without him.

Bryan Jones continues to be a source of intellectual inspiration and I thank him for his suggestions and interest in the project. Michael McCann and Karen Litfin also read and commented on an early version of the manuscript. Their thoughtfulness and lively intellectual exchanges during our meetings were most appreciated. Several friends and colleagues at the University of Washington and Princeton University, including Lisa Miller, Judy Aks, Lenny Feldman, Erica Cosgrove, Lisa Hilbink, and Ana Maria Bejarano, also read parts of the manuscript and provided sound advice (as well as some much-needed laughs).

I am especially thankful to the activists, government officials, and citizens who granted interviews for this book. Their willingness to talk with me about their work not only made this research possible but also made it pleasurable. I admire their passion and commitment. Warren Magnuson at the University of Victoria provided access to the Clayoquot Sound archives and Karena Shaw helped to guide me through the filing cabinets. I appreciate the financial support provided by the Canadian embassy for my research in Canada.

Thanks to Gail Grella at Georgetown University Press and series editors Gerard Boychuk, Karen Mossberger, and Mark Rom for their guidance and helpful advice, along with the constructive feedback from three anonymous reviewers.

Finally, I am grateful to have loving and supportive parents, Robert and Carole Pralle, to whom this book is dedicated. Jill Pralle and Daniel Gutierrez helped me to keep life—and this project—in perspective. Thank you for your friendship.

Acronyms

CASPO	California Spotted Owl (report and guidelines)
CORE	Commission on Resources and the Environment
EIS	environmental impact statement
FOCS	Friends of Clayoquot Sound
FPW	Friends of Plumas Wilderness
FSC	Forest Stewardship Council
INGO	international nongovernmental organization
NDP	New Democratic Party
NEPA	National Environmental Policy Act
NFMA	National Forest Management Act
NGO	nongovernmental organization
NRDC	Natural Resources Defense Council
QLG	Quincy Library Group
SNEP	Sierra Nevada Ecosystem Project
USFS	U.S. Forest Service
WCWC	Western Canada Wilderness Committee

Introduction

On July 1, 1993, environmental activists gathered outside Canadian embassies in England, Germany, Austria, Japan, and the United States holding placards and chanting slogans in an attempt to raise international awareness about Canada's destructive logging practices. These demonstrations composed the first "International Day of Protest" to save the rain forests of Clayoquot Sound, a remote area on the west coast of Vancouver Island, British Columbia. When the campaign to protect the sound was launched nearly fifteen years earlier, few people outside of Vancouver Island were aware of the extensive logging in the region, let alone concerned about it. But by the mid-1990s, Clayoquot Sound had risen from relative obscurity to become a global icon of the forest conservation movement. One environmental activist who witnessed firsthand the rapid expansion of conflict over Clayoquot Sound during the summers of 1993 and 1994 said it was a "little like being on a surfboard with a tsunami coming" (Foy 2000).

A parallel conflict over forest policy was unfolding quite differently in the woods of northern California during the same time period. Here, a group of community activists, dubbed the "Quincy Library Group" (QLG), was attempting to defuse a potentially volatile debate over logging in the Sierra Nevada mountains. In 1993, three activists representing competing interests in the forest debate attempted to end, or at least diminish, the "war in the woods" by developing a forest management plan that purportedly balanced environmental and economic goals. By 1997, Congress had passed a version of the QLG's plan with relatively little fanfare, despite the vigorous objections of a number of environmental organizations. As one opponent of the QLG plan lamented, the issue failed to attract much national attention because it was seen largely as a regional problem (Blumberg, 2001).

This book began as an attempt to explain the different trajectories taken by these two forestry conflicts. Why did citizens around the world mobilize on behalf of saving the roughly 624,000 acres of forest in Clayoquot Sound while very few took note of the 2.5 million acres at stake in northern California? Why did conflict and controversy surround the conflict over logging in Clayoquot Sound but remain relatively contained around the QLG's forest management plan? The puzzle is especially interesting given that the substantive issues at stake were quite similar. Both involved debates over logging and other forest management practices in publicly owned forests. During the 1980s and 1990s, the management practices of the U.S. Forest Service (USFS) and the B.C. Ministry of Forests came under increasing scrutiny from environmentalists, who challenged among other things the privileging of timber production over other uses of the forest and the methods of logging sanctioned by the agencies. In both British Columbia and northern California, environmentalists argued that the pace of logging and the practice of clear-cutting were unsustainable. One focal point for the activists was the viability of the northern and California spotted owls, along with other species who relied on old-growth forests for their survival.

The substantive issues in the two cases were similar enough to suggest that it was not the nature of the conflicts themselves that determined their divergent fates. Moreover, the outcomes in the two cases were not predictable given their starting points. In the late 1980s, the controversy over Clayoquot Sound appeared to be heading in the direction of earlier forest conflicts in British Columbia—one that would attract little public attention outside of the "usual suspects" and that would fail to address broader policy issues associated with the province's forestry practices (J. Wilson 1990). Forest advocacy groups in British Columbia had been mobilizing throughout the decade in various locales around the province. But their campaigns were typically aimed at saving a particular valley or watershed area; the conflicts rarely expanded beyond the regional level. The conflict over logging in northern California, meanwhile, looked as if it might be the second round in a national debate over U.S. forest policy. In the late 1980s and early 1990s, forest policy had exploded onto the national stage when environmental groups sued the USFS over their logging practices in the Pacific Northwest. With similar issues at stake in the Sierra Nevada mountain range, it seemed likely that national attention would now turn to the conflict in California, expanding the scope of the conflict beyond the surrounding region. Rather than follow these expected paths, however, the cases developed quite differently: The Clayoquot Sound case attracted global attention and led to significant provincewide forestry reform while the conflict in northern California remained relatively contained, failing to spark the kind of conflict and controversy found in the Pacific Northwest.

The apparent differences between the two cases, rather than helping to explain the divergent outcomes, added to the puzzle. First, the geographic area at stake in the QLG case was about four times as great as that in Clayoquot Sound, yet it attracted little attention compared to the Clayoquot conflict. Second, old-growth forests are less plentiful in northern California than in British Columbia. The amount of old growth in the Sierra Nevada mountains had dropped from around 67 percent in presettlement days to its current level of around 12 percent (Wildlands Resources Center 1996). Levels of old growth in British Columbia, on the other hand, are estimated to be between 47 and 83 percent (Hoberg 1997). In short, more land was at stake in northern California and old-growth forests are relatively rarer in this region. These factors suggest that the conflict in northern California might have attracted more attention and protest than the conflict in Clayoquot Sound, where the forest area in dispute was smaller and where old-growth forests are more plentiful.

The political context surrounding each case also suggested different paths of development. The forest advocacy movement in British Columbia, while increasingly active, was quite fragmented in the 1980s and early 1990s. As noted, environmental advocacy groups in the province tended to rally around a particular valley or watershed but rarely worked together to challenge forest policy more generally. Forest advocacy groups in the United States, on the other hand, had gained experience and momentum as a result of their victories in the Pacific Northwest. They also had access to the courts and could potentially enlist them as an ally in their struggle to change forest policy; in contrast, Canadian environmentalists had little hope of using the courts because the judiciary played only a minor role in forest policymaking at that time. In short, the political context in northern California seemed more favorable to environmentalists and therefore more vulnerable to conflict expansion.

Of course, institutional differences between the two countries extend beyond the judicial branch and must be considered when accounting for the different outcomes in the cases. Canada's parliamentary system fuses the legislative and executive branches of government, thereby centralizing power in the executive branch; the legislature, dominated by the party (or coalition) in power, does not play the kind of independent role found in the United States. VanNijnatten (1999, 270) concludes that the Canadian system "affords more limited access to nongovernmental actors, as third-party interest groups in Canada have found it difficult to influence these decision makers due to the strictures of cabinet dominance and party discipline at both levels of government." The U.S. system, in contrast, is typically seen as providing interest groups with more access and avenues to influence policy. Because power is divided between the executive and legislative branches, the legislature has considerable autonomy and often acts independently of executive wishes. Moreover, individual legislators are less beholden to party positions, allowing renegade lawmakers to introduce legislation for important constituencies. These features of the U.S. political system create a more adversarial system, one that interest groups can readily exploit.

The two countries also differ in the balance each has struck between federal and provincial or state power. In environmental policy in particular, the Canadian system is extremely decentralized. Provincial primacy has been the hallmark of Canadian environmental policy, although the federal government in recent years has staked a greater claim in this issue area and intergovernmental bargaining is common (Morton 1996). The practical result of decentralization is the relative lack of opportunities for environmental groups to solicit federal involvement in environmental policy when they encounter roadblocks at the provincial level. In the United States, the national government has more authority in environmental matters, due in part to a liberal reading of the commerce clause in the U.S. Constitution; Congress has been able to enact federal environmental legislation and preempt state and local action by claiming the matter affects interstate commerce. Environmental interest groups in the United States, then, have greater opportunity to play different levels of government off one another. If a group fails at the local or state level, for example, it can try to nationalize the issue by going to Congress.

These institutional differences help us understand the strategies of the various interest and advocacy groups in the conflicts. For Canadian environmental groups, "going international" might have been the best option in the face of barriers to reform at the provincial and national levels. In contrast, advocacy groups involved in the conflict in northern California may have enjoyed so many avenues and opportunities that there was no need to extend the conflict very far. This explanation is plausible, and I explore institutional differences between the two cases (and their influence on advocacy group strategies) in later chapters. Nevertheless, an institutional perspective cannot, on its own, explain the specific outcomes in the two cases. After all, none of the battles over forestry in British Columbia before the Clayoquot Sound conflict extended beyond the local or regional level (J. Wilson 1990); why did the conflict over Clayoquot Sound? In the United States, a myriad of domestic institutions, which are relatively open and active in environmental policymaking, may obviate the need for advocacy groups to "go global" with their campaigns. Nevertheless, interest groups regularly try to nationalize campaigns and otherwise raise the salience of an issue. Why did they fail in the conflict over logging in northern California?

If institutional differences cannot fully account for the divergent outcomes, what can? Another possible explanation is a resource-based one. Perhaps environmental groups in Clayoquot Sound were more powerful and resource-rich than their opponents, allowing them to place the issue of logging in Clayoquot Sound on the international agenda. In contrast, those who opposed the QLG plan might have lacked these attributes, thereby explaining their failure to attract more public attention, mobilization, or conflict to the issue. While resource differences are important factors to consider in any discussion of agenda setting and policy change, they could not account for the different outcomes in these cases. First, the more financially powerful players did not necessarily win. In the Clayoquot Sound case, the economic power of the timber industry far outweighed the combined resources of the various environmental groups—local, national, and international—that eventually got involved in the conflict. Despite these discrepancies, the environmental coalition successfully expanded the scope of the conflict and witnessed significant policy changes at the provincial level. Second, it was difficult to compare the resources of the players in any meaningful way, raising questions about the utility of resource-based theories of agenda and policy change. In the QLG case, proponents and opponents disagreed about who had access to more financial resources, raising the broader question of how to make such calculations. Do we examine the resources of opposing advocacy groups at just one point in a policy conflict, or tally them over its duration?[1] Are comparisons more meaningful at some stages in a policy conflict than others? How do we make these choices?

The inadequacy of an explanation based on the nature of the issues themselves, or the material resources of the competing advocacy groups, led me to the public policy literature on agenda setting. E. E. Schattschneider's (1960) early work in this area emphasized the strategic importance of expanding and containing the scope of conflict around policy issues. For those pursuing agenda and policy change, success often depends on enlarging the scope of conflict beyond the initial policy disputants. It is the audience, more often than not, that determines the outcome of any conflict: "The number of people involved in any conflict determines what happens; every change in the number of participants, every increase or reduction in the number of participants, affects the result" (Schattschneider 1960, 2). Because the audience is not neutral in its preferences, the involvement of new participants is likely to shift the balance of power among the original players. The groups who control this process of involvement, Schattschneider suggests, have the upper hand in politics. More recent scholarship on agenda setting examines strategies in greater detail to understand why some issues attract more attention and mobilization than others. The *nonmaterial* resources of advocacy groups and coalitions, primarily their ability to define and redefine issues, emerge as important factors in expanding the scope of conflict, getting issues onto the governmental agenda, and changing public policy (Cobb and Elder 1972; Kingdon 1995; Stone 1988; Baumgartner and Jones 1993; Rochefort and Cobb 1994).

The insights from the agenda-setting literature made sense of the two cases in ways that other frameworks could not. I argue that the strategies of advocacy groups in the areas of framing policy issues, forming alliances, and changing the institutional venues of decision making are the keys to understanding why the Clayoquot Sound conflict expanded to the global arena while the QLG case was confined to the local level. By "strategy," I mean the process of choosing and executing a plan of action to realize policy goals. Strategizing involves selecting targets for action, choosing specific tactics, and paying attention to timing (see Ganz 2000). Our understanding of how groups choose the strategies they do and what makes them successful is often understudied or not well understood by scholars of interest groups (see Lowery and Gray 2004).[2] What motivates groups to pursue certain strategies over others? When and why do they change strategies? How do competing advocacy groups shape one another's strategy? This book attempts to answer such questions and is principally a study of advocacy group strategies, especially in the agenda-setting stage of the policy process. It represents an effort to better understand strategic processes in the area of expanding and containing the scope of conflict around policy issues.

Another goal is to offer "lessons learned" from the case studies that can be applied in other contexts. One important theoretical lesson is that advocacy group strategies cannot be understood without paying attention to the dynamic quality of the policy process generally and the shifting strategies of advocacy groups in particular. The external environment for political action is constantly shifting, and this changing set of opportunities requires advocacy groups to be flexible and adaptable, especially with respect to the actions and reactions of other political actors. Current models of conflict expansion and containment do not always take account of how advocacy groups respond to their opponents' successes and failures as well as the changing political context in which a conflict is unfolding. To account for the dynamic nature of the policy process, I introduce a model of "conflict management." This model recognizes that ongoing political competition pushes advocacy groups to compete on the same rhetorical "turf," to lobby the same audiences, and to pursue (or fight) policy change in the same venues as their rivals. Under these circumstances, a premium is placed on innovation, adaptability, and creative thinking. Sometimes the result, however, is a significant amount of mirroring and matching of strategies by competing advocacy organizations, who are responding to the moves of their opponents.

The following chapters shed light on how advocacy groups negotiate and strategize in increasingly competitive and pluralistic political environments. On the one hand, the opportunities for the exploitation and expansion of policy conflict appear to be growing: Hypermobilized interest groups, sophisticated communications technologies, and the existence of multiple policy arenas increase the prospects for agenda and policy change. At the same time, policy change is often elusive: Advocacy groups take advantage of multiple policy arenas to stymie reform efforts, deep partisan divisions make consensus on policy direction difficult, and entrenched interests continue to occupy center stage in some policy arenas, effectively blocking new participants and perspectives. The system, in short, provides multiple opportunities as well as significant constraints to those seeking agenda and policy change. How these groups go about exploiting these opportunities and overcoming constraints is a critical part of the policy process. This book is an effort to advance our understanding of these processes.

Case Selection

The Clayoquot Sound and QLG cases are important episodes in the history of forest politics in Canada and the United States. The Clayoquot Sound controversy spawned the largest civil disobedience in Canada's history and led to the most significant changes in British Columbia's forest policy in decades. In the 1990s, forest policy in British Columbia shifted from a focus on old-growth liquidation and the maximization of timber production to a more sustainable, ecosystem-friendly approach to forestry. Among the more notable reforms, the provincial government in the 1990s passed the Forest Practices Code, which limited the size of clear-cuts and increased the stringency of regulations on provincial forestland. The government also pledged to protect 12 percent of the land base of British Columbia and initiated a review of timber supply with an eye toward achieving a more sustainable harvest rate (Cashore and others 2001). While it remains unclear whether the B.C. government will sustain this new policy regime, particularly with the election of more conservative administrations, the changes are nonetheless significant. As Hoberg (1996, 288) argues, policy inertia and the inclusion of environmental players in decision making, among other factors, suggest that substantial policy retrenchment is unlikely.

The QLG case, for its part, is sometimes seen as the "poster child" for a growing movement in natural resource management, referred to as "grassroots environmental management" or "collaborative conservation." This movement embraces the resolution of natural resource conflicts through the use of stakeholder collaboration and negotiation. For some, the QLG is a model of collaborative conservation to be emulated; for others, it serves as a warning about the potential problems in such an approach. As one study of the QLG reported, the group is "now possibly the most celebrated and discussed of all natural-resource-focused collaborative groups," and it "made a difference" ("The Quincy Library Group" 2001, 14). The actual policy outputs in the QLG case are somewhat uncertain, however. The QLG saw the enactment of their Community Stability Proposal in Congress, but implementation of the plan was subsequently stalled because of a regionwide forest planning project that was already under way. When the forest service unveiled the Sierra Nevada Forest Plan Amendment in early 2001, QLG members and their supporters denounced the plan because it conflicted with parts of the QLG legislation. Since then, the QLG found an ally in the forest service and the framework was revised to be more in line with the QLG's forest plan. Actual logging projects, however, are now mired in the courts; environmental groups are once again suing the forest service under the National Environmental Policy Act.

While the cases are important political events in their own right, this book is designed to advance our understanding of public policy processes. The cases were chosen because they presented an interesting research puzzle: How did similar initial case conditions lead to such radically different outcomes? While the contexts for the cases were not identical, they were similar enough to raise questions about why comparable policy conflicts developed in quite divergent ways. The analysis explores whether and to what extent existing literature on interest groups and agenda-setting processes can explain this puzzle while applying existing theory to new contexts. The Clayoquot Sound case, because it expanded internationally, helps us extend agenda-setting models beyond the domestic context. Many case studies of agenda setting have been limited to the domestic, particularly the U.S., context. But with the growth of transnational networks and international environmental regimes, the potential for conflicts to expand beyond domestic borders has increased dramatically (see Keck and Sikkink 1998). The QLG case, on the other hand, reveals how advocacy groups pursue strategies of conflict containment in a context notable for its pluralistic and previously expansive nature.

Studies of conflict containment often use examples of closed policy subsystems to illustrate how policy elites deny outsiders access to decision-making venues. But given the more fluid and open nature of many policy subsystems, such studies are less helpful for understanding how advocacy groups try to regain control over an issue that has broken out of its previous boundaries.

Another consideration in case selection was the opportunity to compare public policy processes in two countries. Recently, public policy scholars have called for more comparative studies of agenda setting.[3] Most of the agenda-setting literature has been developed in the context of U.S. politics, raising obvious questions about whether the models can be applied in other institutional settings and how agenda dynamics might differ in other countries. Clearly, different institutional contexts in the United States and Canada will affect the incentives, tactics, and resources of advocacy groups operating within them. Venue shopping, for example, is likely to be easier in federal systems with separated powers than in unitary, parliamentary systems. A comparative study looking at the agenda-setting dynamics around similar policy debates in different countries can help us understand how domestic institutional arrangements affect agenda-setting and policy-change processes.

Research Approach and Data Sources

Research into the strategies of advocacy groups necessarily requires talking to participants to reconstruct the choices and decisions they made. As Hacker (1997, 6) noted, "Studies of agenda setting need to examine the strategies of political actors who attempt to shape the agenda of government, and, in most cases, these strategies can only be fully understood by speaking with the actors themselves." This study relies on interviews with key actors to understand their perceptions of the opportunities and constraints facing them and to analyze why they made the strategic choices that they did. In the Clayoquot Sound case, I interviewed the core group of environmental activists involved in the campaign. For the QLG case, I interviewed key members of the QLG, forest service officials from the regional office in Quincy, California, and individuals from environmental organizations who opposed the QLG. I chose my interview subjects based on preliminary research I did on each case, using media accounts and secondary sources to identify the central players. At each interview, I also requested the names of other important people whom I should contact. Each interview lasted between a half hour and two hours; they were recorded for accuracy. I chose a semistructured interview method that allowed me to change my questions based on the particular role that each interviewee played in the campaign.[4] It also gave the respondents the liberty to move the conversation in a direction that was of interest to them.

While the interviews were invaluable in helping me understand the strategic choices of advocacy groups and other key policy actors, there are limitations to using interviews as the sole source of data for agenda-setting studies. The chief among these is that participants often create post hoc rationalizations for their actions; people may imply that their strategies were more consciously crafted than was the case, or they may ascribe to themselves more noble motives than perhaps they deserve. Hacker (1997, 7) also notes that participants might not be the best judges of what influences their strategic decisions. Less visible influences, such as gradual changes in ideas or broad institutional changes, are not likely to be foremost in the minds of activists and policymakers.

Given the limitations of interviews, I sought additional sources of data to understand and analyze the strategic landscape in the two cases. For the Clayoquot Sound case, I was fortunate to have access to the Clayoquot Sound archives at the University of Victoria.[5] The archives consist of thousands of pages of primary documents relating to the case, including internal memos, e-mail correspondence, newsletters, reports, and press releases from advocacy organizations, government agencies, and industry representatives.[6] I also retrieved materials from the archives of the Forest Alliance (an industry trade group) in their main office in Vancouver, British Columbia. These primary documents provided a firsthand, insider look at the strategic considerations of the various players, in "real time" rather than after the fact. I used media accounts of the Clayoquot conflict to reconstruct key events, to track attention to the issue, and to analyze what problem definitions and policy frames were "winning out" over others.

The archival materials for the QLG case were not as extensive as those for the Clayoquot Sound case, but they were ample enough to verify the claims made by the participants and to extend my analysis beyond what was suggested in the interviews. The QLG has posted several kinds of archival materials on their website, including: interviews with members of the QLG; minutes from QLG meetings; internal memos; organizational press releases; letters from the QLG, environmental groups, USFS officials, and members of Congress; government reports and scientific studies; QLG reports and studies; and assorted commentaries from both supporters and opponents.[7] Of particular importance in the case of the QLG were the congressional hearings testimony and floor debates on the QLG bill. These documents allowed me to assess how the issue was being framed and how policy officials were react-

ing to these frames. Secondary sources for each case were helpful in reconstructing events and interpreting the conflicts.

Plan of the Book

In the first chapter of the book, I lay out a theoretical foundation for the case
studies to follow. The main goal of the chapter is to disaggregate strategies of
expansion and containment based on whether the focus is on policy issues,
actors, or political institutions. This model is then applied to the cases in a
way that highlights the theoretical insights gained from the case studies. For
each case, strategies of issue definition, alliance formation, and venue shopping are examined. These discussions form separate chapters; at times the
same events are revisited but from a different theoretical point of view. In all
the chapters, I draw out the larger lessons about agenda setting that originate
from the case studies.

Part I of the book (chapters 2 through 5) is devoted to analyzing the expansion of conflict over the issue of logging and forest management in Clayoquot
Sound, British Columbia. In chapter 2, I sketch the history of forest policy in
British Columbia, describe some of the features of the forest policy subsystem,
and provide a brief outline of the conflict over Clayoquot Sound. Chapter 3
begins the theoretical analysis with a look at the politics of issue definition. I
find that environmentalists' success in expanding the issue of logging in Clayoquot Sound depended on linking the Clayoquot case to other important values, issues, and cleavages in society; on tailoring their arguments to particular
audiences; and on taking advantage of popular symbols, up-to-date scientific
research, and emerging lines of debate in the global arena.

Chapter 4 continues looking at the Clayoquot Sound case by focusing
on alliance formation and participation patterns. The movement to protect
Clayoquot Sound became a rallying point for a fragmented and diverse forest
protection movement in British Columbia and Canada. Local environmental
groups successfully built regional, national, and then international alliances
of environmental activists, whose numbers and publicity-provoking tactics
upset the traditional balance of power in the B.C. forest policy subsystem.
This chapter examines how these successful alliances were built and why the
timber industry and the provincial government were unable to stop the explo-
sion in participation. In chapter 5, I turn to the venue-shopping strategies of
environmental advocacy groups involved in the Clayoquot Sound conflict.
The chapter explores the incentives and motivations of these groups as they

increasingly sought institutional venues further from the site of conflict and explains how they were able to "win" in these arenas.

Part II of the book (chapters 6 through 9) examines the conflict over forest management in northern California. Chapter 6 provides an introduction to the case by summarizing the key historical developments in U.S. forest policy generally and in the Sierra Nevada region specifically. I also provide background information on the QLG in preparation for the case analysis. In chapter 7, the analysis begins by examining how members of the QLG relocalized the issue of logging on national forests after an era of nationalization in the forest policy arena. I argue that the success of the QLG coalition in containing the issue hinged on their ability to subsume controversial forest issues under the technical issue of forest fires and on their ability to focus attention on their widely respected decision-making process.

Chapter 8 looks at the participation management strategies of the QLG, specifically on their successful effort to shift the lines of cleavage among participants in the forest policy subsystem in northern California. The QLG displaced conflict by replacing the more traditional rivalry between environmentalists and the timber industry with a (somewhat imagined) conflict between grassroots groups and national environmentalists. This strategy disarmed potential opponents long enough that an effective countercampaign could not be successfully waged. In chapter 9, I look at how and why the QLG eschewed traditional policy venues and created a new policy arena at the local level. The QLG's identity was closely tied to its rejection of "adversarial" arenas such as the courts, but eventually the group solicited the support of Congress. The chapter explains why the QLG switched venues and how it was able to contain conflict even as the issue moved to national arenas.

Chapter 10 develops a model of "conflict management" that reflects some of the general lessons from the case studies. This model pays attention to what happens to advocacy group strategies in highly contested, drawn-out policy conflicts. I argue that under these conditions, opposing advocacy groups often directly compete over how to define a policy issue, they must struggle to win the sympathies of the public and allies, and they must do battle in the same venues as their opponents. This puts a premium on timing, targeting, and tactics that help groups gain an advantage over opponents. Similarly, advocacy groups must be flexible and innovative as the policy environment becomes more pluralistic, crowded with competing issue definitions, interest groups, and policy venues.

1

The Expansion and Containment
of Policy Conflict

When Congress started debating the Quincy Library Group Forest Recovery and Economic Stability Act in the spring of 1997, opposition to the legislation by members of the environmental community was palpable. Nevertheless, leaders in the fight against the QLG forest plan were frustrated: They had generally failed to attract the attention of the broader environmental movement, let alone a wider public. The media was taking scant notice of the issue, and the stories that did appear were largely sympathetic to the QLG and their forest management plan. National environmental organizations, for their part, were late to get involved in the conflict, allowing the QLG to set the terms of debate and recruit key allies to their cause. In short, the QLG coalition had restricted the scope of conflict around their policy proposal, managing the issue much more effectively than their opponents.[1]

In British Columbia, on the other hand, environmental organizations wielded the upper hand in the conflict over forest management in the early to mid-1990s and were well on their way to expanding participation in it. Media attention to British Columbia's forest practices was high and generally more favorable to the claims of environmentalists than the timber industry. Groups like Friends of Clayoquot Sound in alliance with Greenpeace International had successfully "internationalized" the conflict over logging in Clayoquot Sound, leaving the logging industry and the B.C. government scrambling to make their case to a global public. The forest advocacy community had, at least for a time, expanded the scope of the conflict, much to the dismay of their opponents.

Controlling the scope of conflict around an issue is a key strategy in politics, because the amount of attention, mobilization, and conflict surrounding a policy problem or proposal affects whether it gets on agendas and how it is resolved. A lack of change in agendas and policies is due in part to the ability of dominant policymakers and advocacy groups to restrict the scope of conflict around a policy issue. These actors may form a policy monopoly where they control both the image of a policy problem and access to the policy process (Baumgartner and Jones 1993). As long as conflict remains restricted in its scope, a small group of stakeholders can largely direct the policy process surrounding an issue. Dramatic policy change under these circumstances is rare unless initiated by a policy monopoly to further the interests of its stakeholders.[2]

Those seeking significant agenda and policy change often invite attention to and participation in a conflict in order to get movement on an issue that has languished in the backwaters of some decision room, has become stalemated by the "usual suspects," or is simply not deemed important enough to warrant governmental attention. E. E. Schattschneider (1960) claims that disadvantaged, "outsider" groups try to expand the scope of conflict surrounding an issue so as to upset the balance of power in a policy subsystem. These individuals or groups may appeal directly to government, attempting to transform a "private" conflict into a public one, or involve a wider public in the debate in order to gain the attention of government officials. As the public becomes aware of a problem and demands action, decision makers face pressure to either break up the policy monopoly or circumvent it. Agenda, if not policy change, is often the result of these pressures.

In short, the emergence of an issue on the public and governmental agenda, as well as its resolution, depends in part on the degree of conflict surrounding a policy problem or proposal.[3] Without conflict, problems will be ignored or addressed by a small group of experts or stakeholders; with conflict, problems are more likely to attract a broader range of participants, including segments of the general public. Put differently, policymaking around issues with and without "publics" will differ (May 1991).[4] For this reason, advocacy groups interested in maintaining or changing the policy status quo will attempt to either restrict or expand the scope of conflict around an issue. While this general point is well understood by policy scholars, additional work needs to be done to clarify the meaning of conflict expansion and containment and to increase our understanding of how these processes work (Kollman 1998). In this chapter, I disaggregate the concepts of expansion and containment and suggest ways that advocacy groups and policymakers succeed at such strategies.

Strategies of Conflict Expansion and Containment: Issues, Actors, and Institutions

What is being expanded or contained when advocacy groups and policymakers attempt to control the scope of conflict around an issue?[5] The policy literature offers several answers: The degree of expansion might refer to the salience of an issue, the intensity of the conflict, the number of participants involved, or how interest groups court the public and policymakers (Schattschneider 1960; Cobb and Elder 1972; Baumgartner 1989; Baumgartner and Jones 1993; Kollman 1998). These various understandings of conflict expansion and containment lead to confusion in the literature; it is not always clear what an author is referring to when she claims that a conflict has expanded.

To clarify what is being expanded and contained, I identify three main focal points around which strategies of expansion and containment revolve: issues, actors, and institutions. One important struggle is between groups who want to raise the importance, visibility, and "publicness" of a problem and those who want to decrease the political significance of an issue. This refers to the expansion and containment of policy *issues*. A second set of strategies is focused on policy *actors*; the key dynamic here revolves around expanding or containing participation in policy conflicts. Depending on their objectives, advocacy groups seek to either mobilize or demobilize various audiences to a conflict (Schattschneider 1960; Baumgartner 1989; Baumgartner and Jones 1993). The final set of strategies focuses on *institutions*, the rules of the game, and the venues in which policy conflicts take place. Advocacy groups seeking change try to advance a policy issue in a new venue or to change institutional rules, while status-quo groups attempt to preserve existing arrangements so as to prevent change (Baumgartner 1989; Baumgartner and Jones 1993; Sabatier and Jenkins-Smith 1993, 1999; C. Wilson 2000).[6] Each of these strategies is examined in detail in the following sections and summarized in table 1.1.

Issue Definition: Using Rhetoric and Symbols to Expand and Contain Conflicts

What makes some policy issues "big" and others "small"? Why are some issues discussed in fairly narrow terms, while others carry broad political implications? What determines the scope of an issue, or its political significance? Successful expansion of the scope of an issue is part strategy, part luck, and part art. Some issues seem predestined to be big—problems that affect large numbers of people, solutions that cost significant sums of public money, and policy changes that represent dramatic shifts from past practices (Baumgartner 1989).

TABLE I.I   Strategies of Conflict Expansion and Containment

Focal point of strategy	Individual components of strategy	Strategies of expansion	Strategies of containment
Issue definition	Framing	Frame problem in broadest terms possible.	Frame problem in narrow terms.
	Linking to other issues	Link problem to other important problems on the agenda.	Deny links to other problems; treat problem in isolation.
	Constructing boundaries	Expand boundaries of problem.	Limit boundaries of problem; categorize people out of issue.
	Problem ownership	Encourage broader ownership; dislodge dominant group claims of ownership.	Limit ownership of problem to original set of policy claimants.
Actors	Scope of participation	Expand number of participants.	Limit number of participants.
	Characterization contests	Label opponents as enemies.	Label opponents as subversive, extremists.
	Conflict or appearance of it	Encourage conflict and appearance of it.	Encourage consensus, cooperation, and appearance of it.
Institutions and venues	Jurisdictions	Expand jurisdictions of institutions and blur jurisdictional boundaries.	Maintain clear jurisdictional boundaries.
	Levels of authority	Move conflict up ladder of authority.	Prevent conflict from moving to higher levels of authority.
	Rules of the game	Relax rules governing access.	Support rules that restrict access.

President Clinton's effort to reform the U.S. health care system, for example, predictably attracted a great deal of public and media attention because it involved a rather large outlay of government funds and would potentially affect millions of Americans. Other issues are "hard" in that they are technically complex, require specialized knowledge, or are highly unfamiliar to the public (Pollack, Lilie, and Vittes 1993; Howlett and Ramesh 2002). These issues tend to attract less attention.

But even these fairly straightforward claims hide many counterexamples. The bailing out of the savings and loan industry in the United States required enormous public subsidies, and yet the issue was apparently too complex and technically defined for it to figure prominently on the public agenda. And nuclear power, a technically complex issue, generated widespread opposition in the United States (Pollack, Lilie, and Vittes 1993; Ladd, Hood, and Van Liere 1983; Gamson and Modigliani 1989). In Baumgartner's (1989) study of thirty educational policy debates in France, he found that the "objective" scope of the issue, measured in the above terms, had very little effect on whether the issue attracted widespread public attention or was decided by a small group of experts. Put simply, issues are malleable, and politically savvy actors are capable of containing a potentially big issue as well as expanding a seemingly small one. To do this, policy actors manipulate the symbols and rhetoric associated with a conflict. As Deborah Stone (1988, 25) remarks, "People fight *with* ideas as well as about them. The different sides in a conflict create different portrayals of the battle—who is affected, how they are affected, and what is at stake. Political fights are conducted with money, with rules, and with votes, to be sure, but they are conducted above all with words." Strategies of issue expansion and containment involve rhetorical battles over the ideas and causal reasoning associated with a policy, fought in the realm of public opinion and media attention. The weapons are words, symbols, and images.

The battles over issue definition emerge when opponents cannot deny the existence of a problem. Faced with overwhelming evidence or public outcry, opponents to policy change will downplay the severity of a problem, define it in highly technical terms, or otherwise limit the discussion of a problem so as to decrease participation and public attention to an issue (Baumgartner 1989; Cobb and Ross 1997; Kingdon 1995). They are likely to face competing efforts by proponents of policy change to expand the terms of debate. Issue expansion efforts are aimed at enlarging the significance of a problem, broadening its political relevance, and otherwise raising the stakes by suggesting that a problem affects a great many people or implicates important values and belief systems.

Issue expansion and containment strategies are part of the larger battle over problem definition (Rochefort and Cobb 1994; Kingdon 1995). Beyond trying to expand or contain the significance of issues, advocacy groups attempt to shape the framing of policy issues more generally. In other words, advocacy groups are not only trying to increase or decrease attention to an issue but are also interpreting events and constructing them in such a way that makes sense to potential participants and decision makers. These frames offer evaluations of current policy and prescriptions for what should be done. Therefore, it is in the interest of advocacy groups to get their framing of a problem accepted by policymakers and the general public so that their solutions seem logical and desirable.[7] For example, law enforcement officials frame the problem of police brutality (to the extent they admit to the problem at all) in individual terms—the policemen who brutalize suspects constitute a few "bad apples" in an otherwise law-abiding police force. This framing calls for little policy action beyond the possible reprimand or firing of individual cops. As long as an individualized frame is accepted, the lack of a broader policy addressing the problem of police brutality is justified (Lawrence 2000).

Of course, no single actor or set of actors has complete control over policy images and frames because they are partially shaped by exogenous factors, including history, individual experience, unanticipated focusing events, and the like. As noted by Rochefort and Cobb (1994, 7), the social construction of policy problems is an indeterminate process involving multiple players "who are constrained by shifts in the site of decision-making as well as accidents of history." Other actors and institutions, such as the media, are also framing issues, asserting causal stories, and making connections among problems (see Gamson and Modigliani 1989; Schon and Rein 1994). As Lawrence (2000) notes in the case of police brutality, occasionally a news story about police use of force—the Rodney King case being the most obvious example—spins out of official control. In such cases, even the most adept actors have trouble managing an issue. In short, issue definition processes are complex and ever changing: "Conflict is inherently spontaneous and confusing, but activists and organized interests attempt to direct its course by strategic maneuvers based on problem definitions" (Rochefort and Cobb 1994, 5).

Proponents of change are either aided or hampered in their efforts to expand the scope of an issue by the structure of opportunities afforded in the political system. Institutions, in other words, shape the prospects for issue expansion, attesting to the interrelated nature of issues and institutions. In closed systems where there is no independent media, no democratic electoral system, and very little access to alternative policy venues, successful issue expansion is unlikely because of the lack of opportunities and arenas for groups to reframe dominant issue images (Baumgartner 1989; Howlett and Ramesh 2002). Sometimes, the rhetoric and images associated with a conflict assume a life of their own as particular problem definitions get lodged in the minds of the public and policymakers alike (see Yee 1996). At other times, a group might redefine an issue in just one venue or for only a brief time following a focusing event.[8]

The basic structure of government and political institutions thus impose the most general constraints and opportunities on groups who wish to expand an issue. But another set of opportunities and constraints operates in the more immediate political environment of policy actors. These include such things as the timing of elections, levels of media coverage of a conflict, unanticipated focusing events, and the political standing of the ruling administration (Baumgartner 1989; Birkland 1997; Kingdon 1995). Whether these opportunities are realized depends in part on the resources of problem proponents, including their entrepreneurial skills, political experience, financial assets, relationships with allies, and their tactical resourcefulness. The following sections highlight three key tactics for expanding an issue—issue linkage, boundary construction, and problem ownership.

Creating Links to Other Issues. One way to contain a problem is to treat it in isolation, denying its connection to other matters of importance. Murray Edelman (1993, 236) suggests that "the treatment of closely connected issues as though they were autonomous" serves the interests of powerful actors. Policymakers may disassociate a policy from related issues or overarching governing ideologies to decontextualize undesirable policy outcomes or government actions. They can deny that the problem was predictable given the government's approach to resolving (or not resolving) policy conflicts. Moreover, policymakers can assume a piecemeal approach to addressing problems rather than consider broad political or economic restructuring based on a holistic understanding of an issue (Edelman 1993, 236). Treating policies in isolation restricts conflict by narrowing the discourse that is used in discussing problems and solutions, by limiting the perceived importance of an issue, and by discouraging involvement of actors who might not see their relationship to the issue in question.

Conversely, groups can expand conflicts by linking them to other public problems and important political debates (Riker 1986; see also Haas 1980). When the public and policymakers connect a previously isolated problem to a broader issue, its significance increases. For example, the gravity of floods and other extreme weather-related disasters grows when they are linked to the larger problem of climate change. The association of climate change— a human-caused problem—to floods suggests that floods are not merely accidents, or acts of God. If human activities are indirectly responsible for the extreme weather patterns, then the public significance of the problem increases simply because we can do something about it.[9] Problems or issues that are linked together raise the importance of each problem simultaneously. Using the same example, the public's perception that climate change is an important issue increases to the extent that it is linked to real, physical events on the ground. The floods, hurricanes, hot weather, and other alleged effects of climate change make the issue more visible and real to the public, thus increasing its scope and significance.

Political actors realize that linking their issue to others can be strategically useful. For one thing, the addition of new issues means new constituents, thus bolstering claims that the original problem affects large numbers of people. Policymakers and problem proponents may find that linking problems allows them to speak of a generalized threat or public crisis, providing a better justification for policy action. Donovan (2001) shows, for example, how lawmakers linked the problem of drugs to crime, thereby raising the salience of drug use to the level of a national crisis even though drug use was declining in terms of raw numbers. Linking issues might also facilitate strategic alliances among groups whose issues are connected to one another. Tarry (2001) provides an example from the U.S. aviation industry that was successful in linking its concerns about tort reform to the concerns of the pilot community. According to Tarry (2001, 584), the pilot's organization provided "significant organizational resources the industry lacked," thereby securing a victory for the aviation industry when the issue of tort reform came before Congress.

Issues also carry with them a set of symbols, metaphors, and images that can be used in the rhetorical battles between problem proponents and opponents. It is far easier to use preexisting symbols and images, ones that have already proved to be culturally resonant, than to fashion them anew. As Gamson (1992, 134) notes, "Issue frames gain plausibility and seem more natural to the extent that they resonate with enduring themes that transcend specific issue domains" (see also Gamson and Modigliani 1989). New issues can also inject new ideas into a debate by suggesting particular causal stories that assign blame, imply consequences, and suggest solutions. These causal stories are implicitly invoked when issues are connected to one another, allowing problem proponents to transfer existing judgments to a new problem with relatively little expenditure of scarce resources. For example, by linking drug use to crime, policymakers can more easily justify a law enforcement approach to drug offenders, advocating for jail time rather than for rehabilitative programs.

Finally, if problem proponents are able to connect their issue to deep cleavages or ideological debates in politics, then the stakes of the issue increase as the battle takes on added significance. The success of antinuclear activists, for example, hinged on their ability to link the issue of nuclear power to core economic values that divide the public (Pollack, Lilie, and Vittes 1993). Linking an issue to *controversial* or polarized debates is key. Indeed, advocacy groups who want to defuse an issue will likely link it to *noncontroversial* issues, thereby decreasing conflict overall and providing a basis for consensus. Given this, we can expect that battles will ensue over what issue linkages (if any) are the most appropriate and what are the nature of those linkages, as various players recognize strategic advantages and disadvantages in associating their issue with others.

Constructing Boundaries. Advocacy groups can manipulate policy images by redrawing the boundaries around policy issues and problems. Issue boundaries refer to the formal and informal lines that designate where a problem ends, how far it reaches, and who has jurisdiction over it. The boundaries around some issues appear to be objective—water travels, therefore water pollution transcends local and state boundaries. All nations share one atmosphere; therefore climate change is a global problem requiring international cooperation. The nature of an environmental problem, in other words, would seem to influence its categorization and the boundaries we draw around it. But issues are subject to manipulation and recategorization. Strategic actors can convincingly argue that a problem, once understood as a "local" issue, is really a national or global one. Less frequent but just as important are cases in which a problem that was once broadly understood is recategorized as a local or regional issue. The boundaries we draw around issues are just as much a construction of our collective understandings as they are "real" in the sense that they accurately represent the real range or reach of a problem.

The ability to categorize environmental problems is especially difficult. Such flexibility in problem definitions is due in part to the fact that many environmental issues can convincingly be constructed as local, regional, or global in their scope. Environmental problems result from activities that are occurring at both the local and global level, and their *effects* are often felt far from the place of origin. For example, local logging companies may harvest old-growth forests, but deforestation is also linked to global consumption of and trade in timber products. Another example hails from the contemporary watershed movement. Promoters of watershed-level management argue that political jurisdictions—such as counties, states, and even nations—are inappropriate for managing natural resources. They encourage new institutional structures that transfer power to stakeholders within watershed boundaries, arguing that watersheds embody more natural decision-making units for allocating and managing resources. But political scientists point out that there is no such thing as "natural" boundaries, that "defining boundaries is a supremely political act. Boundaries that define the reach of management activities determine who and what matters" (Blomquist and Schlager 2005, 105; see also Woolley and McGinnis 1999).

The process of categorizing policy problems—as local, regional, national, global, or the like—is important because these categories help to define who has a legitimate voice in a conflict, who does not, where alliances will be drawn, how solutions are formulated, and how institutions are structured. As Deborah Stone (1988, 25) notes, "Every idea about policy draws boundaries. It tells what or who is included or excluded in a category. These categories are more than intellectual—they define people in and out of conflict or place them on different sides." For example, in the 1980s and 1990s international environmental groups successfully constructed rain forest loss in Brazil as a global problem, first arguing that the Amazon functioned as the "lungs of the earth" and later claiming that the vast rain forest was a significant mitigator of climate change. Consequently, citizens in other countries became interested in the domestic policies of Brazil and urged international institutions to help preserve tropical rain forests. They justified international intervention by claiming that the Amazon was a "world heritage" that ought to be preserved for the global community. However, the government of Brazil (among others) contested this construction of the issue, citing concerns that the North was using this issue to reassert their control over the economies of Latin America (Hildyard 1993; Lohmann 1993; Shiva 1993). The globalization of Amazonia therefore redrew and hardened lines of conflict between the northern industrial countries and southern developing ones.

Kingdon (1995) agrees that categories shape how we view problems. He argues that government will put off as long as possible a change in categories; groups might lose policy privileges or benefits when an issue is recategorized. For example, if the transportation of the handicapped is defined as a civil rights issue, then government agencies must retrofit subways and buses to make them accessible. These changes cost a great deal more than simply treating the issue as one of mobility, in which case separate transportation could be arranged for the handicapped. But a civil rights frame suggests that separate is not equal, and thus handicapped-only transportation would not be an adequate solution to the problem. Based on Kingdon's insight, we can predict that those in favor of the policy status quo are likely to hold on to the old categories, while those seeking change will search for and advocate new categories for classifying policy problems.

Problem Ownership. The battles between groups who are working to expand and contain issues are part of the politics of "problem ownership," a concept that emphasizes the strategic importance of laying claim to a problem and typifying it in ways that benefit one's interests. Ownership of a problem denotes a measure of control over issue definition, which can happen when the defining group wields significant power or when there are few competing definitions (Gusfield 1981). Portz (1994), for example, argues that the Brown and Williamson Corporation "owned" the problems associated with their decision to close several U.S. factories. The company spokespeople convinced affected communities that plant managers were not responsible for the job losses: "Causation was impersonal, relatively simple, and to a degree, accidental" (Portz 1994, 34). Employees accepted that management was merely responding to market forces and therefore did not blame the company for the plant closings.

Problem ownership confers power on those who stand as the authoritative voice concerning the cause of a problem and solutions to it (Rochefort and Cobb 1994, 14). For example, when a national energy shortage is defined as a problem of oil supply rather than consumer demand, oil companies and government agencies in charge of energy supply and trade are empowered. They are given the authority to set prices, develop domestic reserves of oil, and relax environmental regulations. A different definition of the problem—one that stressed conservation—would empower a different set of actors and institutions, resulting in a different set of policy prescriptions. Issue expansion strategies attempt to dislodge dominant groups' claims of ownership, arguing for a broader understanding of the issue that encourages more people to claim a proprietary interest in the issue. Issue containment strategies, on the other hand, seek to limit ownership of the issue to the original set of policy claimants.

Actors: Expanding and Restricting Political Participation

A second way to understand strategies of conflict expansion and containment is to focus on the extent of participation in any particular policy arena. E. E. Schattschneider (1960) noted that most political conflicts involve relatively small groups of individuals or organizations who are actively engaged at the center of a debate. This core group typically consists of those individuals and groups who are directly affected by an issue as well as relevant government agencies and nongovernmental organizations. Outside of this, there exists a large audience that may be drawn into the debate at any moment. If members of the public involve themselves in the conflict they can tilt the balance of power in favor of one side or another, because the audience is not neutral in its preferences (Schattschneider 1960). Presumably, core actors are aware of the public's latent power and take measures to control the participation of outside groups.

Schattschneider suggests that opponents to change will try to limit the attention and participation of the public (see also Baumgartner and Jones 1993). In general, dominant groups prefer to keep the game restricted to the current set of players as long as the arrangement continues to provide them with favorable policies. Why risk expanding participation when one is winning, especially if the results of such an expansion are uncertain? On the other hand, groups and interests on the "losing" side have an incentive to mobilize allies and members of the public in order to change the balance of power between themselves and their opponents. Civil rights groups in the South, for example, appealed to northern white liberals in an effort to involve a national audience in the conflict and, in so doing, overwhelm and isolate southern segregationists (see McAdam 1982).

As the civil rights example illustrates, an important strategy for expanding participation in a conflict involves creating political alliances. Forming alliances—whether formal or informal in nature—may expand conflict by bringing in key constituents whose attention to and participation in the conflict nationalizes or even internationalizes it. But it is not just numbers that matter: Who gets involved is also important. In her study of why groups join alliances, Marie Hojnacki (1997, 83) finds that the presence of "pivotal" players in an alliance encourages others to join. A key strategy in expanding conflict, then, may be to recruit highly visible and powerful individuals and groups with the expectation that their presence will lure additional players.

As individuals and groups join a conflict, a bandwagon effect can take hold wherein momentum gathers and participation increases further. As Baumgartner and Leech (2001, 1206) point out, "Increased participation can be self-perpetuating . . . as advocates both in favor and opposed to the potential action see that the issue is 'moving.'" Importantly, a bandwagon effect may increase *overall* participation in a conflict rather than simply add more players to one side in a dispute. This is why expanding the scope of conflict can be risky: the outcomes are often uncertain. While an advocacy group or policy entrepreneur might see advantages to involving more players, such efforts can backfire by mobilizing previously latent *opponents*. Participation may increase, in other words, but stalemate result.

Advocacy groups and policy entrepreneurs can also try to control participation in a conflict by preventing or breaking alliances. It is possible to check the growth of a coalition by making overtures to potential joiners. A government official, for example, could persuade key groups to stay out of a fight that is of limited interest to them by promising action on another issue to which they are more committed. Such offers can prevent powerful alliances from forming and thus restrict the scope of conflict. If alliances cannot be prevented, they can sometimes be broken or reshuffled once they have formed. Schattschneider (1960) refers to these efforts as strategies of "conflict displacement." Conflict displacement involves shifting the lines of cleavage in a conflict such that existing alliances are rearranged: in common parlance, the "divide and conquer" strategy. The restructuring of alliances, while potentially very difficult, can be a powerful way to control participation in a conflict. When former friends become adversaries, the momentum behind a campaign can quickly dwindle or the advantage can shift to another set of players.

Two additional means of controlling the scope of participation involve attacking the character of one's opponents and publicly encouraging or minimizing a conflict.

Characterization Contests. A common strategy for deflecting serious attention to an issue is to attack the issue itself, by arguing that the problem is unimportant, does not affect a large number of people, or the like. But another means of limiting participation in a conflict involves directly attacking the group who is promoting the issue (Cobb and Elder 1972; Cobb and Ross 1997). Groups who are trying to contain an issue may attach negative labels to their opponents in hopes that the public will discount the claims of policy reformers and disengage from the dispute. However, naming and blaming contests may just as likely result in *more* attention to and participation in a policy conflict. Groups who want to expand conflict vilify enemies to align supporters with the goals of the movement, provide a specific target for action, and supply a compelling rationale for mobilization (e.g., "to defeat the enemy"). Characterization contests are a way, in other words, to raise alarm among potential supporters and the attentive public. Advocacy groups may use such strategies to galvanize members, increase members' commitment to a cause, and create greater group solidarity and cohesion (Vanderford 1989; Edelman 1988).

In some contexts, then, characterization contests will lead to conflict expansion, not containment, as other scholars have suggested. For example, extensive vilification in the pro-life and pro-choice movements has led to open hostility and violence, generating media attention and greater public mobilization around the conflict (Vanderford 1989). Conflicts may increase in intensity and expand in scope because policy opponents are characterized not only as an adversary, but also as the source of the policy problem. In such formulations, a problem is seen as stemming from purposive human action rather than being the result of an accident or the product of complex impersonal forces. These understandings can increase levels of political mobilization and conflict. People are more likely to mobilize when a problem is associated with the actions of specific individuals or groups: The "market" or "global capitalism" hardly provides the same type of clear, identifiable target that is often the prerequisite to political mobilization (see Iyengar 1991; Gamson 1992; Stone 1988).

Encouraging or Minimizing Conflict. Conflict attracts the attention and participation of an audience; as Schattschneider (1960, 1) quipped, "Nothing attracts a crowd as quickly as a fight." Groups who want to increase participation, then, will stress points of disagreement between themselves and their opponents. These groups might stage actions or simply pronounce their disagreements with opponents in order to generate conflict and attract supporters. The environmental group Greenpeace, for example, is well known for this strategy. They regularly hang banners and engage in other forms of public protest activities to advertise their grievances with both industry and government. It follows that if conflict attracts an audience, then groups who are trying to *limit* participation will deny or minimize any disagreements that arise among the original policy participants. Advocacy groups intent on containing participation will use the language of consensus and generally downplay any conflicts that arise so as to decrease the involvement of outside players.

In sum, the scope of political participation is a key factor in shaping the outcomes of policy conflicts. It matters a great deal how many people are involved and who is participating. The mix of individuals, organized groups, and segments of the general public who take an interest in, and actively contribute to, any particular policy debate guides the trajectory of a policy conflict. But it is not just who gets involved—we must also consider where a policy conflict is debated and decided. Strategies of conflict expansion and containment extend to the policy institutions where decisions are made.

Institutions: Expanding Jurisdictions, Changing Venues, Modifying Rules

A final way to understand strategies of expansion and containment is to focus on institutions and the institutional context in which a conflict unfolds.[10] There are three ways to think about institutions in relation to the scope of policy conflict. First, an institution's jurisdiction can expand or contract; second, the locus of decision making can move up or down the ladder of authority; and third, changing the rules that govern access to and participation within institutions can promote or inhibit involvement by a wide array of policy actors. The first two of these strategies involve "venue shopping" by advocacy groups. Venue shopping refers to the activities of advocacy groups who seek out a decision setting where they can air their grievances with current policy and present alternative policy proposals. Groups and policy entrepreneurs often shop for a new policy venue when they are prevented from participating in key decision-making arenas, or when a venue's rules are biased in favor of their opponent. If successful, a change in venue can lead to substantive policy change, due in part to the participation of new actors, the adoption of new rules, and the promotion of new policy images and understandings of issues.

Expanding Jurisdictions. Every decision unit in a political system has a set of issues that lies within its decision-making authority. This is referred to as a political institution's jurisdiction (Baumgartner, Jones, and MacLeod 2000). Jurisdictions often change over time as institutions adopt new issues for their agendas or appropriate elements of existing policies from competing political bodies. For example, the U.S. federal government has recently assumed greater control over education policy with passage of the 2002 "No Child Left Behind Act," which requires states to implement accountability measures that critics claim have derailed state reform efforts (Orfield 2004). Institutions might willingly relinquish control over a policy issue or give up components of it to rival institutional actors. For example, the USFS gave jurisdiction of the Grand Canyon National Monument (later reclassified as a national park) to the National Park Service in 1919, and then battled with the National Park Service over other areas in later years (see Rothman 1997). Pressures to expand the jurisdiction of any particular political institution can come from actors within the institution itself or from outsiders who perceive an advantage if jurisdictions were to change. These outside actors include both advocacy groups and other institutional players. An example from this latter category is provided by Joseph Smith (2005), who examines how Congress expanded judicial review in three amendments to the Clean Air Act, making the courts more appealing venues for challenging environmental policy. According to Smith (2005, 147), a Democratic Congress saw an opportunity to advance their political goals and respond to supporters by increasing the judicial review rights of public interest groups.

Strategies of expansion in the context of institutions involve asking an institution to expand its jurisdiction to a new issue or to aspects of an existing one. Advocacy groups on the losing side of policy are more likely to pursue these strategies. Pesticides policymaking provides a useful example of this type of institutional expansion. In the 1960s, antipesticides groups attempted to expand the judiciary's involvement in pesticides policy when they asked the courts to halt government-sponsored spraying programs for the gypsy moth. In filing their lawsuit, environmental organizations asked the courts to intervene in a policy issue previously left to other political institutions. Although the judiciary had been reluctant to overturn agency decisions in the past, environmental groups had little choice but to venue shop in the courts. The Department of Agriculture and key committees in Congress historically dominated pesticides policymaking, providing few avenues for environmentalists to voice their grievances about pesticides policy (Bosso 1987). More recently, public health activists have turned to the courts in the face of congressional deadlock over tobacco regulation, winning an impressive variety of restrictions on tobacco advertising and marketing (Kersh and Morone 2005).

Strategies of expansion may not involve such formal appeals nor result in authoritative decisions. Advocacy groups might ask an institution to symbolically take on a policy problem or advocate for a particular solution, even if that institution has little formal decision-making authority or is unwilling to use it. Nonauthoritative decisions by an institution—a pronouncement by a judge, politician, or scientist, for example—can confer cultural and symbolic resources on advocacy groups even if they do not redistribute power among groups in a material sense. The mere fact that an institution is taking on or highlighting a new problem, or even better, showing support for an advocacy group's particular position, lends legitimacy to a campaign.

Containing conflict in the context of institutional jurisdictions involves preventing or discouraging the movement of an issue or aspects of it to a new institution. Advocacy groups or individual policy entrepreneurs pursuing containment will try to restrict decision-making authority to venues that historically have held power in an issue area. These strategies will be pursued by actors who benefit under existing policy. Such actors can depend on having supporters in the legislative committees, government agencies, or other venues where decisions are currently made.[11] Alternative institutions might display less support; at the very least, dominant groups will be uncertain about how the new institution will deal with the issue. Other things equal, advocacy groups in this situation would prefer that authority reside in an institution that is at least partially sympathetic to their position.

Changing Venues: Moving Up and Down the Ladder of Authority. Policy arenas exist at the local, state, provincial, national, and international levels. A common strategy in politics involves changing the level where a policy is decided, a change that can have significant policy consequences. The history of federalism in the United States is distinguished by increasing centralization or nationalization of power. Many issues that were once left to the states were either completely or partially taken over by the federal government in the twentieth century. The result is a complex, "extremely intergovernmental" system in which "few functions [belong] exclusively to one level of government" (Bowman 2002, 4). This intergovernmental system allows advocacy groups to search for the level of government where they perceive the most advantages.

Conflict expansion strategies are associated with moving up the ladder of authority—from the local or state level to national institutions (Schatt-schneider 1960; Birkland 1997). Advocacy groups who encounter biases in local or state institutions may solicit the support of the federal government, expanding the conflict by involving a more powerful and authoritative player. The use of these strategies helps to explain the nationalization of many policies in the latter half of the twentieth century. In the 1950s and 1960s, for example, U.S. civil rights groups moved conflict into federal institutions and away from the states where they were at a decided disadvantage compared to their opponents. In the 1970s, the environmental movement followed suit, pushing for the nationalization of environmental policy, including clean air and water policy, endangered species policy, and pesticides policy, among others.

Containment strategies are designed to prevent the federal government from usurping state or local power, or to devolve authority from the national level to the state or local level. Despite a trend in the United States toward centralization and intergovernmental sharing of power, numerous efforts to devolve authority to lower levels of government have been made. In the 1990s devolution proponents in the United States included a wide array of national politicians (mainly Republicans), governors from both parties, and various advocacy groups. This movement culminated in the enactment of devolutionary public policies like the 1995 Unfunded Mandates Reform Act and the 1996 welfare reform legislation (Bowman 2002; Posner 1998). Today, many advocacy groups continue to pursue strategies of devolution even if they do not identify with a larger devolution movement, out of a belief that lower levels of government provide a more favorable decision-making environment than federal institutions.

Changing the Rules of the Game. In addition to changing venues, advocacy groups attempt to change the rules operating in policy institutions. Institutional rules, procedures, and norms create structures of bias that give some interests more institutional access than others. Strategies of expansion are designed to relax the rules governing access to particular venues. Environmental groups in the United States were successful in this respect when the U.S. Supreme Court relaxed the "standing" rule in the early 1970s. Prior to that time, the rule of judicial standing limited environmental groups' use of the courts by requiring them to prove specific and direct harm by the government action in question. In 1973, the Court broadened the definition of "injury" to include general and aesthetic harm suffered by the public at large.[12] This rule change allowed environmental groups to contest a host of agency actions (and inactions) that they considered harmful to the environment; environmental litigants later tried to challenge broad policies of the Bureau of Land Management, but with less success (McSpadden 2000).

Containment strategies can also involve changing institutional rules and norms but with the goal of restricting access to key decision-making institutions and processes. Widespread access runs the risk of expanding the scope of conflict by involving a broad set of players with different interests and viewpoints. Strategies of containment are designed to limit the set of players to those who share a common understanding of the nature of a policy problem and solutions to it. In addition, dominant groups will try to minimize the number of opportunities for outsiders to challenge their authority over policymaking. Examples of using rules or norms to restrict access are best illustrated in the U.S. Congress, where rules and norms dictate how much time is spent debating bills, whether amendments can be added to proposed legislation, and the like.

Interdependencies among Strategies

The above strategies are highly interdependent and work in concert with one another. For example, to increase participation in a policy conflict, groups must use broad and emotional rhetorical appeals that will draw in an audience. Advocacy groups might also redefine an issue when searching for an alternative venue in order to conform to the discourse and norms of the targeted institution. For example, if environmentalists pursue a judicial strategy, they may invoke the discourse of rights or otherwise reframe their arguments in ways that engage the legal system. This might lead to an expansion of the discourse (as when they employ rights talk) or a narrowing of the issue (when they are forced to limit their arguments to a narrow legal issue before the courts). It is important to note that advocacy groups cannot always control these processes because institutions work within a context of embedded traditions and rules that are not always easily manipulated. In addition, institutional actors have interests of their own and independently affect issue definitions as well as the expansion or containment of conflicts.

Strategies of participation and venue shopping are also interrelated. Advocacy groups search for arenas with sympathetic audiences and potential allies. Different arenas of conflict will typically have different combinations of advocates and opponents. As Baumgartner (1989, 218) notes: "Where there are different majorities in different sectors of society (as is often the case because of different intensities of preference), a minority with especially intense feelings can try to shift the debate to that area where it will be best received. Opponents attempt to stop the redirection. No single group of actors controls the process, and each side engages in a rhetorical battle over the terms of the debate and the proper arena for the controversy." At the same time, Baumgartner and Jones (1993) suggest that venue shopping is a way to affect policy *without* necessarily having to mobilize large numbers of people. In other words, advocacy groups may pursue institutional strategies like venue shopping because they do not have the resources to rally large segments of the public around their reform efforts. Shifting venues becomes an alternative route to policy reform.

This last point illustrates the analytic value of disaggregating strategies of expansion and containment. By identifying several different types of expansion and containment, we can more accurately describe how advocacy groups behave in the policy process. Advocacy groups do not necessarily pursue expansion or containment strategies across all three areas simultaneously but "mix and match" strategies depending on their policy goals and their relative success in each area. An environmental group, for example, might expand conflict by involving the federal government but, once successful, could attempt to restrict participation to a select (sympathetic) committee. Other advocacy groups will broaden their rhetoric but with the goal of *decreasing* involvement by the general public. Christopher Plein (1997) uses the example of health care reform to show that expansion of an issue can lead to public confusion and disengagement. Plein argues that opponents to President Clinton's 1993 Health Security Act raised public fears about the proposal by making broad appeals based on people's distrust of big government and preference for private solutions (see also Hacker 1997). The public, which had supported reform, gradually lost interest in the issue and public participation eventually declined.

The case studies in this book illustrate the utility of disaggregating strategies of expansion and containment. The first part of the book examines strategies of issue definition, alliance building, and venue shopping in the Clayoquot Sound case; the second part does the same for the QLG case. In each case, advocacy groups develop distinctive strategies around each dimension of the conflict.

The Expansion of Conflict
in British Columbia Forest Politics

2

Forest Policy in British Columbia and the Conflict over Clayoquot Sound

Forests are central to the ecology, economy, and politics of British Columbia. About two-thirds of the province is forested and is home to a rich diversity of plant and animal species. Forest products are one of the biggest exports in British Columbia, and the forest industry alone is a source of approximately ninety thousand jobs.[1] Beginning in the 1990s, forest management rose to the top of the provincial government's agenda while also attracting increasing international attention. For much of its history, however, forest policy in British Columbia was formulated inside a relatively autonomous subsystem and generated little public controversy overall. In the 1990s, the politics of forest policy broke out of the confines it had operated within in the past, and the province found itself under the watchful eye of an increasingly skeptical public at home and abroad. The conflict over Clayoquot Sound was in the eye of this storm of protest; for opponents, it symbolized everything that was wrong with forest management in the province and became a rallying point for changing forest practices throughout British Columbia.

The first part of this chapter examines the historical and institutional context of forest policymaking in British Columbia prior to the outbreak of conflict in Clayoquot Sound. The discussion focuses first on the origins and maintenance of the forest policy subsystem and then briefly examines the emergence of cracks in the subsystem and resulting changes in forest policy. This discussion sets the stage for understanding the Clayoquot Sound case, the dynamics of which are detailed in the next three chapters. A brief overview of the case at the end of the chapter provides an introduction to the conflict.

The B.C. Forest Policy Subsystem

The Canadian constitution gives primary authority over land and natural resource management to the provinces, such that the federal government has played little role in British Columbia's forest policy and politics.[2] The B.C. Ministry of Forests is the key manager and regulator of provincial lands, often working in close collaboration with timber companies who are granted long-term leases to forest resources. Because most of the land in the province is publicly owned, and about a quarter of the province is suitable for timber harvest, the Ministry of Forests historically has had a great deal of authority over what happens in the woods of British Columbia.

While the decentralization of authority over forest policy in Canada sets it apart from the United States, where authority resides at the national level, the early history of British Columbia's forest policy resembles that of its neighbor to the south. For much of the nineteenth and half of the twentieth century, B.C. forests were logged with little concern or attention to future timber supplies. As a result, a portion of the province's forestland was converted to farms in the nineteenth century (Bryner 1999, 313). In 1912, the province passed its first forestry law, the Forest Act, which established a forest service but did little to stop the widespread practice of logging old-growth forests and replacing them with faster growing second-growth forests. Beginning in the 1940s, however, people questioned the policy (or nonpolicy) of liquidation and conversion, fearing that timber supplies might run out if companies were allowed to "cut and run." In 1947, the provincial government intervened by amending the 1912 Forest Act. The new legislation delegated more responsibility for timber management to private companies but required timber companies to replant logged areas and regulated the rate of cut.

Despite the changes in forest policy, timber harvesting continued at a rapid rate. Hoberg and Morawski (1997, 392) note that the government's policy of sustained-yield forestry actually accelerated the rate of cut in old-growth forests: "The legitimacy of the [forest policy] regime was supported by the concept of sustained-yield forestry, which in British Columbia was used to justify the rapid conversion of old-growth forests to more routinely managed second-growth forests" (see also Howlett and Brownsey 1996). Kamieniecki (2000, 182) believes that professional foresters were "deliberately optimistic" about the sustainability of their policies, convincing "sympathetic policymakers and the public that it was possible to cut trees at a high, sustainable rate."

Kamieniecki's statement aside, it is doubtful whether foresters or anyone else connected to the timber industry had to justify their forestry practices to the public. From the 1950s until at least the mid-1980s, forest policies and practices were largely shielded from public scrutiny. The structure of decision making resembled a Canadian version of the "iron triangle" wherein forest policy was developed in a sheltered environment inhabited by the Ministry of Forests, the Environment and Land Use Committee, and the ten to twelve major forest companies that had tenure rights on about 60 percent of the provincial forests (J. Wilson 1990, 144). Unlike in the United States, the B.C. legislature is not represented in this iron triangle because it historically played little role in forest policymaking (J. Wilson 1990). Rather, the third "leg" of the triangle is occupied by the Environment and Land Use Committee, established in 1969 as a cabinet-level committee whose purpose is to settle disputes among natural resource agencies. This arrangement left even less room for public involvement because the most democratic institution—the legislature—existed on the periphery of the forest policy subsystem.

In many ways, the noninvolvement of the legislature in forest policymaking is unsurprising. Canada's parliamentary system fuses the executive and legislative branches through an electoral system that selects the prime minister and cabinet from the majority party in the legislature; therefore, "There is virtually no significant role played by the legislature independent of the cabinet" (Cashore and others 2001, 20). Similar dynamics operate at the provincial level. But this laissez-faire stance altered somewhat in 1978 when the Social Credit Party adopted legislation espousing a "multiple use" framework for forest management. The 1978 Ministry of Forests Act recognized other (nontimber) uses of the forest, such as commercial and recreational fishing, tourism, wildlife habitat, and the like. While the law recommended that the ministry take such uses into account when managing forest resources, the regulatory framework allowed the Ministry of Forests a great deal of discretion and autonomy in implementing the legislation (Hoberg and Morawski 1997). Not surprisingly, the ministry continued to favor resource extraction over other uses of the forest. Forest policy was largely decided during bargaining sessions between the companies and the Ministry of Forests even after passage of the multiple use legislation (Hoberg 1996). Policy debates, to the extent that there were any, centered on how the revenues from resource extraction should be divided up among the three key stakeholders—government, industry, and timber workers (J. Wilson 1998). At the heart of this stable policy subsystem was the forest tenure system, an arrangement that virtually guaranteed corporate dominance over forest policy.

The Forest Tenure System

Close to 95 percent of the land in British Columbia is publicly owned Crown land, but the centerpiece of B.C. forest management—the forest tenure system—transferred a considerable amount of management authority to the private timber companies themselves. Consequently, the role of the Ministry of Forests in forest management decisions was even more limited than the word "bargaining" implies. The Ministry of Forests delegated so much authority to private interests that even professional foresters (particularly field personnel) had very little influence over decisions relating to management, implementation, or compliance with forest plans. Writing in 1981, Christopher Leman stated, "A key constraint on the authority of field personnel in the Canadian natural resources agencies is that each province has, as a matter of policy, delegated major authority straight to private companies" (Leman 1981, 1). Ted Komoto, a professional forester in the 1970s, admitted that the "dialogue was between industry and the Ministry of Forests, and if industry could convince the Ministry of Forests that the planning was right, then that was the process that was used. We were convinced . . . that we knew what was best" (quoted in Bossin 2000). Such arrangements left little room for public input or criticism.

The forest tenure system in British Columbia is still in place—indeed, it is an institutional legacy that has been difficult for environmental groups to combat (see Cashore and others 2001, chapter 4). The system grants timber companies long-term renewable leases to timber on provincial forests. Tree farm licenses give companies control over particular forested areas for up to twenty-five years, with opportunities to renew their lease every ten years. Timber supply areas guarantee a certain amount of timber volume for fifteen years.[3] The tenure system was designed in part to maintain a continuous supply of timber and generate revenues for the province in the form of stumpage fees and rents. It was also intended to provide companies with incentives to harvest sustainably, given that the tenure agreements require companies to engage in long-term forest planning. In practice, the tenure system has been an important asset for timber companies, who rely on these guaranteed harvest rights to attract investors and secure loans from financial institutions (J. Wilson 1990, 143). With such high financial stakes involved, timber companies have a strong incentive to maintain the tenure system.

Environmental groups charge, among other things, that the tenure system has led to consolidation in the forest industry. When the tenure system was created, it imposed new costs on timber companies and these costs served as entry barriers to small firms (Howlett and Brownsey 1996, 22). Moreover, the long-term nature of the leases solidified the power of the firms who "got there first": By cutting the best (and most valuable) timber, these firms increased their profits and were in a good position to renew their leases and gain new management rights. According to critics, the large firms are "less sensitive to the needs of both environmental and community sustainability"

(Hoberg 1996, 273–74). Multinational firms have less incentive to harvest in a sustainable manner because they have few ties to local communities. Large timber companies also wield considerable material resources, making formidable opponents to those who challenge their practices.

Another problem with the tenure system was that it supported discretionary, ad hoc policymaking. As Hoberg (1996, 280) notes, "Rather than a comprehensive set of rules for the province, policies have been contained in regional guides, management plans specific to a Tree Farm License or Tree Supply Area, and particular cutting permits." Such disjointed policy made it difficult for environmental groups to challenge forest policies or practices because the rules varied from one area to the next; there were no general guidelines for evaluating (or litigating) forest plans. Moreover, the 1978 Forest Act did not provide citizens and environmental groups the opportunity to challenge individual forest plans at the time of tree farm license or timber supply area renewal. In fact, Jeremy Wilson (1990, 159) argues that "the state's commitments to tenure holders were, for all intents and purposes, in perpetuity: the government was under no obligation to re-examine land use options before granting a replacement license."[4]

Public Accountability

The tight policy subsystem inhabited by the Ministry of Forests and the timber industry meant that the public interest in the forests was rarely represented in forest policies or practices. The Ministry of the Environment, Land, and Parks (or Ministry of Environment) and the Federal Department of Fisheries and Oceans allegedly represented the interests of the general public in the preservation of recreational and aesthetic values. However, these agencies remained on the periphery of the forest subsystem, unable to effectively advocate for the environmental point of view. They typically failed to win any battles with the Ministry of Forests due to lack of sufficient resources and political support (J. Wilson 1990).

Like its counterpart in the United States, the B.C. forest subgovernment was subjected to increasing pressures from the environmental movement beginning in the late 1960s. Some relatively high-profile battles in the 1980s over South Moresby Island, the Stein Valley, the Carmanah, and the Valhalla wilderness (along with other areas) led the Social Credit Party under Premier Vander Zalm to set aside some areas as a concession to preservationists. Between 1975 and 1988, the amount of land under protected area status increased by 25 percent, in large part due to the preservation of South Moresby Island and the Valhalla wilderness (J. Wilson 1990, 163). But overall, the strategy of the

Ministry of Forests and their allies in industry was to offer symbolic policy gestures to environmentalists while continuing to dominate forest land-use policy. In fact, the rate of cut in the 1980s increased to about 500,000 acres per year (200,000 hectares) from a rate of 325,000 acres (130,000 hectares) in the 1970s (J. Wilson 1990, 162).

The Ministry of Forests' documents from the early 1980s suggest that they were aware of the need to improve public access to forest planning processes. In response to citizen complaints, the ministry recommended that "resource development of an area should not be allowed to proceed until the [citizen] group has made its recommendations" (British Columbia Ministry of Forests 1982, 2). However, ministry officials had no obligation to establish citizens groups, and the groups (if established) possessed no real decision-making power; they could only make recommendations. Environmentalists also complained that the government restricted public input to minor matters, rather than allow comment on the larger issue of preservation. Writing in 1984, B.C. environmentalist Ken Farquharson wrote: "It is my opinion that public participation only really works where the conflicts being considered can be resolved by minor adjustments to logging . . . and do not compromise the overall intent. Where a public group wishes to change a land use designation, such as to prohibit logging, *I see the public participation process as a trap designed to exhaust the participants* and to shield politicians and civil servants from discomforting confrontations" (quoted in J. Wilson 1990, 157; emphasis added).

The Ministry of Forests' own statements suggest that they were more interested in managing and controlling citizen participation than allowing citizens a significant voice in forest policy. One of the agency's key strategies was to keep conflicts local to ensure that "unnecessarily high profiles be avoided" (British Columbia Ministry of Forests 1982, 2). The ministry's interest in isolating conflicts is evident in the following statement: "In order to make the task of resolving local issues easier, the issues that are regional or provincial in scope *should be isolated* and discussed at the appropriate level. . . . *Removing unresolvable problems from local public involvement* issues will allow the local programs to function more efficiently and with less confrontation" (British Columbia Ministry of Forests 1982, 13; emphases added). The agency's goal was not to involve the public in the development and evaluation of forest management alternatives but to remove controversial issues from the only level where the public had input. Moreover, the ministry admitted that it often did not give citizen groups enough time to review tree farm license forest plans. This put citizen and environmental groups at a decided disadvantage because they were often left asking for reductions in the annual allowable cut in plans that had already been approved (British Columbia Ministry of Forests 1982, 22).

In short, up until the late 1980s, the Ministry of Forests was able to maintain its primary role in decision making while appearing to consult the public and loosen its grip on forest policymaking. Jeremy Wilson (1990) argues that the ministry and the timber industry actually *consolidated* their power in the 1970s and 1980s. During this period, the Ministry of Forests convinced the B.C. government to adopt a model of land-use planning that designated most of the Crown land as "forestland" and thus brought it under the control of the Ministry of Forests rather than other cabinet agencies. According to Wilson (1990, 163), the government rejected "alternative models of land use planning that would have given agencies with environmental protection mandates the resources needed to bargain on a 'between equals' basis with MoF [Ministry of Forests] officials." In addition, timber companies received direct benefits from the 1978 Forest Act in the form of compensation for land that was withdrawn for parks and wilderness areas. This financial arrangement had a chilling effect on the designation of new provincial parks.

This brief overview of the B.C. forest policy subsystem suggests that the historical institutional context favored a government-industry alliance oriented toward the rapid liquidation of old-growth forests and extensive harvesting of second-growth forests. The Ministry of Forests was granted considerable autonomy and discretion to carry out its timber harvesting programs, with little oversight or input by other agencies—indeed, the timber industry had far more access to land-use decision making than did other cabinet officials. The tenure system also supported the forest subgovernment in that it consolidated power into the hands of a few large timber firms and fragmented policymaking so that environmentalists had no clear target or standards to oppose. Finally, the public interest was largely shut out of decision-making processes or was consigned to citizens groups who had little actual authority.

Cracks in the Subsystem and the Conflict over Clayoquot Sound

The forest policy subsystem by the end of the 1980s was strong but increasingly vulnerable. Mobilization by environmentalists throughout the decade had raised questions about whether forest policy and practices were always in the best interests of the public. New ideas based on environmental values challenged the ministry's singular focus on resource extraction, leading to some government concessions in the form of wilderness set-asides. But rather than appease environmentalists, these concessions seemed to raise the expectations of forest advocacy groups, some of whom were calling for a comprehensive approach to wilderness preservation and forest management.

The New Democratic Party (NDP) capitalized on the increased salience of the forest issue and growing public support for a more balanced forest policy. The proindustry, neoliberal Social Credit Party had dominated electoral politics in British Columbia since 1980 but came under increasing criticism by the social democratic NDP during the 1991 election.[5] Among other things, the NDP attacked the government for failing to resolve the conflict over forest management. When the NDP assumed power in October 1991 they promised to bring about "peace in the woods" (Cashore and others 2001, 39). As it turned out, the NDP stood watch over the most explosive forest conflict in the history of the province: the conflict over logging and forest management practices along the west coast of Vancouver Island, in and around Clayoquot Sound. The conflict over Clayoquot Sound subsequently led to the most significant legislative changes to forest policy and practices in British Columbia's history.

Clayoquot Sound and the Origins of Conflict

Clayoquot Sound lies on the west coast of Vancouver Island in British Columbia, Canada. The ecology of the area is typical of the Pacific Northwest, with mountains, ocean, islands, beaches, and forests creating a varied and rich environment, home to marbled murrelets, bear, cougar, wolves, salmon, and large tracts of old-growth forest. Clayoquot Sound is home to eight of eleven large valleys on Vancouver Island that still have intact temperate rain forests; in fact, the roughly 624,000 acres of forest in Clayoquot Sound make it one of the largest remaining coastal temperate rain forests in the world.

Clayoquot's rich forest resources were attractive sources of timber, and plans were announced in the late 1970s to log Meares Island, a pristine island that provides the scenic backdrop for the small town of Tofino in the heart of Clayoquot Sound. Local environmentalists formed Friends of Clayoquot Sound (FOCS) in 1979 in response to timber company MacMillan Bloedel's logging proposal.[6] Due to the proximity of Meares Island to Tofino, the decision to log the island rallied the local community against the provincial government and MacMillan Bloedel. Because the clear-cuts would be visible from the town, local leaders including the mayor and city council supported environmentalists and native groups, fearing a negative influence on the tourism economy if the logging plans went ahead as planned.[7]

The earliest stage of the Clayoquot conflict resembled previous wilderness battles in British Columbia, ones in which environmentalists argued for the preservation of a particular valley or set of valleys, rather than challenge the province's forestry policies at large (J. Wilson 1990). The local antilogging coalition raised two concerns: the potential effect of logging on Tofino's views, and the possible contamination of the town's water supply.[8] The antilogging coalition wanted reassurances from MacMillan Bloedel that the logging would not be visible from downtown Tofino and would not adversely affect Tofino's drinking water. At this point in the campaign, the issues were narrow and localized, but they served to unite the somewhat fragile antilogging coalition, one that included radical environmentalists, First Nations, and local business and political leaders. The debate was also narrow because environmentalists had not yet connected the Meares Island issue to other logging in the sound.

MacMillan Bloedel responded by reassuring the community that very little logging would be visible from Tofino for twenty years and that current regulations were adequate to protect water resources. The company agreed, however, to investigate options for managing the logging on Meares; in 1982, MacMillan Bloedel entered into a two-year-long negotiation process with a coalition of antilogging interests, timber workers' unions, and local native populations. The Meares Island Planning Team, as it was called, presented three options to the Environment and Land Use Committee of the provincial government. However, before the committee had decided on a plan, MacMillan Bloedel pulled out of the negotiations. Environmentalists and Nuu-chah-nulth First Nations subsequently left the negotiating tables to jointly conduct blockades on Meares Island. Eventually, the Nuu-chah-nulth obtained a court injunction barring logging on the island.

While the Meares Island issue was being considered in the courts, environmentalists turned their attention to other areas of the sound that were slated for logging. Blockades and arrests at Sulpher Pass in 1988 and in Bulson Creek in 1991 intensified the conflict. Meanwhile, the provincial government was experimenting with consensus-based negotiation ("task forces") in an effort to find agreement among the various stakeholders. But consensus proved elusive, and environmental groups eventually abandoned the Clayoquot Sound task forces. The government also gave up, reverting to policymaking "the old fashioned way, at the highest level of government in a hard-fought, intense, and lengthy cabinet debate" (Hoberg 1996, 277). In April 1993 the provincial government under the leadership of Premier Michael Harcourt announced its own solution to Clayoquot Sound, a solution that failed to resolve the conflict.

The Clayoquot Sound Land Use Decision
and the Globalization of Conflict

The 1993 Clayoquot Sound Land Use Decision called for the preservation of about one-third of the sound and allowed logging in the remaining two-thirds. Environmentalists were outraged at the decision and soon the conflict exploded beyond the provincial level. In response to the government's decision, grassroots groups mobilized some of the largest nonviolent protests in North America, with more than twelve thousand protesters from Canada and around the world coming to the sound in the summer of 1993, eight hundred of whom were arrested for blocking logging roads. The protests focused regional and national attention on the destruction of Clayoquot Sound, putting industry and the provincial government under Premier Harcourt on the defensive.

By 1994, the issue of Clayoquot Sound had expanded to the global arena; international criticism was directed not only at the logging of Clayoquot Sound but also at British Columbia's forest management practices more generally. Environmental activists initiated a markets campaign aimed at pressuring international consumers to boycott B.C. wood products. They also generated a series of public protests in major European and American cities, and in cities as far away as Japan and Australia. In response, the Harcourt government launched a sophisticated public relations campaign to improve Canada's image abroad; Harcourt himself took upward of half a dozen trips to Europe and the United States to talk directly with foreign consumer companies, government officials, and the public.

In the mid-1990s, the B.C. government responded to the pressure by agreeing to new forestry regulations. In July 1995, it accepted more than four hundred recommendations from the Scientific Panel for Sustainable Forest Practices in Clayoquot Sound. The government had appointed the scientific panel two years earlier in response to the Clayoquot protests; the goal was "to make forest practices in Clayoquot not only the best in the province, but the best in the world," a nod to the increasingly globalized framing of the issue. Among the more notable provisions, the government agreed to reduce the size of cutblocks, the practical effect of which was to prohibit the practice of clear-cutting (Hoberg 1996). More importantly, perhaps, the panel embraced ecosystem-based planning in the forests; as FOCS explained it, this marked a dramatic shift from traditional planning methods which were aimed at providing a high volume of timber to local mills (Langer and others 1998). As shown in figure 2.1, the volume of timber cut in Clayoquot Sound in the 1990s decreased significantly from almost a million cubic meters in 1988, to

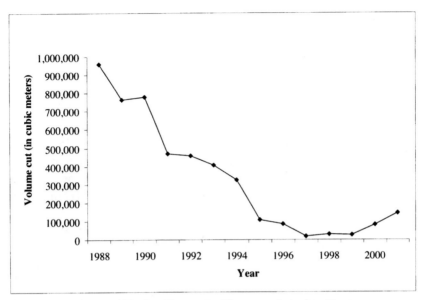

FIGURE 2.1   Annual Timber Harvest in Clayoquot Sound, 1988–2001

less than ninety thousand cubic meters in 1997, to about twenty-four thousand in 2000.

The B.C. government also passed a comprehensive forest management law that governed practices throughout the province. The 1994 Forest Practices Code contained the most stringent restrictions on logging enacted in British Columbia. In fact, the legislation was far stricter (at least on paper) than comparable legislation in other Canadian provinces, the United States, Europe, and Australia (Kamieniecki 2000).[9] Among other provisions, the legislation provided for independent auditing and monitoring of forest practices, increased public access to forest policy decision-making and implementation processes, and gave the government stronger enforcement tools. The code established a Forest Practices Board to represent the public interest in forest policy, to audit government and industry forest management practices, and to investigate complaints. In addition, it set up a Forest Appeals Commission to review policies under the new legislation. Finally, the law increased fines for noncompliance from two thousand to one million dollars a day and gave the government the authority to suspend the logging operations of companies who break the law (Kamieniecki 2000, 181).

The Forest Practices Code also required forest companies to engage in planning on a much larger scale than in the past—up to a hundred thousand hectares, the size of large watersheds. The plans, moreover, had to take into account biodiversity objectives and consider noncommercial values of the forest; in the words of the code itself, sustainable forestry must maintain "a balance between productive, spiritual, ecological, and recreational values of the forests to meet the economic and cultural needs of communities, including aboriginal peoples" (quoted in Kamieniecki 2000, 181). The plans detail how and where logging will occur and how riparian areas will be protected; they also include sivicultural plans, among other requirements. Importantly, the plans are subject to public review and comment, and they must be approved by the forest district manager (Bryner 1999, 316). These regulatory changes coincided with a "timber supply review" in which the government recalculated the annual allowable cut levels on public lands downward (Hoberg 1996; Cashore and others 2001).

The remarkable changes in forest policy in British Columbia during the 1990s is evidence of the weakening of the B.C. forest policy subsystem, one characterized by a tight relationship between the government and the timber industry along with an almost singular focus on timber production. The Clayoquot Sound conflict forced the issue of forest management high onto the agenda of the Harcourt administration, and public attention at home and abroad exposed the unsustainable policies of the past. Environmental groups, once far on the periphery of the forest policy subsystem, had gained considerable power.

The policy changes enacted in the 1990s did not end the conflict in Clayoquot Sound, but they did shift the focus of the debate somewhat toward implementation and enforcement issues. FOCS and other environmental groups in the province kept a close eye on the implementation of the new regulations, charging that the Ministry of Forests was purposefully neglectful in their enforcement. For example, in 1996 FOCS and Greenpeace blocked logging in the Bulson Valley after accusing the government of failing to abide by the Clayoquot scientific panel's recommendation that a full inventory of forest values be conducted before logging. Partly in response to these protests, First Nations called for a meeting with all stakeholders to try to find a peaceful solution to the Clayoquot conflict. Environmentalists subsequently suspended their protest activities (if only temporarily) and focused on bringing international recognition to Clayoquot Sound through its designation as a UN Biosphere Reserve. (UNESCO granted the designation to Clayoquot Sound in 2000.)

The scope of conflict became far less expansive as the 1990s drew to a close. In 1999, Greenpeace Canada, Greenpeace International, Natural Resources Defense Council (NRDC), Sierra Club of British Columbia, and Western

Canada Wilderness Committee (WCWC) signed a memorandum of under-standing with Iisaak Natural Resources, a joint forestry venture between First Nations and MacMillan Bloedel. The memorandum committed environ-mental groups to promote Iisaak's products and to engage in further coopera-tive efforts. Iisaak, for its part, agreed to respect the role of First Nations in forest management decisions, protect nontimber values of the forests, and work toward forest certification. Notably, the memorandum deemed the Clayoquot Valley "eehmiis" (meaning "very precious") and declared certain pristine areas off-limits to logging. While significant, environmental groups did not pursue government legislation to formally protect these pristine areas; according to one activist, the lack of formal protection is now "causing us a headache" (Wu 2006).

The activism of the 1990s profoundly changed forest politics in British Columbia. Hoberg (1996, 288) noted these changes in his analysis of B.C. for-est policy: "The transformation of B.C. forest policy achieved by the Harcourt NDP [New Democratic Party] marks a profound change in B.C. politics and policy. While the forest industry maintains some profound advantages in terms of political resources, the environmental movements and its allies in the NDP have succeeded in bringing greater balance between values of environ-mental sustainability and the pro-development values that have historically dominated policy in this area." The most recent evidence of this power shift came in February 2006 when the B.C. government announced the estab-lishment of more than one hundred new protected areas (encompassing 3.3 million acres) on the central and northern coast of British Columbia (the so-called Great Bear Rainforest). This agreement, representing one of the largest single wilderness set-asides in North America, has increased the amount of B.C. protected land to 13.8 percent of the province.

The historic announcement signified an enormous victory for envi-ronmentalists, many of whom had turned their attention to the Great Bear Rainforest after the conflict in Clayoquot Sound died down. Environmental groups such as Greenpeace, ForestEthics, Rainforest Action Network, and the Sierra Club of British Columbia continued a Clayoquot-style markets strategy to pressure logging companies elsewhere in the province. The compa-nies, facing boycotts by more than eighty companies—including Ikea, Home Depot, and Staples—eventually negotiated an agreement with environmen-talists (ForestEthics 2006). The agreement between the environmental coali-tion and the logging industry was then rolled into the government's land-use plans for the region and codified in legislation. According to Ken Wu of WCWC, "The Great Bear Rainforest campaign in large part was an extension of the Clayoquot Sound campaign and its reverberations in the European markets (and less so because of the political pressure within B.C. from the electorate)" (2006). In short, the conflict over Clayoquot Sound continued to affect B.C. forest politics long after it disappeared from the front pages of the newspapers.

The next three chapters detail the strategies used by environmental activists in the Clayoquot Sound conflict, as well as the counterstrategies employed by their opponents, in order to understand the transformation in the B.C. forest policy subsystem.

3

Constructing the Global

Issue Expansion in Clayoquot Sound, British Columbia

The expansion of conflict over old-growth logging in Clayoquot Sound, British Columbia, is a dramatic example of how issues can transform from local or regional problems into global ones. For many years, local antilogging groups on Vancouver Island battled the forestry industry in relative obscurity. In the 1980s, environmentalists faced off against prologging forces in a succession of isolated valleys in British Columbia—the Caramanah, the Walbran, the Bulson, the Stein. The conflict in each case was intense, yet relatively contained to those with a direct interest in forestry issues. Moreover, the scope of the debate was limited. As Jeremy Wilson (1990, 155) argues, the wilderness debate in British Columbia during this time was "'about' a limited list of wilderness area candidates nominated by environmentalists rather than about all the province's remaining wilderness." However, by the mid-1990s, things had changed dramatically. The forest practices of British Columbia and Canada at large were being debated in the halls of the United Nations, the government of British Columbia had embarked on a provincewide forest management plan, and Clayoquot Sound, as one newspaper article put it, was "en route to becoming the global icon of the conservation movement" (Lee 1993b, A1). The debate was far more expansive, the conflict widespread.

How did the issue of Clayoquot Sound achieve global notoriety and attract widespread participation? How was the environmental community able to expand the issue against competing pressures by industry and the government to restrict it? What accounts for their success? This chapter uses the framework developed in chapter 1 to analyze strategies of issue expansion and containment in Clayoquot Sound. The chapter first details the rhetorical strategies of environmental groups as they attempted to broaden the importance, significance, and scope of the issue. The second part of the discussion focuses on the strategies of opponents, who tried to contain the issue in the face of increasing international scrutiny of British Columbia's forest practices.

As the discussion will illustrate, advocacy groups who want to expand an issue must do two things simultaneously. First, they must convince the public, or segments of it, that a problem exists and that it warrants their attention. This is not always an easy task; as scholars of agenda setting note, competition for space on the public agenda can be quite fierce (Downs 1972; Hilgartner and Bosk 1988; Kingdon 1995). Even if the public recognizes a problem, citizens might not see the relevance of an issue to their lives. The problem may be viewed as relatively isolated or esoteric: It is not a "crisis" that commands immediate action (see Cobb and Elder 1972; Rochefort and Cobb 1994). In addition to drawing attention to a problem, advocacy groups must persuade the public to view the issue in a particular way. More specifically, advocacy groups try to direct the public's attention toward those aspects of the issue that favor their framing of the problem and their preferred solution. Simply put, a successful issue expansion campaign both attracts a wider public and elicits sympathy from it.

Nor surprisingly, strategies of issue expansion or containment sometimes fail (Baumgartner 1989; Howlett and Ramesh 2002). But what factors influence success or failure in the context of a particular policy debate? I argue that the successful expansion of the Clayoquot Sound issue both nationally and internationally stemmed from three main factors. First, environmentalists effectively linked the Clayoquot issue to other important issues, values, and cleavages in society. These linkages encouraged a broader public to view the conflict and its resolution as bearing on larger ecological processes and political debates. The stakes in Clayoquot Sound were raised, in other words, by linking the problem of logging in Clayoquot Sound to global processes and by connecting potential solutions to underlying democratic values. The environmentalists' second secret of success was their ability and willingness to tailor their message to specific segments of the public rather than use one general frame for talking about the problem. This increased the effectiveness of their campaign when they went abroad to court foreign audiences. Finally, timing was important—environmentalists took advantage of popular symbols, up-to-date scientific research, and emerging lines of debate in the global arena. Their opponents attempted to manage the issue, but with varied success. In the end, the provincial government and industry acknowledged that better forest management in Clayoquot Sound and British Columbia was salient in both Canada and the international community, suggesting that environmentalists had successfully expanded the debate.

The incentive to expand the issue of logging in Clayoquot Sound stemmed in part from the desire of local environmental activists to mobilize citizens and organizations in Canada and beyond. Chapter 4 examines more closely these patterns of participation; this chapter examines the rhetorical strategies that helped environmentalists enlarge the scope of political participation in the conflict.

Issue Definition and Expansion in Clayoquot Sound

Forest advocacy groups in British Columbia attempted to expand the issue of old-growth logging in Clayoquot Sound in a political environment that historically favored a more narrow definition of the issue. Until the 1980s, the issue of forest management was largely seen as a technical issue best left to the "experts"; debate, to the extent that it existed, centered on whether particular valleys should be protected as wilderness areas. The success of environmentalists in expanding the issue to a broader audience and in contesting the "liquidation-conversion" paradigm of the government-timber industry alliance stemmed in part from their ability to credibly link the issue to other important symbols, policy issues, and political debates. These linkages became a battleground for environmentalists, the provincial government, and the logging industry, all of whom attempted to gain control over the definition of the Clayoquot issue by debating the nature and validity of these linkages.

Environmentalists involved in Clayoquot Sound constructed links to at least three important issues in the course of the campaign, namely (1) rain forest protection and biodiversity, (2) native rights, and (3) democratic governance and participatory processes. Each of these is examined below, with particular attention paid to how various parties to the conflict used these issues to shape the terms of debate surrounding Clayoquot Sound.

The Rain Forests of Clayoquot Sound

One important set of issues linked to Clayoquot Sound were those of rain forest destruction and biodiversity loss. The destruction of tropical rain forests, particularly in the Amazon, has long been a subject of debate in the international arena and a concern of Western environmentalists in particular. A cursory examination of the Canadian Index, a guide to Canadian newspaper stories, indicates that media attention to rain forest issues in the 1980s and 1990s was high, particularly with respect to the Amazon rain forest in Brazil. Not only was attention high, but also the arguments, symbols, and frames that supported an expansive definition of the problem were firmly in place by the time Clayoquot environmentalists appealed to the public. International environmental organizations, with the help of conservation biologists, had been making three main arguments that helped to globalize the issue of rain forest destruction. First, they argued that protection of the rain forests was crucial to preserving the biodiversity of the planet, given the huge biological storehouse contained in these forests. Second, environmental groups suggested that rain forests functioned as "lungs of the earth," a particularly effective globalizing symbol, if not completely accurate according to scientists. Third, forest loss was linked to climate change, a connection environmentalists used to further their claim that deforestation contributed to global environmental problems.

Environmental groups involved in the protection of Clayoquot Sound tapped into this rich inventory of framing devices by advertising that Clayoquot Sound was one of the last undisturbed temperate rain forests in the world. The designation of temperate rain forests, as opposed to tropical ones, helped environmentalists because it highlighted the uniqueness of these particular forests. With fewer temperate rain forests worldwide, the pressure to preserve them was seen as even greater. For their part, scientists disagreed about what exactly defined a temperate rain forest, and how these forests compared to tropical ones in terms of biodiversity (see Ecotrust, Pacific GIS, and Conservation International 1995). Indeed, very little scientific research on temperate rain forests existed when the Clayoquot Sound campaign began in the early 1980s.

Environmental activist Maureen Fraser admitted that environmentalists initially knew very little about the ecology of these forests: "What people knew about the ecology of temperate old-growth rainforests you could have put into a tiny little slim volume. We were learning as we went, because research had not been done. People did not know what was in a temperate old-growth rainforest. All we knew was that's a very big tree and we think it is very old and that was about it" (quoted in Bossin 2000). Despite gaps in their knowledge, environmentalists embraced the terminology and symbols associated with rain forests, and as research accumulated, they stressed the biological density of temperate rain forests, arguing that they store more organic matter than even tropical forests.

Clayoquot activists first had to educate British Columbians and Canadians about Canada's rain forests. As Sergio Paone, a forest campaigner for

FOCS, remarked, "At that time [early 1990s] . . . a lot of Canadians did not know we had rain forests in Canada. They hear 'rain forest' and they immediately associate it with tropical rain forests. . . . We needed to get through to them that there are rain forests other than tropical and you have them in Canada" (1999). The main groups involved in the Clayoquot Sound campaign—FOCS, WCWC, Greenpeace, Ecotrust, the Valhalla Society, and others—were quick to describe British Columbia's forests as ancient, full of old growth, and as temperate rain forests. As Tamara Stark of Greenpeace Canada admitted, "We [environmental groups] agreed to talk about the rain forest because people have an understanding that rain forests are fragile. We had valley-by-valley fights [in the 1980s and early 1990s] and although people would get to identify with the valleys, they would not see it as a large, fragile ecosystem, like they do with the Amazon. . . . We talked about it strategically and thought it was really important for people to identify this place as a large, pristine wilderness, an intact area" (2000).

As suggested in this quote, the association with rain forests promised to raise the stakes of the issue by suggesting that Canada, like Brazil, had a global treasure worth preserving. Valerie Langer of FOCS made explicit their strategy: "We are going to raise temperate rainforests to the level of concern that tropical rainforests have. And focus the attention on Canada the way that attention has been focused on Brazil and Sarawak" (quoted in Hamilton 1993, A1). Steve Sawyer, a Greenpeace International and Greenpeace Canada board member, claimed during the height of the controversy, "The Clayoquot is rapidly gaining the kind of international focus that the forests haven't had since the Amazon itself" (quoted in Lee 1993b, A1). And Paul George of the WCWC later attested to the effectiveness of the strategy: "The temperate rainforests became as sexy as the tropical ones. We proved that they were way more biodiverse than people had thought" (2000).

The timing of their appeals proved auspicious. As Linder (1995, 225) notes, timing often helps explain why one set of arguments prevails over another. In this case, Canada had recently signed the UN Convention on Biological Diversity at the 1992 United Nations Conference on Environment and Development in Rio de Janeiro, Brazil. Clayoquot environmentalists recognized the strategic power of using the convention to raise the stakes in Clayoquot Sound and hold Canada to its ecological principles and promises. Valerie Langer of FOCS emphasized the importance of this tactic specifically, and of "messaging" more generally: "We started to attach our message to the Biodiversity Convention that was signed in Rio in 1992. We built on the hopes people had that something had changed—that all the governments of the world had gone to Rio and signed a Biodiversity Convention and we had legitimate expectations that something would change" (Langer 2000a). Langer and other Clayoquot activists capitalized on the contradictions between Canada's words, or pledge, and its actions. Zald (1996, 268) argues that cultural contradictions can be important components of framing processes. When movement activists point out the contradictions between the stated values of their opponents and their actions, movements can "reframe grievances and injustices and the possibilities of action."

The environmentalists' strategy had the added benefit of reminding the public that rain forests were critical to the long-term health of the planet. The scientific concept of "biodiversity" is not new, but "it has become more influential recently as a category for defining and organizing responses to many specific problems" (Fiorino 1995, 148–49; see also Noss and Cooperrider 1994). Indeed, forest activists were rather adept at using biodiversity as a vehicle for preserving forests—a logical extension, perhaps, of the spotted owl argument for saving old growth.[1] Ken Lertzman and his colleagues (1996, 122) note that environmentalists in British Columbia "shifted the focus of their defence [sic] of old-growth ecosystems, supplementing long-standing arguments that stressed the scenic and recreational values of wilderness with the claim that the conversion of old-growth forests led to loss of natural biodiversity." Environmental groups outside British Columbia also picked up on the biodiversity theme. The Kenya Consumers' Organization in Africa, for example, raised the issue in a letter to Premier Harcourt: "We are concerned [about Clayoquot Sound] because *the adverse consequences of such action is global*. . . . We the Kenyan Consumers urge you to do your utmost to preserve these forests for posterity, *in the interest of biodiversity and the general well-being of the global village*" (Kenya Consumers' Organization 1993; emphases added).

By focusing on the long-term, global consequences of large-scale logging, environmentalists increased the importance of what was happening in their own backyard to both the public and policymakers. In addition to the localized negative effects of clear-cutting—such as erosion, destruction of salmon habitat, degradation of drinking water, and losses in tourist dollars—there were now perhaps irreversible global consequences.

Merging Native Rights with Forestry Policy

In British Columbia and Canada at large, the issue of aboriginal land claims gained increasing importance during the 1970s and became a highly contentious issue in the 1980s (Tennant 1996). At this time, the provincial administration was being pressured by the federal government and the courts to end their long-standing tradition of nonnegotiation with native tribes over land claims.[2] These pressures continued throughout the 1980s as a series of legal cases and direct actions by First Nations kept the issue on the government's agenda (Howlett 2001; Tennant 1996). The issue of native land claims figured prominently in the conflict over Clayoquot Sound. The treaty rights of the Nuu-chah-nulth tribe were a major issue in the initial 1984 confrontation over Meares Island; some argue that the issue was first and foremost about aboriginal title to the land.[3] At this point in the conflict, environmentalists and local native populations shared a common interest, symbolized by the fact that Tla-o-qui-aht and Ahousaht natives invited environmentalists to join them during the Meares blockades after negotiations with timber company MacMillan Bloedel broke down.

The early connection between environmental and native issues was, according to FOCS cofounder Mike Mullin, "a very important reason why Meares [the campaign to protect Meares Island] caught the provincial, then the national, and the international imagination. It gave people something to believe in, an example of something they wanted to see" (1999). Mullin describes how FOCS went to Victoria accompanied by native leaders, dugout canoes, and other native cultural artifacts. It was the native culture, he claims, that originally attracted people to the presentations, providing FOCS a platform from which to talk about forestry and environmental issues. "And we were painting this picture that healthy environmentalism coincides with Native self-interest, which I still believe," he added (Mullin 1999).

The involvement of native people allowed environmentalists to argue for aboriginal rights along with forest protection, providing a clear avenue for issue expansion by broadening the sense of who was affected by provincial logging plans. Indeed, the high visibility and salience of native issues made them attractive to environmentalists. A series of polls conducted in late 1993 showed that while a majority of British Columbians supported continued (albeit limited) logging in Clayoquot Sound, 63 percent of the respondents supported an outright ban of logging in areas with outstanding native land claims.[4] The poll data suggest that the additional issue of aboriginal rights figured prominently in the public's disapproval of the provincial government's forestry practices.

The issue of native rights was highly salient outside of Canada as well. The displacement of native people from around the world and the loss of cultural diversity as a result of industrialization and Westernization are global issues that generate ongoing concern and mobilization. The support of native groups arguing for their rights has become an important legitimizing symbol for environmental organizations; it provides a means of broadening the forest issue to include human rights as well as environmental goals. As Hoberg and Morawski (1997, 408) note, "Environmentalists [in Clayoquot Sound] sought to ally themselves with First Nations, using arguments about aboriginal title to buttress the legitimacy of their environmental claims." At a time when environmentalists were increasingly being accused of ignoring the human element in their singular pursuit of ecological protection, making connections to human rights issues was especially important.

As the conflict over Clayoquot continued, tensions between environmentalists and First Nations grew and became matters for public consumption. Chapter 4 will detail these changes in alliances, but suffice it to say that the provincial government took advantage of these rifts. In February 1994, then premier Harcourt traveled to Europe with the intent of preventing a European boycott of B.C. wood products. Accompanying him was Nuu-chah-nulth leader George Watts, who stood by Harcourt and argued that a boycott of Canadian pulp and paper would cripple native economies, criticizing Greenpeace in particular for downplaying the potential effect on local native communities. In doing so, Watts helped Harcourt in his effort to link the government's position to the legitimizing symbol of native rights.

The provincial government attempted to co-opt the symbols of environmental activists, suggesting that as the power of environmental groups increased, the government competed to attach itself to resonant symbols and popular issue positions. Such strategic maneuvering is common. Richard Merelman (1966, 553) observed some time ago, "Most major political conflicts within any policy area may be seen as the attempt by partisans to attach the available legitimacy symbols to the policies they advocate and to sever the relationships between these symbols and the policies of their opponents." In the Clayoquot Sound case, both environmentalists and the government eventually agreed that the issue of forest management was tied to the "problem" of First Nations. The links between the two issues were well established through environmentalists' actions and rhetoric, by the provincial government, and by First Nations themselves. This represents a significant change, for the government was no longer treating these as separate and unrelated problems, as had been the case during much of the 1980s (see Hoberg and Morawski 1997). Ultimately, it served government interests to deny the connection. As Kingdon (1995, 112) reminds us, government's "first instinct is to preserve the old categories as long as possible" because someone is bound to lose from the new categorization.

Once the government of British Columbia acknowledged the centrality of aboriginal rights in forest policy, they could no longer define forestry in completely technical or commercial terms. The issue of native land claims brought with it broader discourses of rights, emphasizing the moral dimensions of the debate. Consider, for example, an editorial by Karen Charleson (1993, A19) in the *Vancouver Sun*, where she demands that the B.C. government remedy past "insults of seized lands and waters, stolen resources and degraded streams" and act in a "just and moral fashion." While Charleson denounces environmentalists' efforts to convert tribal land into provincial parks, she nevertheless extols the virtues of preservation: "It seems only natural to want to preserve [the] beauty [of the sound]. A need to protect natural wonder, a desire to never see the perfection marred—I think this is a quite basic human feeling" (Charleson 1993, A19). The discourse of aboriginal rights often includes references to the land in terms of its ecological and spiritual value to First Nations. Such rhetoric broadens the issue of logging, moving it away from a utilitarian focus on jobs and timber production.[5]

The role of First Nations in linking the issue of logging to aboriginal title is particularly interesting, as their actions—perhaps more than the efforts of environmentalists—worked to secure the connection. It is significant that First Nations asserted their land claims through an anti-clear-cut logging stance, a choice that may reflect the early alliance between environmentalists and First Nations. As the campaign to end clear-cutting gathered support, native leaders may have seen a strategic advantage to framing their claims in these terms. It is important to note, however, that the First Nations in Clayoquot Sound opposed the methods of harvesting employed by MacMillan Bloedel, not logging per se. In an advertisement responding to the 1993 Clayoquot Sound Land Use Decision, First Nations indicated support for logging in some areas of the sound but voiced opposition to "methods of logging that threaten our unique way of life and destroy sacred sites" (Nuu-chah-nulth First Nations 1993). In the judiciary's 1989 Meares Island ruling, appeals court judge Justice Seaton validated First Nations' claims: "The proposal is to clear-cut the area [Meares Island]. Almost nothing will be left. I cannot think of any native right that could be exercised on lands that have been recently logged" (quoted in Bossin 2000). Clear-cutting, in other words, abrogates native rights to land because it interferes with other uses of the land, including sustainable forestry.

The government, environmentalists, and First Nations eventually shared a common story line about forests and First Nations, even though they held different positions within this common frame, interpreted the meaning of the story somewhat differently, and continued to disagree (sometimes vociferously) about particular issues. Maarten Hajer's (1995, 66) notion of a "discourse coalition" is helpful in characterizing the nature of these relationships: Discourse coalitions, he argues, "differ from traditional political coalitions or alliances . . . in its emphasis on the linguistic basis of the coalition: story-lines, not interests, form the basis of the coalition." Hajer's concept of a discourse coalition alerts us to the possibility that political opponents might agree to talk about issues in similar ways even if their interests in the issue remain opposed. The rival groups might not even recognize their agreement; in the Clayoquot case, environmental groups, First Nations, and the Harcourt government certainly did not see themselves as being in coalition with one another. But this is secondary to the fact that they agreed to talk about First Nations rights and forestry policy together. The fact that the provincial government, First Nations, and environmentalists did not always have the same policy interests, then, might be less important than their discursive convergence—their sometimes tacit and sometimes explicit agreement that the issues were intertwined. As will be shown below, there was increasing convergence on a variety of issues related to Clayoquot as the conflict developed.

Clayoquot as a Tool for Reinvigorating Democracy

The third set of issues linked to Clayoquot focuses on the processes used to resolve the conflict, as opposed to substantive aspects of the forestry issue. One of the most notable features of this issue linkage is that environmentalists were not the key actors making the connection. Rather, the link between the resolution of the Clayoquot Sound conflict and larger issues of democratic governance was made largely by government officials who hoped that the conflict resolution process in Clayoquot would stand as a model for natural resource conflicts elsewhere in the province. The B.C. government inadvertently drew attention to the conflict in Clayoquot Sound by heavily promoting its attempts at conflict resolution. Promises of democratic, stakeholder negotiation resonated outside the confines of the forest policy subsystem, attracting public attention and raising expectations.

To understand the government's actions, it is helpful to realize that the Canadian government during the period of the Clayoquot conflict was experiencing a "crisis of legitimacy in the Canadian administrative state that [went] far beyond Clayoquot Sound or BC" (Hoberg 1996, 274). Hoberg argues that whereas the federal and provincial governments used to derive their legitimacy through "norms of representative and responsible government," this understanding had been undermined by the perception that elections and voting often failed to adequately translate the public's concerns and preferences into policy. People were calling for "direct participation by those most affected by decisions" (Hoberg 1996, 275). The B.C. government initiated a rather elaborate series of task forces and other participatory mechanisms with the proximate goal of resolving the Clayoquot land-use conflict and with the longer-term goal of reestablishing their democratic governing legitimacy.

The first efforts were by anyone's calculations dismal failures. The 1989 Clayoquot Sound Sustainable Development Task Force, for example, disbanded shortly after its creation. Its progeny, the Clayoquot Sound Sustainable Development Strategy Steering Committee, fared no better when environmentalists resigned in 1991 over their objection to the decision to log Bulson Creek, a relatively pristine watershed in Clayoquot Sound. The steering committee proceeded without environmental representatives, but the legitimacy of the process was compromised without the participation of a key interest group. From the environmentalists' perspective, these negotiations were nothing but exercises in "talk and log"—while the talks were going on, the industry continued to log.

In 1992, the NDP under the leadership of Premier Harcourt embarked on another experiment in consensus-based land-use planning with the formation of CORE, or the Commission on Resources and the Environment. The goal of CORE was even more ambitious than the Clayoquot Sound committee in that its task was to develop sustainable development plans for the entire province. In theory, this would end the valley-by-valley conflicts that had taken their toll on all parties. The Clayoquot Sound region was exempt from CORE, somewhat ironically, given that the Clayoquot conflict largely prompted its creation.[6] Nevertheless, Clayoquot was publicly connected to CORE, in part because environmentalists were calling for the inclusion of Clayoquot Sound in the CORE process. Many activists refused to participate in the CORE discussions on the grounds that the most important conflict on Vancouver Island had been excluded from the process (George 2000; Langer 2000b).[7] Policymakers also linked the two issues, along with some activists. For example, Robert F. Kennedy Jr., writing in the *Vancouver Sun*, argued for the importance of both CORE and Clayoquot Sound: "Clayoquot's symbolic value is most important. Governments around the world have accepted Premier Mike Harcourt's assurances that British Columbia will protect its last ancient rainforests through an innovative land-use planning process: the Commission on Resources and the Environment. . . . In CORE, the government has made a giant investment of human talent and economic resources to resolve British Columbia's forestry crisis. In the process, British Columbia has created a model that may be used to protect important ecosystems around the globe" (Kennedy 1993, B4). Kennedy went on to suggest that any backtracking on the part of the government from the CORE process would be due to pressure from the timber industry. He raised the stakes in Clayoquot Sound by arguing that it was not only important ecologically but was also a symbol and test case for whether governments could resist industry pressure and involve multiple interests in forest decision-making processes. In short, Clayoquot Sound was both substantively and procedurally important.

Most studies of issue expansion assume that if an issue expands, it is because those seeking policy change have actively framed it in expansive terms. What is notable about the expansion of Clayoquot—at least through its association with deeper debates about the democratic responsiveness of the B.C. government—is that environmentalists had little to do with it. Notwithstanding Kennedy's remarks, many key environmental activists denounced the government's efforts to resolve the conflict, calling them "task farces" and stating they were flawed from the outset, "doomed to fail," and making other derogatory remarks about the various commissions. For them, the significance of Clayoquot was not embodied in these stakeholder processes. The main proponents of CORE were government officials, suggesting that other actors—even those who might prefer to keep an issue contained—can play a role in issue expansion. The government, perhaps unintentionally, raised the political significance of the conflict in Clayoquot Sound by associating it with larger issues of democratic governance.[8] As Hoberg (1996, 274) notes, "The Clayoquot Sound decision-making process was a failed test of an innovative and promising experiment in democratic governance." Its failure might have simply served to increase the visibility of the conflict.

In short, the global importance of Clayoquot was acknowledged by all parties, even if they had different reasons for doing so. For the government, Clayoquot was a test case for whether forest conflicts could be resolved using a multistakeholder, consensus-based decision-making process—an approach that would take the conflict off the streets and out of the international spotlight.

The Credibility of Issue Linkages

The above discussion illustrates how issues expand in their scope and significance through their credible associations with other problems in society. In policy debates with high levels of conflict, opposing groups often compete with one another over what issue linkages are most appropriate, engaging in a process of attachment and denial. In general, status quo–oriented groups have an interest in denying issue linkages altogether so as to contain conflict and participation. But containment strategies are sometimes unsuccessful. Under such conditions, both proponents and opponents of policy change compete to attach themselves to popular symbols, or otherwise manage an issue's image by strategically linking the problem to other problems or solutions in society.

A question that remains is why some issue linkages are credible and others are less so. What factors and circumstances, in other words, lend credibility to the claims of political actors who are trying to link an issue to others? One consideration is whether advocacy groups reference familiar, previously accepted connections. Preexisting arguments and frameworks make it easier for groups to engage audiences and expand debates. For example, the credibility of the link between environmental and native issues in Clayoquot Sound was enhanced to the extent that similar alliances and linkages had been formed in other locales around the globe. Within these frameworks, extraordinary aspects of an issue may increase its chances for expansion (see Cobb and Elder 1972; Rochefort and Cobb 1994). For example, the new focus on deforestation by an industrialized, northern country contributed greatly to the expansion of the Clayoquot issue. Environmental advocacy groups had long targeted developing countries in their rain forest protection campaigns. Officials and even activists in these countries often challenged such campaigns on the ground that they portrayed Brazil and other developing countries as environmental "outlaws" while paying scant attention to the environmental problems in industrialized countries. The focus on Canadian forest practices challenged the positive images associated with more "responsible" northern industrialized countries, which were allegedly years ahead of the South in terms of forest management. In short, the novelty of the temperate rain forest issue, combined with its tacit critique of northern assumptions, helped to propel the issue into the international spotlight.

Evidence of these effects can be found in the response of environmental organizations around the world to the Clayoquot Sound conflict. For example, eight major U.S. environmental organizations, including the Sierra Club and the National Audubon Society, sponsored an advertisement in the *New York Times* in early 1993, noting that most global attention had focused on the alarming rate of tropical rain forest destruction in Brazil. "Few people realize that an even greater level of environmental devastation has taken place in British Columbia," the advertisement reads, going on to proclaim that "Canada's dirty, secret war against its forests is about to reach a critical watershed" (Conservation International and others 1993). The Organization for Peace and Disarmament in Southern Africa wrote directly to Premier Harcourt, asking, "If affluent British Columbia fails to save its rain forests, how can we expect other countries like Zimbabwe, under severe pressures of poverty and debt, to save theirs?" (Siziba 1993). The question suggests that Clayoquot was defined as a critical test case for conservation efforts elsewhere, due in no small part to the fact that it was located in a highly developed country that could allegedly afford to protect its rain forests.

The Clayoquot case also suggests that when it comes to the credibility of issue frames, the choice of venue matters. Some ways of framing an issue—linking forestry to economics and jobs, for example—resonate at a local and regional level but may fail when presented to an international audience far removed from the economic realities of the locale. Linking a local conflict over logging to a global problem such as biodiversity loss, however, works very well on the international stage, particularly in countries such as Germany where high proportions of the populace belong to environmental groups and identify with ecological values. One of the strengths of Clayoquot environmental groups was their ability to tailor their messages to particular audiences and arenas, a point that I explore further in the next chapter.

Using Metaphors and Images to Expand Issues

If there is a bias in studies of problem definition, it is toward the written and spoken word. Problems, after all, are constructed largely through words. But images and pictures also play an important role in the construction and presentation of issues, particularly in a highly media-saturated, television-oriented society.[9] The activists interviewed suggested that images were just as important as, if not more important than, words in terms of raising awareness and support for the campaign to protect Clayoquot Sound. Environmental groups such as FOCS, WCWC, and Greenpeace provided the public with visual images of the rain forest throughout the campaign, an indication of their belief in the power of visual images to shape the public's understanding of the conflict. For example, to raise public awareness about the existence of the temperate rain forests and the threats posed by continued logging, WCWC published three books, seven posters, and more than one million copies of educational pamphlets with full-color photos. In April 1993, WCWC constructed a "Witness Trail" through some pristine old growth in Clayoquot Valley so that visitors could see for themselves the magnificence of the forests. And in the fall of 1993, the group extracted a large cedar tree stump from Clayoquot Sound (dubbed "Stumpy"), which toured Canada and Europe, its size an indication of the grandeur of British Columbia's forests.

Valerie Langer of FOCS claimed that visual images of the rain forests were a key factor in garnering both domestic and international support. She and photographer Garth Lenz produced a slide show featuring Lenz's photographs of Clayoquot Sound; in 1993 and 1994 they toured Canada and Europe, presenting the slides to interested audiences, key international environmental groups, and even the European Parliament. According to Langer,

"We really worked on our presentation to make it beautifully, visually stunning, and we had text that went along with the images that was emotional while incorporating key facts" (Langer 2000a). Langer emphasized the importance of attaching the group's more radical message to popular and culturally resonant images of beautiful landscapes: "When we are working on wilderness campaigns, and in Clayoquot Sound . . . we utilized a kind of language and messaging which attached our more radical message about . . . the industrialization of wild areas to the sense of beauty and landscape and what that means to people. So, we were not starting off our campaign by saying that clearcutting and industrialization is a horrible thing . . . we started in with what people could hear" (Langer 2000a). According to Langer, images of intact rain forests were more effective in gaining the attention and support of the Canadian public than were images of clear-cuts, which made Canadians "shut down" and feel guilty.

Images of clear-cuts and associations with rain forest destruction were nevertheless effective in getting the attention of government and industry officials. When Colleen McCrory of the Valhalla Society coined the phrase "Brazil of the North" in reference to Canada's logging practices, she set off a storm of fury. "Brazil of the North" made use of preexisting images associated with burning rain forests and a "third world" approach to natural resource management. It became a particularly popular catchphrase and had a long shelf life, reappearing long after McCrory first coined it in the early 1990s. Figure 3.1 shows the number of times the phrase appeared in articles, editorials, and letters to the editor in major Canadian newspapers, magazines, and wire service reports from 1990 to 2005. Note that the most mentions appeared in 1993, not the year McCrory first made her accusation, but the year when the government announced its Clayoquot Sound Land Use Decision and when thousands of people engaged in civil action to protest the decision.

The phrase "Brazil of the North" also surfaced in environmentalists' literature, at the 1992 Earth Summit, in the foreign press (including a 1991 German television program), and in the responses of government officials, most of whom vehemently denied the association. As one article in the *Vancouver Sun* states, "'Brazil of the North' attempts to burden Canadian forestry with the condemnation already heaped on Brazil. It is a provocative denunciation. It is embarrassing and has got more than a little rise out of the Canadian forestry industry" (Armstrong 1992, A17). It also got the attention of government officials who, according to one activist, "were outraged that they were being compared to a third world country that is notorious for demolishing their rainforest. . . . That [phrase] really struck a cord with them" (Mychajilowycz 1999). Indeed, the federal and provincial governments jointly spent nearly

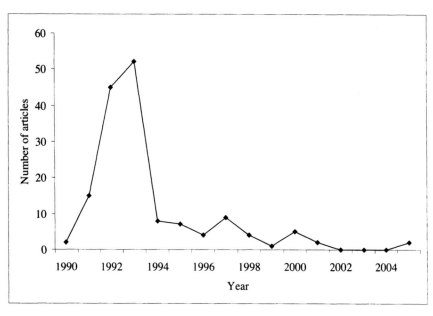

FIGURE 3.1   Frequency of Mentions of "Brazil of the North" in the News Media
Source: Compiled by the author from LexisNexis Academic Universe. Search words were
"Brazil of the North" in combination with "Canada."

$6 million countering the negative international image of Canada sparked by
the "Brazil of the North" slogan.

The "Brazil of the North" metaphor was a powerful means of transferring
disturbing images from one location to another. It helped expand the issue
beyond British Columbia's forestry practices, implicating Canada at large
even though the federal government has very little formal control over what
happens in British Columbia's forests (95 percent of which are publicly owned
and controlled by the province). As the conflict developed, Canada itself
became the focus of much protest and opposition, along with MacMillan
Bloedel and the provincial government of Premier Harcourt. In Greenpeace's
European campaign to protect Clayoquot Sound, for example, the organization rarely made distinctions between British Columbia and Canada; their
banners implored Canada to stop destroying the world's rain forests, even
while they were trailing the premier of British Columbia and protesting at
MacMillan Bloedel offices. Environmentalists and reporters continued to
use the phrase in reference to other environmental conflicts around Canada
throughout the 1990s.

The credibility of the "Brazil of the North" metaphor was enhanced by
pictures of individual clear-cuts and aerial photographs of Vancouver Island

that showed that nearly two-thirds of the island had been clear-cut logged. Even before the international markets campaign was firmly established, environmental organizations in Canada invited European politicians and international activists and journalists to witness the extent of forest destruction for themselves by sponsoring flights over Vancouver Island with the U.S.-based group Lighthawk and taking visitors on hikes in clear-cut forests. As one source notes, "The groups emphasized large, ugly, recent clear-cuts in their tours. They did not show similar areas after replanting and a decade of new growth" (Stanbury and Vertinsky 1997, 19). Patrick Anderson of Greenpeace International was unapologetic about their use of images, admitting that the Clayoquot Sound campaign in Europe did "not need a lot of text" (quoted in Lee 1993a, A1).

One reason images are so effective in creating associations is because they simplify information. A clear-cut forest looks rather similar to land that has been deliberately burned for agricultural uses, as is the case in the Amazon rain forest. The Amazon rain forest is not a source of commercial timber so much as a destination for peasants who are desperately seeking a means of subsistence through ranching or farming. The land is rarely replanted, unlike land used for forestry, a difference that Prince Philip of England pointed out when he visited Canada. These differences became the basis for Prince Philip's denial that Canada is truly the "Brazil of the North" (MacQueen 1992, A9). Industry seized on his statement and even wrote a letter to the *Vancouver Sun* chastising the paper for failing to give adequate attention to Prince Philip's remarks. What they did not realize perhaps was the power of images—in the end, the different reasons for forest destruction were not as important as the similarities in the images.

Public relations specialists working for the timber industry found that Greenpeace's pictures of clear-cuts often overwhelmed their own verbal attempts at combating the images. The Forest Alliance, a nonprofit advocacy group for the forest industry, acknowledged the power of these images after seeing them firsthand. Members of the alliance followed Valerie Langer and Garth Lenz when they toured the United Kingdom with "Stumpy," the old-growth stump from Clayoquot Sound.[10] In the Forest Alliance's report to members, they admitted that their arguments fared better in the absence of the visual images: "Radio debates proved the most effective medium for the Forest Alliance to challenge Greenpeace. In the absence of its slide-show, the Greenpeace/Friends of Clayoquot Sound argument was easily and effectively countered. Not surprisingly, Stumpy had more success in print and on television. . . . *Greenpeace can be very effective when the focus is on the visual.* In forums where issues can be developed more substantively, and in the absence of emotional appeals, pro-forestry arguments play very well" (Forest Alliance of British Columbia 1994, 6; emphasis added).

On his European tour, Premier Harcourt insisted that Greenpeace's pictures of clear-cuts were outdated, taken before British Columbia enacted "world class" forestry standards: "We know there have been some bad practices in the past," he said, "and that's why I was elected—to bring about change" (quoted in Bohn 1994, B3). Similarly, Bill Gilmour, a forester for MacMillan Bloedel, insisted that the clear-cut shown in a Valhalla Wilderness Society–sponsored poster was larger than clear-cuts today, and that "right next to it [the clear-cut], we've got an old-growth stand that has been recommended for preservation. And next to that is a great example of what good logging looks like by today's standards. . . . Brazil should be so lucky" (quoted in Bohn 1992, A5). Another critic blamed the media for advancing inaccurate information via pictures and images: "Before and after logging shots have been the TV's favourite [*sic*] fodder. The contrast is dramatic. When repetitiously linked with shots of people mindlessly chanting, 'Save the Clayoquot,' the false message is conveyed that barren-looking, ugly hillside is the permanent legacy of logging. Any knowledgeable reporting, concerned with conveying the truth, would have included some pictures of hillsides ten, twenty, forty or fifty years after logging" (Barnett n.d., 15).

The critics' protestations were largely lost on those who saw the pictures: Clear-cuts, after all, are clear-cuts. The emotional effect of the visual image was not blunted by knowledge that the cuts had been made years before or that the trees would eventually grow back. Indeed, this was one "objective" aspect of the issue that worked in environmentalists' favor because clear-cuts do not begin to regenerate and resemble a forest for decades. However, the provincial government soon joined in the image game, as they showed photographs of their own to members of the European Parliament. These were photographs of second-growth forests in British Columbia, and Gordon Smith, Canada's ambassador to the European Union, claimed that "visiting European parliamentarians were dumbfounded when they saw some B.C. lush second-growth, which they couldn't distinguish from first-growth" (quoted in Lautens 1994, A23).

Mapping the Issue

Visual images of rain forests and clear-cuts were not the only site where image wars were being waged. Various actors in the Clayoquot conflict also used maps and mapping techniques to shape the definition of the problem and attempt to gain political advantage. Maps became an important tool and site of struggle over the fate of British Columbia's forests generally and Clayoquot

Sound in particular; they represented not just places but ideas, and competing advocacy groups battled over these ideas.

Environmental groups designed maps that reflected and constituted their
particular construction of the issue, taking advantage of satellite mapping
technology that is increasingly within the grasp of nongovernmental organizations. In the early 1990s, Ecotrust Canada and Conservation International
embarked on an ambitious mapping project covering the west coast of North
America, from northern California to Alaska. In their maps, conventional
political boundaries such as the border between the United States and Canada
are secondary to ecological and cultural ones. The maps highlight the boundaries and features of the landscape that Ecotrust and other environmentalists
deemed important. For example, the region is defined as unique and as a rain
forest by its average annual temperature and rainfall, both of which help to
distinguish it from interior landscapes. Notably, ecologists do not typically
define biomes by temperature or levels of precipitation but look at differences
in vegetation structures and in wildlife. Because temperate rain forests do
not differ significantly from drier forest types on these standard dimensions,
environmental organizations devised another way to distinguish them.

The maps also provide a basis and rationale for transnational actions and
alliances among environmental groups. Ecotrust's maps connect coastal areas
across provincial, state, and national boundaries via their ecological similarities, thus providing citizens in the entire region a common interest and stake
in the management of these forest ecosystems. The maps are a representation
and reaffirmation of what environmental groups in the Pacific Northwest had
been arguing for decades—that their region constituted a unique biome and
should be managed on this scale. While environmental groups in Clayoquot
were not arguing for another "Cascadia Alliance" where formal jurisdiction
over the area would be shifted to a regional governing body, they tried to
cultivate a sense of connection among the coastal communities. This strategy
would prove useful once the campaign sought participation by U.S. environmental groups.

Ecotrust admitted that they used maps in their campaigns to protect
specific valleys in British Columbia. Ian Gill was convinced that maps helped
them in their campaign to protect the Kitlope watershed, a large area in the
middle of British Columbia's coast. In an editorial for the *Vancouver Sun*, he
describes how mapping is a relatively recent addition to the environmentalists' tool chest: "Harcourt's government made an informed decision to protect the Kitlope, and much of the information about the area came by way
of maps. It has long been held as axiomatic that information is power, and
in B.C.'s debate over land use, that power is increasingly vested in maps.

Until recently, the capacity to map has been the preserve of governments, or industry, for the simple reason that they have the ability to pay. That means government and industry also had the power to dictate form and content" (Gill 1995, A15). By drawing maps that emphasized criteria of importance to them, Ecotrust "discovered" that the Kitlope was the biggest intact watershed of its kind in the world, prompting the Harcourt administration to set it aside as a provincial park.[11]

Maps were also important tools in conflict over Clayoquot Sound. Local environmental activist Mike Mullin recalled how FOCS was trying hard to link the issue of Clayoquot with other logging activities around the island and province: "Much of the argument about Clayoquot Sound involves the context of the entire island—with three-quarters of it [Vancouver Island] cut, then this portion becomes even more important" (1999). By literally extending the boundaries of the issue, the importance of Clayoquot Sound as one of the few remaining undisturbed areas increased. Mullin accused industry and provincial representatives of using maps to deemphasize the problem of logging on Vancouver Island. When he represented Tofino at the Clayoquot Sound Sustainable Development Strategy Steering Committee meetings, he claims to have seen maps of the whole of Vancouver Island only once (1999).[12] Apparently, industry and government leaders realized that this broad view of the island hurt their cause, for it clearly showed the devastation wrought on Vancouver Island as a result of decades of industrial logging. After this initial strategic blunder on the part of opponents, their maps showed only specific cuts in and around Clayoquot. These maps minimized the problem of logging because the clear-cuts were surrounded by green areas representing the original forests in the Clayoquot region.

The type of maps produced by various parties to the conflict, including First Nations, industry, the provincial ministries, and environmental groups, reveal much about how these groups viewed the issues surrounding Clayoquot. For MacMillan Bloedel, the relevant borders were those established by the Ministry of Forests through tree farm licenses. In the early stages of the conflict, MacMillan Bloedel held onto this legal definition of the issue, one that reflected the provincial government's historical treatment of the forests as commodities, and the land as the quasi–property rights of timber corporations. During the Meares Island campaign, MacMillan Bloedel held onto this rather narrow understanding of the issue. It would be years later that Linda Coady, vice president for environmental affairs at MacMillan Bloedel, admitted that an overly legal framing of the issue was inadequate in the face of the changing public demands: "Just obeying the laws is not enough," she admitted, "because the law runs about five years behind social expectations" (quoted in Bossin 2000).

The courts recognized this legal definition of the issue during the mass trials of Clayoquot protesters who had disobeyed a court injunction against blockades. In these trials, the government introduced as evidence the map of Tree Farm License 44, which covered a significant portion of the sound. The map established the area where MacMillan Bloedel held harvesting rights and where the injunction was in effect. According to one source, "This map was essential to the Crown's case. . . . It formed a mental picture which would predetermine the judge's understanding of the various events and places related to the protests" (Loys Maingon, in Berman and others 1994, 158). Whether and to what extent the map actually influenced the judge is impossible to say, but the court's acceptance of the map and the exclusion of others is revealing. It legitimized MacMillan Bloedel's rights to the area, as well as reinforcing its legalistic definition of the issue.

The B.C. government maps of the 1993 Clayoquot Sound Land Use Decision reveal the particular concerns and positioning of the province. The government viewed land-use conflicts as matters of land allocation; the key decision revolved around how to parcel out the land to the various user-groups. The maps represent a pluralistic conception of the issue and suggest that for the government, Clayoquot Sound was first and foremost a political problem. The maps included in a government-sponsored mailing to more than a million households in British Columbia, for example, reflect the management orientation of the agencies. They partition the area based on the type of activities allowed, focusing on the "inputs" rather than on the potential effect of the decision on the area's ecology. Specifically, the maps illustrate three different land-use designations: Protected areas where no logging is permitted; special management areas where logging will be managed so as to not adversely affect wildlife and scenic corridors; and general integrated management areas where more intensive logging will be allowed to continue, albeit with new regulations. The maps provide very little information on how the government designated these areas and whether the designations conform to current scientific research. Instead, the designations appear to be based on political rather than ecological considerations—environmentalists are given some areas, loggers others, and the remaining areas are to be divided among various users with a particular eye toward not adversely affecting the tourism sector. With these maps, the provincial government was attempting to convince the public, the media, and more specialized audiences that the 1993 decision was a "balanced" one "that recognize[d] environmental values in Clayoquot Sound and the need to provide jobs and economic stability for local communities" (British Columbia Government Communications Office 1993, 2).

In contrast, Ecotrust's maps emphasize the limits on logging in Clayoquot, based on government data and the recommendations of the Clayoquot Sound scientific panel. A series of ten maps published by the organization act as filters, mapping the constraints on logging to protect such things as sensitive hydro-riparian ecosystems, unstable slopes, and cultural values. The final map shows the areas potentially available for forestry—small islands in a sea of protected areas (Ecotrust Canada 1997). There is no attempt to balance the needs and interests of various user groups; rather, the maps refer to the alleged limits of the land, defined in terms of ecosystem sustainability. Indeed, the maps barely acknowledge any human needs or activities in the area with the exception of native peoples and a few recreational areas. These maps reinforce environmentalists' construction of the Clayoquot problem as primarily an ecological one.

Managing the Issue: Official and Industry Strategies

The analysis presented so far shows how the conflict over Clayoquot Sound gained in significance and scope over the course of the campaign, eventually becoming something of a global cause célèbre. For many activists, Clayoquot Sound became the line drawn in the sand, a crucial fight against a myopic view that saw forests principally as a source of timber and a logger's paycheck. Environmental groups used expansive rhetoric and powerful images to broaden the significance of the issue, linking logging in Clayoquot Sound to problems of rain forest destruction, loss of global biodiversity, and unrecognized native rights claims. By the mid-1990s, their framing of the issue was gaining ground as both the provincial government and MacMillan Bloedel acknowledged the global ecological significance of the region and the centrality of native rights to the issue.

This is not to suggest, however, that industry or the provincial government gave up trying to manage the debate in ways favorable to their interests. Indeed, they made significant efforts to contain the issue to the extent that was feasible given the high degree of criticism at home and abroad. Their first line of defense, as already mentioned, involved distancing themselves from the problem. One paid advertisement by MacMillan Bloedel features a picture of a dinosaur, with bold text declaring, "Some opinions on British Columbia's forests are a little out of date," and smaller text that champions the company's new forestry practices (MacMillan Bloedel 1994, 19). MacMillan Bloedel admitted that in the past, it had made some mistakes, but that "new science and changing social values" require changes in forestry practices (MacMillan Bloedel Public Affairs Office 1994, 6). In designating these values and knowledge as "new," MacMillan Bloedel was trying to legitimize past practices by suggesting that they conformed to the science and values of the day. Moreover, the company implies that forest practices are largely determined by science and public values rather than politics, power, or economic imperatives, a proposition that environmentalists would no doubt reject.

Premier Harcourt, for his part, took advantage of the fact that he and his party (the NDP) had just recently come into power, having won leadership of the province from the Social Credit Party in 1991. In a letter to Vice President Al Gore, in which he responds to a negative advertisement in the *New York Times*, Harcourt's strategy of divorcing himself from the Social Credit Party is transparent: "We acknowledge that . . . we are dealing with a legacy of past practices that were deemed appropriate by previous administrations but that were not always optimal. However, by now it is surely a matter of public record that my government has put the health and well-being of the land at the top of the agenda" (Harcourt 1993, 11). Distancing strategies were coupled with rhetoric about the future. The public was encouraged to embrace a new era in which British Columbia would lead the world in sustainable forestry management. In short, the government and industry attempted to regain control over the issue by insisting that the complaints of environmentalists were being addressed and that the forestry practices at the heart of the conflict were a thing of the past. Nicholas Hildyard (1993, 30) argues that mainstream interests at the 1992 Earth Summit used similar tactics in order to capture the debate and contain conflict: "The past disappeared from view, discreetly curtained off from scrutiny. The public was asked to look towards the future and with it, a new age of environmental awareness in which industry—now aware of the environment—had put its house back in order to the satisfaction of the earthworm and corporate executives alike. Industry's record was thus wiped clean: the fox could now be put in charge of the chickens."

Environmental activists fought this characterization by claiming that very little had changed in the woods. FOCS and other environmental groups produced pictures of areas that had been logged under the Social Credit Party and during the Harcourt administration. Not surprisingly, the photographs are almost identical, each showing logged-out landscapes. Environmental groups also cast doubt on whether the government, particularly the Ministry of Forests, could be trusted to enforce the new Forest Practices Code, given its historic ties to industry. Finally, they questioned whether the public could trust MacMillan Bloedel, a company with a substantial criminal record.[13]

Another containment strategy involved shifting the debate away from questions that environmentalists were asking to questions that industry and the government favored. During the Clayoquot campaign, environmental groups successfully expanded the range of inquiry into provincial forest practices— they not only questioned methods of logging and the high rates of cut but also asked whether old-growth forests should be logged at all. Their answer, not surprisingly, was that old-growth areas should be off-limits to any future logging, even if it was conducted in a "sustainable" manner under "world class" standards. The call for complete preservation of old growth worried the government and industry, who had been operating under the doctrine of "multiple use"—a doctrine that acknowledged nontimber values of the forests on paper, but in practice favored logging above all else.

Years of preferential treatment and relative freedom from public scrutiny help to explain the government and industry's alarm when environmentalists called for alienation of the forestland into preserves. Mike Apsey, deputy minister of forests, predicted this trend long before others and warned in a 1983 speech to the B.C. Professional Forests Association, "If we permit the Balkanization of the forest land base into single-use fragments . . . we will have failed in our most basic duty" (Apsey 1983, 10). A decade later MacMillan Bloedel was trying to shift the debate back to forest management issues and away from more basic preservation questions. In a presentation to industry officials, Linda Coady (then director of government affairs for MacMillan Bloedel) said that in the long term, the company must respond to the environmentalists' challenge by "fighting fire with fire," which means MacMillan Bloedel must "find a way to elevate debate from '*should* we do it?' to '*how* do we do it?'" (Coady 1993). In short, MacMillan Bloedel tried to regain control over the issue by shifting the discussion to more technical issues concerning methods of logging and away from the deeper, value-based question of whether logging should occur at all.

Noncontradictory Argumentation?

Initially, environmentalists and their opponents practiced what Baumgartner and Jones (1993) call "noncontradictory argumentation." The two sides appeared to be talking past one another because each focused on particular aspects of the forestry issue where their arguments were most convincing. Environmentalists, for example, attempted to shift the focus away from the economic aspects of forestry by framing the Clayoquot issue in terms of rain forests and biodiversity. When the debate was centered on economics, the timber industry had the upper hand: The industry generates about $4.5 billion in tax revenue for the province, is the largest employer in British Columbia, and in some coastal areas, employs anywhere from 45 to 60 percent of the total population (Bryner 1999, 313; Hoberg and Morawski 1997, 391). Generally speaking, environmentalists had the advantage when the focus of the debate was on the negative ecological effects of forestry, while the logging industry had the advantage when the issue was framed in economic terms.

What is notable about the Clayoquot Sound conflict, however, is the high degree to which both sides directly engaged with one another's arguments. Environmentalists started to question the positive images associated with logging—such as freedom, independence, hard work, industry, and strong communities, to name a few. In some cases, they offered up images of dependency based on the notion that timber sales on public land are below cost. This tarnished the image of the independent, self-reliant logger. Similarly, environmental groups have suggested that the logging industry—and more specifically, the industry's harvesting methods—is, metaphorically speaking, a dinosaur whose day has come and gone. Environmentalists have thus challenged the image of progress and growth with which logging has been historically associated.

In the Clayoquot controversy, Ecotrust Canada and other environmental organizations found a middle ground between ignoring the claims of their opponents and directly contradicting them: They stressed the compatibility of community economic development and environmental sustainability rather than address forestry's aggregate economic contribution to the province. In short, they indirectly countered the economic arguments of their opponents by focusing on economic sustainability at the local level. Their economic arguments gained credibility as Clayoquot Sound became internationally known. As the Clayoquot debate expanded, the tourist industry was becoming an ever more significant component of the local economy. Tourists had been coming to Clayoquot Sound in significant numbers ever since the federal government established Pacific Rim National Park (just south of Tofino) in 1971. But tourism to the area increased about 18 percent per year between the late 1980s and mid-1990s—to an estimated half a million visitors annually in the 1990s, half of whom came from outside British Columbia (Ecotrust Canada 1997). Many activists living in Tofino attribute this increase to the Clayoquot logging controversy and the publicity it generated.

For its part, industry tried to focus public attention on the economic contributions of forestry to the Canadian economy, but its strategies worked better in some venues than others. At home in British Columbia, for example, the government and industry's arguments about jobs and the economy were compelling to the extent that people realized the economic contributions of the logging industry. And some evidence suggests that British Columbians were not only aware of the economic importance of forestry but also were reluctant to support environmental measures that might negatively affect the provincial economy. A 1993 independent public opinion poll found that two-thirds of the respondents considered forestry to be the most important industry in the province. A slight majority also opposed old-growth logging bans if they led to employment losses. And finally, nearly 75 percent of the respondents thought that economic development was as important as environmental protection (Baldrey 1993).

For the audience in British Columbia, it seems, the trade-off was the familiar one of jobs versus the environment. But to the European public, who felt no particular affinity with the four hundred loggers in Clayoquot Sound who might lose their jobs, the choice was much easier. Premier Harcourt initially failed to grasp this fact. As Langer relates, Harcourt started out his European tour by focusing on jobs and how the environmentalists are "out to get your family":

> But it fell completely flat in Europe. They [the government] did not read the European public at all. Not at all. We did our research—we found in England that people who take any interest in environmentalism like fuzzy animals, and in Germany they love forest lands, like the Black Forest. . . . So, when we went to England we had all these photos of the animals of the rainforest and when we went to Germany we had these landscape photos, and whatever you said about jobs fell flat. Because we said *the four hundred jobs that would be lost in Clayoquot Sound are not worth the lives of these animals* (Langer 2000b; emphasis added).

The international markets campaign of the mid-1990s opened up a new set of issue frames for environmental groups. By targeting consumers of B.C. wood products, environmental activists offered incongruous trade-offs and framed the issue as one of consumer choice. The activists were essentially saying that if jobs were not worth the destruction of the forests, then the paper products made from the forests and sold in Europe and the United States were even less worthy. The trade-off appeared increasingly absurd—would the public prefer old-growth forests or phone books and toilet paper? In their European campaign, Greenpeace offered this: "When you blow your nose in Europe you are blowing away the ancient rainforests of Canada." In response, MacMillan Bloedel tried to reassure their customers that the old-growth forests were too valuable to turn into paper products. Only the wood "not of

sufficient quality for solid wood operations" is used in pulp and paper operations, the company claimed in a memo to purchasers (MacMillan Bloedel
Public Affairs Office 1994, 4). But for those who saw only the Greenpeace
banners, the trade-off implied in these slogans could elicit one answer only; as
shown in chapter 4, such appeals helped to draw in the international audience
and expand participation in the conflict.

Eventually, Harcourt and industry officials recognized a need to address
the issues in environmentalists' terms, at least when speaking to an international public. As international criticism mounted in the mid-1990s, they
started referring to British Columbia's new "world class" forestry standards.
They noted that the Clayoquot Sound Land Use Decision conformed to the
UN Convention on Biological Diversity recommendations that 12 percent of
a region's land base be permanently protected. More striking is MacMillan
Bloedel's reaction to the Clayoquot campaign in Europe. After the company's
initial strategy of shifting the debate failed, it embarked on a full-fledged campaign to counter Greenpeace's claims.[14] Here again is an example of discourse
convergence: Certainly, environmentalists and the government continued to
disagree about whether the standards were in fact "world class." But the fact
that the government and industry were attempting to justify their logging
practices to the global community with reference to international biodiversity
standards, rather than shift the debate to the issue of jobs and the Canadian
economy, signifies at least a partial victory for environmentalists.

The Clayoquot Sound case suggests a more general theoretical proposition. That is, it suggests that political actors will not only venue shop in
order to find an arena where the rules are less biased, but also to find a more
receptive audience for their rhetorical claims.[15] Advocacy groups will look
for venues based on whether the arena provides fertile ground for their discourse strategies. Some arenas are more attractive because groups can more
easily advance their particular issue frames in them; the credibility of their
opponents' competing frames may be particularly low in these arenas. Other
things being equal, groups will shop for venues where their frames resonate
and appear credible compared to their opponents'.

Conclusion

This chapter has explored a trend in environmental politics, one in which
increasing numbers of environmental problems are constructed as global
ones. Environmental activists, scientists, and writers have convincingly argued
that the effects of environmental problems are often felt far from where they

originate. Some environmentalists claim that *all* environmental problems are global in scope, possibly because they perceive a strategic advantage in making such arguments: "Clearly, environmentalists look more important if, instead of complaining about a local grievance, they can lay claims to global concerns. They benefit from upping the stakes" (Yearley 1996, 61). If some groups benefit from the globalization of environmental issues, then others potentially lose when environmental problems are constructed so broadly. Battles over the construction of environmental problems, wherein some groups argue for the expansion of an issue while others attempt to contain it, can be expected under these circumstances.

The Clayoquot Sound case is a vivid example of how issues can expand from fairly localized, contained issues to global ones. Environmental groups initially voiced their grievances in local terms, their main concerns being the effect of logging on Tofino's tourism economy and its drinking water supply. The local focus attracted a critical mass of citizens determined to preserve Meares Island, but the campaign did not extend to other parts of the sound nor did it question the province's forestry policies at large. In its early days, the conflict over Clayoquot Sound resembled previous wilderness campaigns in British Columbia. Looking back on these campaigns at the end of the 1980s, Jeremy Wilson (1990, 162) writes, "Different [environmental] groups throughout the province have simply nominated areas of special concern. . . . The logic of political mobilization confronting the movement has led it to concentrate on specific areas with strong emotional appeal rather than on wilderness preservation generally."

As Wilson (1990, 162) goes on to explain, this particular framing of the debate favored government and industry interests: "It obscures the fact that they [environmentalists] are asking for preservation of only a small fraction of the remaining wilderness and it renders them vulnerable to attacks depicting them as greedy and unreasonable." Preservationist groups were geographically scattered around the province and focused on their backyards rather than on the province as a whole. Consequently, they were partly responsible for the piecemeal approach to preservation in the 1980s. But the real culprits, according to Wilson, were the government and its allies in industry who actively contained the wilderness issue.

Activists in the Clayoquot Sound campaign fought this containment strategy and eventually won, due in part to their issue framing strategies. Their success points to a number of general observations about processes of issue definition and policy framing. The Clayoquot case confirms that framing is best viewed as a contested, negotiated, and "process-driven phenomenon" in which activists are "actively engaged in the production and maintenance of meaning for constituents, antagonists, and bystanders or observers" (Snow and Benford 1997, 458). The Clayoquot activists did not accept existing, rather narrow frames that characterized previous wilderness battles in British Columbia but sought to expand the scope of conflict by broadening the significance of the Clayoquot issue. To do so, they linked the Clayoquot Sound conflict to issues that resonated with audiences in British Columbia, in Canada, and eventually in Europe, the United States, and elsewhere around the world.

The environmentalists' strategy is an example of what Snow and Benford (1997) call "frame extension," or the attempt to reach audiences who are not immediately recognizable as potential constituents by appealing to their particular values and interests. The Clayoquot activists proved more adept at frame extension than their opponents as the environmental groups successfully modified their rhetorical appeals when the venue or audience changed. They took advantage of emerging scientific and global discourses whereas their opponents initially resisted altering their own message, failing to understand that such alterations were necessary when the conflict moved to new policy arenas. As Snow and Benford (1997) note, successful framing efforts require that a movement (or countermovement) stay abreast of changes in the larger culture and then transform their frames based on these developments.

The fact that provincial officials and industry representatives eventually shifted their discourse suggests a second theme related to issue definition strategies. The literature on issue definition and policy framing at times references "dominant" or "winning" frames, but it is not entirely clear how to determine when one frame has won out (even if only temporarily) over another. To evaluate the competition over issue definitions and policy frames, we must examine any transformations in discourse by the various competing groups. In the Clayoquot Sound case, provincial officials in particular adopted some of the language and rhetoric of environmental groups, even though they continued to disagree with these groups about the extent and nature of the logging problem. While these disagreements were by no means trivial, the government's acceptance of certain components of their opponents' arguments—for example, that the problems of native rights and forestry were connected, and that Canada's logging practices ought to conform to global standards—is notable. It suggests that environmentalists' understanding of the issue gradually filtered into the "slogans and symbols of the general culture," a key feature of winning frames, according to Zald (1996, 270–71).

The next chapter examines how environmental activists used the increased salience and attention to the conflict in Clayoquot Sound to forge alliances and involve a wider public in the conflict.

4

From Local to Global

Expanding Participation in Clayoquot Sound

The conflict in Clayoquot Sound began as a local issue concerning Mac-Millan Bloedel's plans to log Meares Island. The industry and government's response to the Meares conflict was not unlike their reaction to land-use conflicts prior to it: They made some concessions to environmentalists but offered these concessions "in the context of a strategy aimed at containing the movement" (J. Wilson 1990, 154). In the immediate wake of the Meares Island conflict, it looked as though the old patterns of containment might once again prevail. But by the end of 1993, when representatives from five Greenpeace offices around the world risked arrest in Clayoquot Sound, when three U.S. congressmen wrote a letter to Vice President Al Gore urging U.S. action to protect Clayoquot Sound, and when Japanese environmentalists started a boycott of B.C. forest products, it was clear that the government and industry had failed to contain the movement. How did participation in the conflict expand from a small group of highly committed local activists to an international ensemble of transnational environmental organizations, Hollywood celebrities, and European politicians?

This chapter examines the strategies and tactics used by environmental advocacy groups to expand participation in the Clayoquot Sound conflict. It also analyzes the strategies of their opponents, who initially tried to contain participation in the conflict and later competed with environmental groups for allies and sympathetic audiences. The discussion focuses largely on processes of alliance building and the activation of "reference publics." In focusing on building alliances and coalitions, I depart somewhat from recent research that assumes the presence of two or more competing "advocacy coalitions" in any given policy conflict.[1] Sabatier and Jenkins-Smith's (1993, 1999) Advocacy Coalition Framework claims that advocacy coalitions form around a shared set of normative commitments and causal perceptions about a policy and work together to translate these beliefs into public policy. The process of forming alliances and involving new actors in a coalition, however, is largely unexplained in the model.[2] To understand how conflicts expand, we must explain how coalitions form, including why organizations choose to join an alliance with other organizations (or not). To further this goal, this chapter explains the incentives on the parts of advocacy groups and organizations to engage in coordinated political activity.

I use Michael Lipsky's (1968, 1146) definition of allies as "third parties [who] are induced to join the conflict" and whose "value orientations . . . are sufficiently similar to those of the protesting group that concerted or coordinated action is possible." Allied groups try to activate "reference publics"—the constituents—of officials who are capable of delivering policy benefits. According to Lipsky, reference publics do not formally join alliances with advocacy groups as much as put pressure on public officials to respond to the protesters. A third category of actor, namely that of "reluctant participant," can be added to this list. These individuals and groups do not formally join alliances with the protesting group, nor do they use their influence to pressure decision makers to publicly respond to the protesting group. Rather, reluctant participants take action in response to an advocacy group's tactics in ways that the group can use as evidence of its strength and power.

The extraordinary success of B.C. forestry activists in building alliances, activating reference publics, and expanding the scope of participation more generally was due to three factors. First, the timing of the Clayoquot campaign made it easier to build alliances at home and abroad. As will be shown, the forest advocacy movement in British Columbia was well developed by the early 1990s but lacked a central focus: The Clayoquot campaign provided that focus. Internationally, transnational environmental groups sought a new angle on the rain forest issue in the face of declining issue salience; Clayoquot Sound's rain forests offered a new twist on the issue because of their location in an industrialized country. Second, the leaders of the Clayoquot campaign induced others to join the conflict by tolerating multiple strategies and tactics, allowing groups and individuals to participate in numerous ways and to see their contribution as unique and necessary. Finally, leaders in the movement also kept the conflict over Clayoquot alive by regularly "moving the goalpost"; the continuing controversy provided a compelling rationale for groups and individuals to participate and it kept the issue in the news media.

Strategies for Expanding and Containing Participation

The issue definition strategies discussed in the previous chapter were designed in part to mobilize, demobilize, empower, and disempower segments of the policy community and the general public. Environmental advocacy groups argued that the logging of Clayoquot Sound amounted to a global problem because of the rarity of the old-growth ecosystem and its importance in preserving global biodiversity. These arguments provided a means for attracting key international allies, expanding the size of the environmental coalition, and increasing the pressure on the B.C. government to preserve Clayoquot Sound. More generally, issue redefinition is a key factor in changing the number and range of policy participants in a policy conflict.

However, expanding or limiting political participation requires more than just shifting the public's perception of an issue. Put differently, issue redefinition is a necessary but not always sufficient means for expanding participation. Ideas can certainly inspire and incite people, but sustained action in support of these ideas requires resources, organization, and leadership, among other things. Some minimal level of resources is necessary in order to simply communicate with potential allies and sympathetic audiences. Moreover, advocacy groups must provide an organizational structure to channel the involvement of new actors. And finally, leadership is necessary to build a coalition, create an organizational structure, and take advantage of opportunities. In the absence of these factors, increased attention to an issue will be fleeting, widespread participation is unlikely, and policy change is rare. As A. Paul Pross (1993, 145–46) notes, "Unaggregated demand . . . tends to occur sporadically and on a piecemeal basis. Often it is sufficient to achieve or avert specific decisions . . . but it rarely influences public policy." To play the policy game, individuals and groups must "band together," "share costs," "maintain continuity as the process unfolds"—in other words, "organize."

In addition to building organizational capacity, advocacy groups who want to increase participation must often maintain or intensify the conflict surrounding a policy issue. These groups face a dilemma: While they struggle to achieve their stated policy goals, they must also dissuade the public from being reassured by symbolic victories. Apathy on the part of the public, due to the belief that the problem is being taken care of, can prevent further expansion in the scope of participation (Downs 1972). Competing advocacy groups, then, are not only fighting over the scope of participation but also over how the public perceives the conflict. Advocacy groups who want to limit the public's involvement will try to minimize the appearance of conflict. To keep the public from joining, the fight must be concealed and the public reassured that the grievances of challenging groups are being addressed. The "politics of consensus" involves keeping internal conflicts out of the public arena, minimizing intergroup conflict, and offering reassurances to attentive publics.

Another challenge facing advocacy groups who want to expand participation has less to do with the practical work involved in attracting supporters and more to do with justifying the involvement of new players. It is relatively easy to defend the participation of stakeholders, defined here as individuals and groups who are most immediately affected by a policy decision and groups who have historically played an important role in a policy arena. For example, citizens who live near national forests are seen as having a right to participate in decisions concerning the management of those forests, particularly if they are dependent on them for their water supply, recreational opportunities, or livelihoods. But when new players enter into a conflict, traditional participants often challenge their right to get involved. As a result, advocacy groups trying to expand the scope of participation must rhetorically justify the participation of new actors and allies.

The efforts of environmental advocacy groups to expand participation and the attempts by their opponents to contain it are examined in three different phases of the Clayoquot Sound conflict. The initial phase of the Clayoquot campaign lasted from 1979 (the beginning of the Meares Island campaign) until 1989, when the first government-sponsored Clayoquot Sound stakeholder group met. The second phase from 1989 until 1993, considered here as "Phase Two" of the domestic phase of the conflict, was characterized by the creation of regional alliances. The final period, from 1993 until at least 1999, can be considered the international phase of the conflict. While these dates do not mark clear boundaries, they serve as a way to highlight the dominant activities at different points during the protracted conflict.

The Domestic Campaign, Phase One: Building Local Support and Capacity

FOCS and their allies went public with their forest preservation campaign beginning in the early 1990s, but the campaign did not expand overnight. For at least a decade, environmentalists negotiated with the "usual suspects," working at the local level to try to slow down logging in Clayoquot Sound. The Clayoquot activists generally failed in their efforts during these early years, but they laid a foundation for the subsequent global movement to protect Clayoquot Sound. Valerie Langer of FOCS noted that they "did things in the right order" by building a strong local movement before taking their campaign to the global political stage and international marketplace (2000b). The early years of the campaign were important for a number of reasons: Local environmentalists made an important alliance with First Nations; they solidified the local movement and built their organizational capacity; and they made a name for themselves in the forest activist community. Each of these factors paved the way for subsequent increases in the scope of participation in the Clayoquot campaign.

FOCS was founded in 1979 and started out like most grassroots environmental groups—with a core group of committed activists, very few resources beyond the passion of its members, and no permanent office or funding source. But by 1984, FOCS had united with First Nations, the Chamber of Commerce, and local politicians, each of whom had a strong interest in limiting the logging on Meares Island. These early alliances were important for the development of the local environmental movement even though the coalition later broke down. In fact, the alliance between environmentalists and First Nations was rather short-lived, raising questions about the commonality of interests between the groups. Among other things, the fact that First Nations did not oppose all logging caused rifts between environmental groups and First Nations. A 1990 Nuu-chah-nulth brochure on the "land question" made it clear that if given jurisdiction over the land, the tribe would develop the resources: "New areas would be open for economic and resource development, and employment opportunities for Native people would be created which would increase our spending power in the overall economy" (Nuu-chah-nulth Tribal Council 1990). Environmental groups like FOCS, however, eventually opposed all commercial logging in the sound.

In subsequent years, local environmentalists and First Nations tended to be "allies of convenience," working together when it was strategically useful but without the same degree of allegiance or common purpose as during the Meares campaign (Mychajilowycz 1999; Mullin 1999). For example, after the provincial government's 1993 decision on Clayoquot Sound, native leaders regularly met with FOCS, Greenpeace, WCWC, and the Sierra Club of Western Canada in order to discuss strategies for opposing the decision. While First Nations generally did not approve of the confrontational tactics used by some of the environmental groups, they also did not agree with the 1993 Clayoquot Sound Land Use Decision.

Environmental leaders admit that they were largely responsible for the tension between FOCS and the First Nations: Valerie Langer, director of FOCS, said, "We [environmentalists] started out with a very romantic vision of what native was and what they were going to want. . . . We made a huge number of mistakes because we didn't actually do the work to figure out we had a very complicated relationship—we had overlapping goals in some areas and extremely divergent goals in other areas" (Langer 2000b). Mike Mullin also admitted culpability, emphasizing the importance of the initial coalition while acknowledging the subsequent fallout: "The Natives came to resent us, because to a certain extent we did manipulate and use them, in minor ways" (1999).

The break in alliance between FOCS and the First Nations was damaging but not crippling to the local environmental movement. Mullin noted, for example, that FOCS's early alliance with natives helped them attract attention to the campaign, particularly among urbanites in Victoria and Vancouver. The general public was largely unaware of the rocky relationship between the two groups—for much of the public, it was enough that aboriginal rights were connected to the Clayoquot conflict. The association helped local environmentalists recruit European supporters even after they had experienced some tensions with native groups. Maryjka Mychajilowycz claimed that the Europeans were "just crazy" about First Nations and suggested that European interest in the Clayoquot Sound conflict was due in part to native involvement in the issue (1999). In short, the early association between local environmentalists and First Nations helped to increase awareness and participation in the Clayoquot conflict despite the fact that the formal alliance between the groups was short-lived.

Another important development during this first phase of conflict was the expansion and solidification of a diverse local environmental movement. The organizational structure of FOCS, described by one of the founders as "anarchic," was extremely decentralized. Meetings were open to the public, decided by consensus, and egalitarian in that all input was taken seriously and virtually no decisions were imposed by a select minority of members (Mullin 1999).[3] This organizational structure proved advantageous because the group benefited from multiple points of view and from a sense of ownership over the organization by participants. This helped FOCS develop its "strategic capacity," which manifested itself later in the group's innovative tactics and effective seizing of political opportunities. Ganz, in his study of two labor groups, notes that organizational structures that allow for the generation of multiple points of view and ideas tend to produce better ideas. The more ideas generated, the greater likelihood that good ideas will be among them (Ganz 2000, 1013).

The group's openness to a number of different strategies and tactics also encouraged activists of all stripes to join. For Sergio Paone, a forest campaigner for FOCS, this eclecticism is what attracted him to the group. He was "proud of the fact that we are a small group that uses many different strategies and tactics" (Paone 1999). There was never an attempt to label some activists as less committed if they were not willing to risk arrest (Langer 2000b). FOCS also grew for the simple fact that the community could only support one environmental group; there was only one organizational home for self-identified environmentalists. This alone increased FOCS's capacity given that all available resources were channeled into one organization.

A number of blockades and other direct actions helped to raise the profile of FOCS and to increase awareness about Clayoquot Sound within the B.C. environmental community. The 1988 Sulpher Pass blockades lasted from June until September, capturing attention when at least thirty-five people were arrested during the summer, twenty of whom spent time in prison for violating an injunction against protesting. The Meares Island campaign also brought tourists to the area. According to Mullin, this was important to the campaign, because people who visited Clayoquot Sound went away "inspired and connected," and presumably more willing to fight for it. Mullin went so far as to say, "At every step in the process, all we really needed to do is say, look for yourself. The place has sold itself" (1999).

The ongoing conflict over land use in Clayoquot eventually led the Tofino Chamber of Commerce and Tofino District Council to ask the B.C. Environment and Land Use Committee for a quarter of a million dollars in funding to develop a strategy for sustainable development in Clayoquot Sound. In 1989, then premier Vander Zalm announced the formation of the Clayoquot Sound Sustainable Development Task Force. Thus began a series of task forces and government efforts to resolve the Clayoquot conflict. The second phase of the conflict is notable for these efforts and for the expansion of the Clayoquot campaign as environmentalists soon grew disillusioned with the task forces and the government's unwillingness to craft an acceptable solution to the conflict.

The Domestic Campaign, Phase Two: Building a Regional Coalition

In the early 1990s, local environmentalists made significant efforts to broaden participation in the Clayoquot controversy by reaching out to other B.C. environmental groups and to the Canadian public. The structure of the B.C. forest preservation movement—namely, its pluralistic, fragmented, and specialized nature—presented some challenges to building a coalition. However, the timing of the Clayoquot campaign, combined with the entrepreneurial skills of local environmental leaders, ultimately led to a loose coalition of groups who were committed to the Clayoquot issue. The next section examines the structure of the B.C. forest movement with an eye toward understanding the opportunities and challenges it presented to those trying to form domestic alliances around the Clayoquot issue.

The Structure of the B.C. Forest Movement

Even before the Clayoquot Sound campaign, British Columbia had the largest environmental movement in Canada and boasted a number of groups dedicated exclusively to wilderness preservation and forest advocacy.[4] Many of these organizations had formed around rather narrow campaigns to protect pristine valleys, such as the Valhalla Wilderness Society and the Save the Stein Coalition. The movement was fragmented both geographically and in terms of its campaigns, wherein wilderness groups focused on their backyards, challenging particular logging plans but not the province's overall approach to timber management and wilderness preservation (J. Wilson 1990). During the early 1990s when FOCS was trying to expand its campaign, other groups around British Columbia were focused on saving the Carmanah Valley, the Walbran Valley, and other special areas, thus fragmenting the movement. Steven Recchia (1998) makes a similar point about Canadian environmental groups generally, claiming that local, grassroots groups in the 1980s organized around single issues, to the detriment of building a broader national movement organized around general issues.

William Browne (1990) argues that as organizations create "issue niches" within a policy arena, they are less likely to cooperate or form alliances with others. Specialization creates less incentive for groups to join alliances because they do not necessarily see their interests as overlapping with others. Moreover, advocacy groups might feel that their survival is dependent on their ability to maintain autonomy from other groups. As Hojnacki (1997, 63) notes, "Because groups want at least some degree of autonomy, they will probably prefer to devote resources to efforts that enhance their own reputations rather than devoting substantial resources to efforts that lessen their organizations' distinctiveness." This is especially true for groups providing public goods and offering nonmaterial benefits to their members, inasmuch as such groups often have to compete with one another for public attention and membership (see Olson 1965). In short, interest groups compete not only with their opponents but also with their friends: "Such competition appears to be a day-to-day affair for most interest organizations," note Lowery and Gray (2004, 169).

Joe Foy of WCWC echoed some of these concerns when he explained why his group is reluctant to enter into alliances with others: "Because we can become too tightly bound, instead of allowing the individual groups to do what they are best at. Oftentimes, it is like a three-legged race—you can't go as fast and as far because you are too concerned with what others are doing. . . . Another issue is that you end up with spokespeople who are talking for our members, and it may not be what we would say" (Foy 2000).

Ken Wu also expressed misgivings about joining alliances based on WCWC's desire to remain independent and distinct. WCWC does not form coalitions on general issues like forest preservation in British Columbia, he explained, because often "you end up taking the position of lowest common denominator, which is the weakest position. There are other groups out there who like to piggyback on the reputation or resources of the larger groups" (Wu 2000). Other environmental leaders noted that joining alliances imposes additional tasks on nonprofit groups where the staff is already overworked. As Ian Gill of Ecotrust Canada explained, "As we matured organizationally, we found that we did not have the time to sit in on endless strategy sessions, talking about the same things" (Gill 2000).

Individual organizations within the B.C. forest movement embraced a wide array of political strategies and tactics; this characteristic of the movement might also have thwarted efforts to build coalitions. Such diversity in tactics and overall approaches can easily cause tensions within a coalition because different members have conflicting ideas about the most effective route to change. Some groups might be morally opposed to radical tactics like road blockades while the more radical groups could accuse the others of being too conservative or conciliatory. As noted in table 4.1, the environmental organizations involved in the preservation of Clayoquot Sound embraced rather different strategies. WCWC relied largely on public outreach and education, circulating dramatic images of forests and clear-cuts to their members in hopes that constituent outrage would lead to wilderness set-asides. The Clayoquot Biosphere Project conducted scientific research and made intellectual arguments for wilderness preservation rather than emotional appeals. Ecotrust Canada had a different focus altogether—they worked in native communities in an effort to develop sustainable local economies. And then there were highly eclectic groups like FOCS who spearheaded road blockades on the one hand and sent representatives to stakeholder meetings with industry and government officials on the other.

Interestingly, though, the eclectic and independent nature of the B.C. forest groups proved an asset as the Clayoquot conflict intensified. Far from causing problems, the plurality of the movement was one of its greatest

TABLE 4.1   B.C. Environmental Organizations Involved in the Clayoquot
Campaign, 1989–93

Organization	Location	Primary strategy	Level of involvement[a]
Friends of Clayoquot Sound	Tofino, B.C.	Eclectic: nonviolent direct action, education, grassroots lobbying	Very high
Western Canada Wilderness Committee	Vancouver, B.C.	Education, citizen lobbying, did not condone illegal acts	High
Sierra Club of Western Canada	Victoria, B.C.	Education, outreach, government lobbying	Moderate
Valhalla Society	Slocan Valley, B.C.	Research, public outreach	Low to moderate
Clayoquot Biosphere Project	Tofino, B.C.	Scientific research	Low

Sources: Compiled by the author based on interview data, organizational materials, and media reports.

[a]The level of involvement captures the extent to which the preservation of Clayoquot Sound was the primary focus of the group in addition to the visibility of the group's involvement. This was assessed based on interviews with key activists who were asked about their own and others' level of involvement and by examining media stories during this time period.

strengths, according to the activists interviewed for this study. Valerie Langer noted that many of their allies—such as WCWC, the Sierra Club of Western Canada, and the NRDC—did not participate in the blockades but that this strengthened the movement because "the different skills, the different tactics that groups are willing to work with is extremely useful" (2000b). Similarly, Ian Gill recognized that his work with Ecotrust Canada would not have been possible if FOCS and others had not "woken up industry with their radical tactics" (2000).[5] Social movement scholars call this the "radical flank" effect, whereby the presence of social movement organizations willing to embrace radical tactics like violence and civil disobedience can provide legitimacy to more moderate groups (see, for example, Gamson 1975).

Social movement scholars also attest to the benefits of having a diverse set of organizations that embrace a variety of tactics. McCarthy and Zald (2002, 553) call this the "supply side" argument: "The more SMOs [social movement organizations] there are and the more diverse the mix of organizational forms, the greater the rate at which the SMOs of a movement will be able to mobilize adherents. . . . In addition, the more diverse a movement is in the tactics and goals that animate its SMOs the greater the rate at which adherents will be mobilized."

In short, diversity within a coalition can be an asset rather than a problem. Tolerance for diversity allows groups to maintain autonomy within a coalition. Organizations that might be reluctant to join an alliance because they fear a loss of independence are reassured that they can maintain a strategic niche for themselves. More importantly perhaps, diversity helps individual organizations see their role in the alliance and their usefulness to the coalition. If all groups excel at lobbying, then there is little reason for yet another lobbying group to join a coalition. However, a direct action or public education group has an incentive to join because they can carry on the fight in different battlefields and policy arenas. Greenpeace International admittedly delayed their own entry into the Clayoquot conflict because "FOCS was doing the blockades, WCWC was doing trail building and trying to build up local support, and the First Nations were helping by lobbying government. . . . We did a lot of brainstorming regarding what we could do, how we could play to our strengths" (Stark 2000). Greenpeace eventually found their niche in the Clayoquot campaign, but the group's interest in defining a specific role for itself in the campaign suggests that an advocacy group's decision about whether to join an alliance is contextual. That is, its decision depends in part on the organizational universe around it and what roles are already being occupied within the coalition. This is especially likely if one of the goals is to expand the scope of conflict into different arenas and broaden participation to a more diverse set of actors.

The tremendous tolerance for diversity within the environmental community also helped the Clayoquot coalition maintain a strong and unified presence in the face of increasing opposition from industry and the B.C. government. The Clayoquot coalition consciously kept any internal disagreements out of the public eye. For example, when Greenpeace, WCWC, Sierra Club of British Columbia, and NRDC negotiated a memorandum of understanding with MacMillan Bloedel and First Nations in the late 1990s, FOCS (who opposed the memorandum) did not criticize its allies as much as stand aside and explain its reasons for not signing the agreement. As Mike Mullin explained: "We did not want a public split between the environmentalists. I am not going to stand up and say that Greenpeace is bad. Personally, I think what Greenpeace and Sierra Club did was outrageous because they signed the MOU [Memorandum of Understanding] without any kind of membership dialogue. . . . They have betrayed their memberships. But I am not going to tell that to the media" (Mullin 1999). By 1999, when the memorandum was signed, these groups had been working with one another for at least six years. Still to be fully explained, however, is how and why B.C. environmental groups coalesced around the Clayoquot campaign in the early 1990s.

Providing a Focus for Activism: Coalescing around Clayoquot

In the early 1990s, the B.C. forest movement's attention gradually converged on Clayoquot Sound, and by the summer of 1993 when the mass protests began, Clayoquot was *the* forest campaign in Canada. There are a number of factors that help to explain the increasing attention to Clayoquot Sound. First, as Langer put it, "We were at the right place at the right time" (2000b). As pointed out in chapter 3, Clayoquot environmentalists took advantage of the public attention to and expectations generated by Canada's commitment to the 1992 UN Convention on Biological Diversity. Earlier campaigns to protect pristine valleys did not benefit from this heightened sense of urgency and attention to biodiversity. Ken Wu also noted that by the early 1990s the issue of ancient rain forest destruction was salient for British Columbians, who had witnessed numerous battles for old-growth protection in South Moresby Island and elsewhere (2000). The public, in other words, was primed by the time that Clayoquot activists expanded their campaign to the B.C. public and later to the international community.

A second reason why attention turned to Clayoquot was the unusual amount of government effort that was directed at resolving the conflict, evidenced by the seemingly endless Clayoquot task forces—new task forces formed right on the heels of failed ones. As a result, there was some degree of "watching and waiting" within the B.C. forest movement, as Clayoquot became the test case for the government's ability (and willingness) to change its forest practices to accommodate ecological values. If a satisfactory solution could not be reached in Clayoquot Sound, then there was little hope for any other threatened wilderness areas. As Tamara Stark of Greenpeace Canada said, "I think Clayoquot became the icon of the forestry movement and a symbol of what was at stake elsewhere. If we couldn't do it in Clayoquot then it felt like we should just hang up our hats" (2000). In short, Clayoquot Sound came to represent the B.C. forest community's larger hopes and fears about the future of sustainable forestry and wilderness preservation in the province.

A third reason for the increasing public attention to Clayoquot Sound was the lack of resolution of the conflict. FOCS's increasing demands led to almost constant conflict: Once the group met its goals, the leaders would regroup and decide what to ask for next. Put differently, the Clayoquot coalition continued to raise the bar in Clayoquot. They began with the goal of simply reducing the timber harvest. Once that was accomplished, they demanded that the size of clear-cuts be limited to one hectare, and then they finally called for an end to all commercial harvest (Stanbury and Vertinsky 1997). As Valerie Langer admitted, "We were always moving our goal posts, which can lead to criticisms" (Langer 2000a). The ongoing conflict, though, provided a greater incentive for others to join the fight. As environmentalists' demands escalated, there was a growing sense that Clayoquot was the place to "shut down the industrial machine" (Gill 2000).

Baumgartner and Jones (1993, 190) note that it is often difficult for groups to generate mobilization around an issue, but "with each success comes a greater likelihood of further success . . . as the positive feedback mechanisms begin to enter operation." As attention to an issue grows, a larger audience is drawn to the fight, generating resources for further expansion in the scope of participation. "Political bandwagons build up power, as politicians and interest group leaders become active in a new cause as it gains popularity" (Baumgartner and Jones 1993, 17). Moreover, the battle becomes more interesting, significant, and "winnable" as participation increases. Simply put, there is an excitement in being part of something "big." In addition, individuals have a more compelling reason to join because success seems more likely as the number of participants in the movement increases (Klandermans 1984).

Ken Wu of WCWC confirmed that both of these dynamics were at work in his own decision to join the Clayoquot conflict. In the early 1990s, Woo was a member of a University of Victoria group that was campaigning to preserve the Walbran Valley (an area much closer to Victoria than Clayoquot Sound). In 1993, he abandoned the Walbran campaign in order to work on Clayoquot:

> I was really wrapped up in the Walbran in 1991 and 1992—that was my focus. Then, in 1993 I heard more stirrings about Clayoquot Sound, and at the time I thought, well, there are a lot of temperate rainforests but I have to focus, and the Walbran is where it is at. Then I saw more and more coverage [of Clayoquot] and more people gathering for civil disobedience workshops and eventually I went to one in May 1993. About one hundred people were at the training. *I got caught up in the upswell, because you want to be a part of something big.* Let's see—we had thirty people working on the Walbran and three hundred working on Clayoquot Sound. . . . I got caught up in the excitement (Wu 2000; emphasis added).

Wu recognized that Clayoquot provided a common focus for a forest activist community that was well developed but rather scattered and isolated in its campaigns. Moreover, to the extent that Wu's experience was shared by other activists, the Clayoquot campaign seems to have captured some resources from other forest campaigns around the province as it grew in popularity.[6] This was particularly the case during the summer of 1993 when thousands of citizens converged in Clayoquot Sound during the "summer of protest."

The Clayoquot Compromise and the Politics of Protest

In the first three months of 1993, B.C. forest activists prepared for Premier Harcourt's impending announcement on the fate of Clayoquot Sound. They used the upcoming event as a way to educate the public about the conflict, to increase pressure on the provincial government to come up with an acceptable forest management plan, and to prepare their opponents and the public for mass protests if the decision was unfavorable. One of the highlights during the months leading up to the Clayoquot Sound decision was a rally at the B.C. provincial legislature, wherein more than four hundred protesters broke into the building and chanted slogans so loudly that the throne speech was delayed. The timing of the protest, coming less than a month before the government promised to announce its decision, was deliberate. "The protest really put it [Clayoquot Sound] on the map" said one of the organizers, Paul George (2000).

On April 13 the government announced the Clayoquot Sound Land Use Decision, which protected one-third of the sound and allowed logging in the other two-thirds. The disappointing decision led FOCS and other leaders in the movement to shift their strategy by fully engaging in the "politics of protest." As shown in table 4.2, activists had been blocking logging roads and risking arrest in the sound since 1984. But these protests typically attracted a small population of committed activists who were at the core of the movement. The idea behind the 1993 summer protests was to broaden participation by attracting individuals who were sympathetic to the cause but who had not yet participated in any significant way.

The mass blockades were a bigger success than even Valerie Langer had anticipated: Earlier in the year she told a reporter that they were hoping to attract one thousand sympathizers. By the end of the summer twelve times that many people had been to Peace Camp in Clayoquot Sound, and close to nine hundred citizens were arrested in the blockades. The scale of the protests and extent of civil disobedience were unprecedented in Canadian history. The

TABLE 4.2   Logging Blockades in Clayoquot Sound, 1984–93

Date(s)	Location	Arrests and other notable aspects of blockade
Nov. 1984–Mar. 1985	Meares Island	First logging blockade in Canadian history; native and nonnative participants
June 1988–Sept. 1989	Sulpher Pass	35 arrests
Sept. 1991	Bulson River Road	6 arrests
July 5, 1993	Kennedy River Bridge	First day of mass blockades
July 1993	Kennedy River Bridge	Blockades on almost a daily basis, resulting in at least 100 arrests including the arrests of MP Svend Robinson, the "Clayoquot grandmothers," and two young boys
Aug. 9, 1993	Kennedy River Bridge	More than 1,000 join blockade; 309 arrests
Aug. 18, 1993	Kennedy River Bridge	"Youth Voices for Our Future" blockade; 18 young people arrested
Aug. 19, 1993	Kennedy River Bridge	"Senior's Day"; 12 elderly citizens arrested
Sept. 7, 1993	Kennedy River Bridge	242 arrests
Nov. 9, 1993	Kennedy River Bridge	Greenpeace International blockades; 7 international protesters arrested
Nov. 10, 1993	Kennedy River Bridge	19 arrests, including Newfoundland fishermen

Source: Compiled from the Clayoquot Sound chronology, part of the Clayoquot Sound archive project at the University of Victoria. To view the entire chronology and references to the original sources, see the Clayoquot Sound archive at www.cous.uvic.ca/clayoquot.chronolo.htm.

blockades attracted a wide array of Canadian citizens, international activists, and celebrities from the United States, Europe, and Australia. Some of the protesters went back to Toronto and other Canadian cities to form "sister" Clayoquot organizations; these groups later organized direct actions in eastern Canadian cities, further expanding the conflict.[7] In short, the blockades expanded the scope of participation and increased the level of organization both nationally and internationally.

The success of the blockades is largely attributable to the entrepreneurial skills of Valerie Langer, Tzeporah Berman, and other leaders of the movement. FOCS made a conscious decision to keep the protests "on the ground" and nonviolent. That is, they did not encourage tactics, such as tree sitting, that are associated with more radical groups like Earth First! Such actions, they thought, might alienate the average Canadian and would certainly limit participation; not everyone would be willing to perform these more danger- ous and physically demanding activities. As Ken Wu explained,

> Valerie Langer understood how to structure a movement for maximum involvement by the public. She deliberately stayed away from the hard core tactics like sitting in trees or setting up tripods and instead encour- aged people to lock arms, *creating a very accessible form of protest* where people just stood or sat on the road. . . . It wasn't just a physical barrier but a conceptual one as well—it does not seem as radical to stand on a road. . . . *It made the protests not too far out of the comfort zone of the aver- age Canadian* (Wu 2000; emphases added).

One of the goals of the blockades was to show the strength of the movement by bringing in large numbers of people so their opponents could not claim (as they had in the past) that a "small but vocal minority" wanted to halt logging in the sound. But an equally important goal was to change the face of the Clayoquot campaign by involving different types of people. Put dif- ferently, organizers were trying to transform the image of the movement so that the media and their opponents could not easily dismiss or delegitimize it. As it turned out, the 1993 protests did attract the "usual suspects"—the young "hippy crowd" as Langer put it—but it also brought in a broader range of people in terms of age, experience, and socioeconomic status. Ken Wu noticed the change in the crowd, guessing that about 70 percent of the people were not your "typical" protester (2000). Langer claims the protests received positive press, even from the conservative papers, because "people from all walks of life" were there and "put their liberty on the line" (2000b).

The 1993 Clayoquot protests attracted an unprecedented level of media attention. As shown in figure 4.1, the aggregate number of stories concerning the Clayoquot Sound conflict increased dramatically from 16 stories in 1992 to 690 stories in 1993. Most of the coverage was from the *Vancouver Sun*, but national and regional newspapers such as the *Toronto Star* and the *Ottawa Citizen* also carried stories on the protests, while the national newsmagazine *MacLean's* ran an eight-page cover story on the Clayoquot controversy. Figure 4.2 indicates that the April 13 Clayoquot Sound Land Use Decision prompted an increase in coverage, but the real growth in media stories was due to the demonstrations and protests during the summer months.

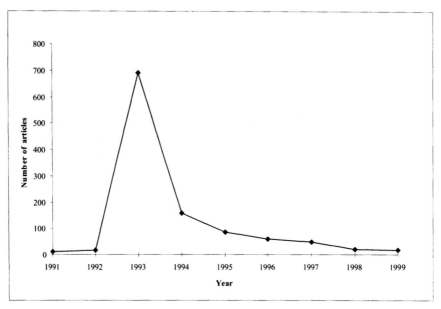

FIGURE 4.1   Annual Coverage of Clayoquot Sound in Canadian Newspapers, 1991–99

Source: Compiled by the author from LexisNexis Academic Universe.

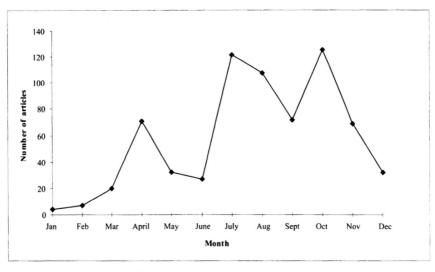

FIGURE 4.2   Coverage of Clayoquot Sound Events, 1993

Source: Compiled by the author from LexisNexis Academic Universe.

Some individual protesters attracted a disproportionate amount of media attention. For example, member of Parliament Svend Robinson generated numerous stories when he participated on the first day of protests. Not only was he a national political figure, but he was also a member of Harcourt's own political party, the NDP. The intraparty conflict generated by Robinson's public protests helped to expand the scope of conflict as it tapped into partisan themes and ongoing rivalries between the federal and provincial governments in Canada. Robert Kennedy Jr.'s visit to Clayoquot Sound during the blockades also attracted considerable media attention and was welcomed by both native leaders and environmentalists. Kennedy's involvement was a sign that the campaign was quickly becoming something of a global cause célèbre.

One of the goals of advocacy groups who engage in protest is to increase their public exposure through the media (Lipsky 1968, 1144). Protest leaders are trying to activate segments of the public, who will then put pressure on officials to grant the protesters' demands. If the citizens are not aware of the movement or its goals, then they cannot effectively lobby government officials. Advocacy groups, in other words, must activate a bystander public that may be geographically far removed from the site of the conflict and politically unaware of the specific issues at stake. As McCarthy and Zald (2002, 538) put it, "In modern societies, which are usually large with dispersed communities, the conditions and injustices that SMs [social movements] wish to rectify are not directly experienced or perceived by bystanders." The media are used to amplify the message of activists and reach these bystanders. In the absence of media coverage, demonstrations may build solidarity and cohesion among activists, but they do not alert third parties to the power of the movement and the content of its demands.

Phase Three: The Globalization of Clayoquot Sound

Even during the domestic phase of the Clayoquot conflict, B.C. forest activists were courting European environmental groups and European politicians as potential allies. However, international participation (like domestic participation) broadened and intensified in 1993; in less than a year, the battle to preserve Clayoquot Sound had largely moved to the international arena. There were two main targets in this phase of the campaign: First, leaders in the effort to preserve Clayoquot Sound recruited international nongovernmental organizations (INGOs), and second, they (along with the newly recruited INGOs) targeted consumers of B.C. forest products.[8] To understand how and why these actors entered the conflict, we must consider both the strategies of domestic leaders of the movement as they courted transnational and international actors and the incentives of the INGOs themselves as they considered whether to put their energy and resources into the campaign.

Recruiting Transnational and International Environmental Organizations

At this point, the incentives of Clayoquot activists to "go global" should be well understood. Faced with a seemingly intransigent provincial government and industry, Clayoquot activists sought to involve more players whose participation would put pressure on the B.C. government to change forest policy and induce the forest industry to change its logging practices, independent of official policy. In March 1993, Valerie Langer and photographer Garth Lenz made their first trip to England and Germany, armed with images of Clayoquot Sound's wildlife and rain forests. Their intent was to spark the interest of European environmental organizations, and to a lesser extent, the general public. Langer and Lenz's tour, hosted by the Women's Environment Network in the United Kingdom, included visits with some of the larger European Union environmental groups, including World Wildlife Fund, Friends of the Earth, and Greenpeace Germany. FOCS subsequently asked Greenpeace International for its help in pursuing a full-fledged international public relations and markets campaign.[9]

The advantages of an alliance with Greenpeace International are obvious from the point of view of FOCS and the other B.C. environmental groups: Greenpeace International would bring substantial material resources to the campaign, as well as name recognition, international clout, and political connections.[10] Put differently, Greenpeace's involvement promised to increase the scope of the conflict and link the local campaign with a global audience (see Princen and Finger 1994). But what did Greenpeace International have to gain from the alliance? The scholarship on transnational environmental networks sometimes neglects to ask how international organizations choose—out of the innumerable local, regional, and national environmental conflicts going on at any given time—their specific campaigns and priorities.

One way of conceptualizing the relationship between grassroots or domestic nongovernmental groups (NGOs) and INGOs is to look at it as a mutual exchange relationship. International NGOs bring material resources, name recognition, and media attention to local or domestic environmental movements, not to mention access to a wider audience (Princen and Finger 1994). But domestic NGOs also offer benefits to transnational and international organizations. Local groups provide legitimacy to transnational environmental organizations who might be accused of inappropriately interfering in the domestic affairs of any particular country. An alliance with a domestic environmental organization is one means of countering or mitigating such criticisms.

In the Clayoquot Sound case, international environmental groups like Greenpeace International, the Rainforest Action Network, Conservation International, and the National Resources Defense Council had several compelling reasons for joining the Clayoquot conflict. First, the substantive nature of the issue proved attractive to these groups. The fact that Clayoquot Sound addressed temperate, as opposed to tropical, rain forests lent novelty to the campaign and provided an opportunity for INGOs to raise their profiles by pursuing a new angle on an existing problem (namely, global forest destruction). Greenpeace saw that they could fill a niche in the international forest movement, one crowded with prominent INGOs who were focused almost exclusively on tropical rain forests. The Rainforest Action Network, for its part, would use the conflict over Clayoquot Sound to keep the issue of rain forests on the international agenda at a time when tropical rain forest destruction was losing some momentum as an issue (Stanbury and Vertinsky 1997).

Another important feature of Clayoquot Sound was that it was located in a wealthy, northern industrialized country. This fact alone made the Clayoquot campaign attractive because it helped INGOs like Rainforest Action Network look more "balanced" and less biased in their forest campaigns (see Stanbury and Vertinsky 1997, 21). Langer explained the attraction of Clayoquot to INGOs this way: "One of the problems campaigning on forest issues in the tropics is that you come up against poverty and feelings of guilt—'How can you rich western nations tell us that we can't log our forests after you have logged all of your own?' That is very difficult to overcome. And then *all of a sudden there was a rainforest issue that the public could mobilize around that would keep ancient rainforests in the public psyche, but it was in a rich country"* (Langer 2000b; emphasis added).

Finally, the timing of the international campaign made it easier to recruit U.S.-based environmental organizations. By 1993, the conflict over old-growth forests in the Pacific Northwest had reached a temporary resolution after U.S. environmental groups successfully used the courts to shut down much of the logging in the states of Washington and Oregon. Clayoquot Sound, and later the Great Bear Rainforest (in northern British Columbia), provided these groups with a new focus and campaign, something they needed in order to retain their members and maintain their organizations more generally (Stanbury and Vertinsky 1997).

In short, joining the Clayoquot Sound campaign offered many strategic benefits to existing international and transnational environmental groups.[11]

What is notable about the Clayoquot campaign, however, is that it also resulted in the formation of new transnational groups and coalitions. The Clayoquot conflict suggests that particular campaigns can be the breeding ground for the development of new advocacy networks. Table 4.3 lists the transnational organizations and coalitions that were founded as a result of, or in response to, the Clayoquot campaign and that now constitute its organizational legacy.[12]

The coalitions listed in table 4.3 developed a sophisticated markets campaign, designed to put economic pressure on MacMillan Bloedel by convincing industrial consumers of MacMillan Bloedel's pulp and wood products to cancel their contracts with the company. The coalition attempted to shame large companies like Scott Paper, Pacific Bell, and the *New York Times* by advertising that old-growth forests were being destroyed to make tissue paper, phone books, and newspapers. The threat of a boycott prompted Scott, United Kingdom, to cancel their contract with MacMillan Bloedel in February 1994 and Kimberly-Clark (maker of Kleenex in the United Kingdom) to do the same soon after. In Germany, several publishers including *Der Spiegel* magazine signed a letter disavowing clear-cutting as a method of logging and pledged to buy paper from non-clear-cut forests (Stanbury and Vertinsky

TABLE 4.3 Clayoquot-Inspired Environmental Organizations and Alliances

Name of organization or coalition	Affiliated groups	Comments
Forest Action Network	Branches in United Kingdom, Switzerland, California	Began as a B.C. environmental group that subsequently opened offices abroad.
Ecotrust Canada	Conservation International; Ecotrust (Oregon)	Opened in order to expand campaigns into British Columbia; Clayoquot became a major (but not exclusive) focus.
Clayoquot Rainforest Coalition, Coastal Rainforest Coalition	Rainforest Action Network, Greenpeace, NRDC, Coalition for Forests, Pacific Environment & Resource Center, FOCS	Later renamed the Coastal Rainforest Coalition. Currently works on variety of coastal forest campaigns.

Source: Compiled by the author from interviews, internal organizational documents, and press releases.

1997). An analysis of why Clayoquot activists switched from political venues to economic ones is presented in the next chapter. The following section considers how environmental activists secured the cooperation of several key customers of British Columbia's forest products.

Targeting Consumers and Customers

Typically, political participation is conceptualized as involving a public act, such as when protesters block roads or interest groups run advertisements in newspapers about an issue or campaign. For groups who want to expand participation, such public acts and pronouncements are particularly important for demonstrating unity and strength to their opponents. They want to show, in other words, that more people are on their side. This is particularly true for politically marginalized groups, who try to indirectly influence elites by expressing their increased political strength, support, and resources (see Lipsky 1968; McAdam 1982; Piven and Cloward 1979).

The goal of environmental leaders in the Clayoquot markets campaign was somewhat different from their previous efforts to expand the scope of participation. While they sought the participation of corporations doing business with MacMillan Bloedel, they did not expect these companies to become allies in any way, or to become surrogate spokespeople for the preservation of Clayoquot Sound. The most important goal was to simply get these corporations to cancel their contract with MacMillan Bloedel so that the company would feel economic pressure to stop logging in Clayoquot. Langer explains the difference in tactics this way: "We often think of getting people *on side* when what we need is people *in sync*. You don't have to make friends with everyone in order to build a campaign—some organizations and politicians need to be on your side, but in fact you can have people who hate you who are still in sync because they do not want your campaign targeted at them. They may not agree but they might change" (Langer 2000a).

One type of alliance formation is based on positive inducements, such as when FOCS courted international environmental groups who stood to gain from the alliance. Another kind of participation is based on negative inducements or threats. Some actors reluctantly participate in a conflict because they want to avoid something, such as negative publicity and consumer boycotts. The best possible scenario for activists is to get such participants to publicly support the protester's goals, such as when Greenpeace asked the Axel Springer publishing house (in Germany) to sign a declaration disavowing MacMillan Bloedel's destructive logging practices. But such statements are not necessary, as Langer explains:

> The *New York Times* did not want to cancel their contract with MB [MacMillan Bloedel] because they had had a long-standing purchasing relationship with them, and we wanted them to make a public announcement about their decision to cancel the contract. But they said [they cancelled the MacMillan Bloedel contract] for a different reason, not related to environmental concerns, even though it was obvious that the protests had had an effect. They did not "go public" but that was okay because they still made the decision that we wanted them to make in order to pressure MB on the inside (Langer 2000b).

Of course, threats are only effective to the extent that the threatened action (in this case, a boycott) is likely to occur. In this case, Greenpeace had a history of organizing successful boycotts and its participation was therefore critical to the markets campaign; a boycott threat by FOCS (even if they had had the time and resources to organize one) would not carry nearly as much weight.

The markets campaign raised alarm in the forest industry and among B.C. politicians, who were afraid it might expand to cover all B.C. forest products and severely affect the provincial economy. The industry and the B.C. government spent millions of dollars in Europe countering Greenpeace's claims and urging European companies to continue to buy B.C. forest products. Indeed, for several years prior to the globalization of the Clayoquot campaign the provincial government and the forest products industry had been attempting to limit and manage the scope of conflict around Clayoquot Sound. It is to their efforts that we now turn.

Oppositional Strategies for Controlling Conflict and Limiting Participation

The antilogging momentum created in the early 1990s by Clayoquot activists did not go unnoticed or unmet by the provincial government, MacMillan Bloedel, and timber workers. Taken together, they used a variety of tactics to contain the conflict, ranging from protests at the B.C. legislature by loggers and unions to sophisticated public relations campaigns by MacMillan Bloedel. These tactics can be grouped into three overarching strategies. First, the provincial government attempted to manage and channel participation by establishing multistakeholder task forces that limited the role of the public. When these largely failed to contain participation in the conflict, industry, loggers, and the provincial government questioned the right of "outside" individuals and groups to participate. Finally, they made alliances of their own and lobbied foreign governments in an effort to weaken the alliances and support base of environmentalists. Each of these counterstrategies will be examined briefly, along with the reactions of the Clayoquot coalition.

Channeling and Containing Participation

One of the provincial government's first strategies for containing the Clayoquot Sound conflict was to organize a series of sustainable development task forces. These consensus-based stakeholder groups were seen as an innovative tool for improving public participation in forest planning. As noted in chapter 3, the provincial government's proximate goal in creating these task forces was to resolve the conflict in Clayoquot Sound; its longer-term goal was to increase the legitimacy of the government more generally by directly involving the public in land-use decisions. Under the best scenario, the task forces would help change the forest planning process from a top-down and insular decision-making process toward a more open and representative one. It will be argued here, though, that the task forces fell short of this lofty goal and actually worked to contain participation.

To understand how the task forces contained participation, we must consider the political context in which they developed, the structure of the task forces, and actual participation patterns. Prior to and during the time that the task forces met, forest activists in British Columbia had been staging protests and blockades and otherwise engaging in very public forms of political participation. Membership in the task forces, on the other hand, was restricted to stakeholder representatives. More specifically, participation was sector-based—each seat on the task force was occupied by a major stakeholder (such as tourism, the forest products industry, native groups, loggers' unions) or a government group (Burrows 2001). On the surface, these groups represented the main stakeholders with a stated or specific interest in the Clayoquot issue, but in practice it limited the involvement of the public at large and nonaffiliated (unorganized) individuals who might have a general interest in the outcome.

The question of who was invited to sit on the task forces was a point of contention for some forest activists. Maryjka Mychajilowycz of FOCS complained that the 1989 Clayoquot Sound Sustainable Development Task Force was "taken away from the locals" when then premier Vander Zalm brought in people from Port Alberni and Ucluelet, which are timber-dependent towns near Clayoquot Sound. "They broadened the geographical scope of Clayoquot Sound to include the interests that traditionally have logged it," said

Mychajilowycz (1999). Others took a different tact by arguing that the boundaries of Clayoquot Sound should be enlarged so that people from urban areas could participate. As one citizen said during a public workshop held by the Clayoquot Sound Sustainable Development Strategy Steering Committee, "If stakeholders from outside of Clayoquot Sound are to be included, then also the thousands of people living in Vancouver, Victoria, and elsewhere should also have been considered. Because many, many people come here for their holidays and find this a special place and love it, and they don't have a voice in this process" (quoted in Clayoquot Sound Sustainable Development Strategy 1992, 4). In time, groups and individuals from around the globe claimed a stake in Clayoquot Sound. A multistakeholder process, no matter how inclusive, could not possibly accommodate this widespread and geographically scattered community of interest.

The task forces also constrained the role of those who had the privilege of sitting at the table, given that the agenda in many cases was predetermined. For example, while the Clayoquot Sound Sustainable Development Strategy Steering Committee was negotiating a long-term land-use plan for the sound, a panel of officials from the Ministry of Forests and Ministry of Environment allowed logging in Bulson Creek, a watershed that environmentalists claimed was pristine and therefore ought to be preserved. The environmental representatives were outraged that such decisions had been made without their input and subsequently resigned from the steering committee over the issue. As Hoberg (1996, 276) notes, the legitimacy of the task force was tainted thereafter: "Once the official environmental representatives left, the committee lost its most forceful and legitimate advocates of the preservationist position."

In short, the multistakeholder task forces were primarily a way for the provincial government to manage the conflict, rather than allow for full and widespread participation. Douglas Amy (1987) makes a similar point when evaluating the efforts by the U.S. government to mediate disputes among stakeholders in environmental conflicts: "[Conflict management] should not be confused with requirement for public participation. The key word is *management*. In cases where public groups are fighting with the Federal government, better conflict management means better control over the participation process" (Amy 1987, 151–52). The B.C. government tried to use the task forces to channel participation into less adversarial arenas. They also attempted to delegitimize more public forms of participation, such as protest activity, by referencing the task forces. Premier Harcourt, for example, praised the CORE process by saying, "We have provided a way for those [environmental] demands to be heard in an open, public process and we encouraged all interested groups to come to the negotiating table, voice their concerns and be part of the solution" (quoted in Bohn 1993a, B2). Harcourt suggests that the system was open and responsive to environmentalists: The protests, then, must be irrational acts, rather than rational responses to a closed and limited decision-making process.

In addition to questioning the rationality of the protests, opponents raised questions about the character of the Clayoquot protesters. The next section examines these efforts and similar tactics that questioned the right of "outsiders" to participate in the Clayoquot conflict.

Characterization Contests in Clayoquot Sound

Cobb and Ross (1997) note that a common strategy for containing conflict is to discredit the groups and individuals who are promoting agenda or policy change. The intention behind these characterization contests is to destroy the credibility of an advocacy group so that the public neither takes its demands seriously nor enlists in the advocacy group's cause. These contests may involve questioning the right of particular individuals or groups to participate in a conflict, rather than questioning their character per se. The other side of characterization contests entails promoting or improving one's own image in order to secure public support, recruit allies, or simply build trust so that the public does not question the current policy status quo.

Loggers were some of the first groups to negatively characterize the Clayoquot environmental activists. They tried to dismiss their opponents by arguing that the Clayoquot environmentalists constituted only a "tiny minority of individuals—some of whom are not residents of the coast" (Share the Clayoquot Society 1989). After the mass protests, when it was clear that the opposition was not "tiny," loggers raised the familiar objection that the protesters were "cappuccino-sucking, concrete-condo dwelling, granola-eating city slickers" who had little knowledge of the issues in Clayoquot Sound (quoted in Lee 1994, A1). The protesters were also branded as criminals when they failed to abide by an injunction barring road blockades, then exposed as "welfare" recipients after a British Broadcasting television crew showed several Clayoquot arrestees collecting welfare checks after being released from jail.

While these character attacks on protesters were not uncommon, the attacks were increasingly directed at transnational groups and international actors who intervened in the Clayoquot Sound conflict. The provincial government, the timber industry, and loggers questioned whether such "outsiders" had a legitimate right—and enough knowledge—to participate in the conflict.[13] These charges were levied at some of the high profile individuals who visited Clayoquot Sound and later lobbied for its preservation. For example, when the Australian rock group Midnight Oil held a concert at Peace Camp in Clayoquot Sound, one Ucluelet resident responded this way: "It's really aggravating to us to have someone come over from Australia and form an opinion without visiting local people to hear the efforts we have made toward a compromise" (quoted in Lee 1993a, A1). Doug Pichette, a Ucluelet logger, criticized Robert Kennedy Jr.'s participation in the Clayoquot conflict based on both his outsider and elite status: "I've worked hard for forty-four years and now I've got to listen to an outsider who had life given to him on a silver platter tell me what's wrong with my economy and government. Who does he think he is?" (McNish 1993, A5).

Loggers and logger unions were not the only ones to fear or distrust the participation of transnational and international actors. The provincial government also charged transnational and international environmental groups with inappropriately meddling in the affairs of British Columbia, going so far as to call Greenpeace the "enemy of British Columbia and Canada." Premier Glen Clark made this charge when Greenpeace released a report titled "Broken Promises," which detailed the ongoing problems in British Columbia's forests. Tamara Stark of Greenpeace Canada recalls the incident: "We released the report in Canada but also internationally, because we happened to be at the United Nations at that time, and that is what prompted the comment— suggesting that anyone who goes outside of Canada and dares to criticize it is an enemy of the state—even though I was a Canadian" (Stark 2000).

The discourse of sovereignty was embedded in many of these remarks. Consider, for example, a statement by Interfor, another prominent logging company in Clayoquot Sound. The company wrote a letter to the *New York Times* after the newspaper ran an antilogging advertisement sponsored by U.S. environmental groups:

> The ad in your paper urges the American people to involve their federal government in this [the Clayoquot Sound] issue. Is it fair to ask *a distant and insufficiently informed public and government* to overturn all the work that the citizens of British Columbia and of Clayoquot Sound have done? I think not. *Our forest policies and practices are under the legal and moral jurisdiction of the people of British Columbia and rightfully so.* I sincerely hope that the American people and government realize that Canadians are a thinking people, capable of making their own decisions on environmental protection (Lowenberger 1993; emphases added).

Not only does Interfor directly appeal to norms of sovereignty, but it also implies that the Clayoquot forest planning process was extensive and inclusive—as such, there is no need for additional input from the American public.

The appeals to sovereignty were effective in some circles. One journalist suggested that Premier Harcourt's image in British Columbia improved after his 1994 European tour. Seen as "indecisive and lacking in passion back home," Harcourt's defense of B.C. forestry and counterattacks on Greenpeace appealed to the patriotic Canadian: "It helps that [Harcourt] has been able to . . . create an external enemy to rage against: those 'eco-imperialists' of the Greenpeace ilk who are going to suck the brains out of ordinary British Columbians and tell them how to think" (Sheppard 1994, A19). Ken Wu echoed these thoughts when he reflected on how Greenpeace International's entry into the campaign changed things: "It [Greenpeace's involvement] became leverage for the media and logging companies . . . they were able to play on the xenophobic, anti-foreigner card. . . . It was very well crafted so it really hurt Greenpeace and the environmental movement through public perception. If crafted right, it can resonate among a lot of people" (Wu 2000).

The expansion in the scope of conflict provided an opportunity for the B.C. government and the forest products industry to wage a countercampaign based on the norms of sovereignty. Despite globalization, appeals to sovereignty remain a powerful means of containing conflict and limiting (or at least questioning) the participation of international actors in the domestic affairs of other countries. The B.C. government and MacMillan Bloedel's appeals to sovereignty would have been more successful in the Clayoquot Sound case in the absence of extensive mobilization *within* British Columbia for the preservation of Clayoquot Sound. It was rather difficult to credibly argue that pressure was coming entirely, or even chiefly, from outside forces given that a local group, FOCS, had spearheaded the campaign.

The power of the sovereignty claim was also blunted by the fact that MacMillan Bloedel was a multinational corporation with offices in several countries and with customers across the globe. In fact, Clayoquot environmentalists questioned the very notion of outsiders and insiders in an era of economic globalization. Maryjka Mychajlowycz pointed out that global corporations have superseded national governments; "provincialism," she claimed, is a thing of the past when it comes to economics, as evidenced by the recent buyout of MacMillan Bloedel by a U.S. timber corporation (1999). Other activists argued that consumers—no matter where they live—have a democratic right to choose what they want to consume. Robert Kennedy Jr. used this defense when his organization, the NRDC, was criticized for having no roots in Canada. He argued that because the United States imports timber products from British Columbia, the U.S. consumer has a clear stake in the issue—and a responsibility to protect "one of the prettiest and wildest places on Earth" (quoted in McNish 1993, A1).

The timber industry and the B.C. government did not hold a monopoly on characterization contests. Environmentalists also attacked their opponents, creating a common enemy around which their supporters rallied. In particular, environmentalists turned the tables on their opponents after environmental protesters were called "criminals" during the 1993 mass arrests. Langer explains how they recast the timber industry as the "true" criminals: "We then started saying, who are the real criminals? We had this array of people [in the protests]—your father, your brother, your cousin, your grandmother—people were getting arrested who people could identify with, and so we started saying that obviously these people are not criminals. So who are the real criminals? So we started to [invite people to] think about *corporations as being nefarious, and being evil, the dark force.* And that is how we started to shift things" (Langer 2000b; emphasis added). The logging industry and the B.C. government were well aware of the mounting criticism and their increasingly poor public images; they spent millions of dollars trying to improve their reputation in Canada and abroad. Their goal was to neutralize potential opponents, undercut environmentalists' supporters, and attract much-needed allies.

Recruiting Allies and Undercutting Environmentalists' Support

When advocacy groups are successful at expanding the scope of conflict and attracting supporters, we cannot assume that their opponents will simply stand by while the balance of power shifts away from them. Rather, we can expect that they too will recruit allies and launch a campaign to win over, or at least neutralize, the audience to the conflict. This process of switching from containing participation to managing participation may take some time, however. Advocacy groups who pursue "insider strategies" may be unfamiliar with outsider tactics (see Kollman 1998). The timber industry in British Columbia, for example, had been accustomed to conducting its business outside the watchful eyes of the public. If it had to answer to the public in the past, the public was a much smaller one—a particular community of loggers or environmentalists, but certainly not citizens and suppliers in Germany and Australia. As MacMillan Bloedel spokesperson Dennis Fitzgerald lamented after a particularly heavy week of European protests, "We know how to manufacture pulp and paper, but we don't know how to manufacture public opinion on an international scale. Hell, we can't even manufacture it on a provincial scale" (quoted in Lee 1993b, A1).

Fitzgerald's protestations aside, internal documents from MacMillan Bloedel reveal that the company was well aware that it had to begin lobbying the public. In a presentation made by Linda Coady (MacMillan Bloedel's director of government affairs at the time) on the communications aspects of the Clayoquot conflict, she compared the current orientation of the company to where they had to be in the future.[14] Among her list of items were a number of phrases suggesting that MacMillan Bloedel had been rather insular and closed in the past: The company had adopted an "indifference to community," had operated under "closed management," with "poor labor relations" and "no native support." It was "focused internally/isolated" and "seeking a low profile." The company had to shift, she suggested, so that it had "community support, transparent management, employee enthusiasm, and native participation." MacMillan Bloedel had to "network" and engage in "self-promotion." In short, MacMillan Bloedel would have to make alliances, seek public support, and neutralize potential opposition. In a particularly revealing phrase, Coady advises that MacMillan Bloedel should not "go out into the woods alone . . . support from local communities, labour, natives will be pivotal" (Coady 1993, 8–11).

This document and others suggest that the Clayoquot conflict provided MacMillan Bloedel with an opportunity for political learning. As May (1992) explains, political learning occurs when advocacy groups discover the efficacy (or inefficacy) of particular strategies for enacting or preventing policy change. "As policy advocates improve their awareness of the relationship between the political strategy they employ and its impact on the political prospects for a given proposal being enacted, they become more sophisticated in their policy advocacy" (May 1992, 339). Political learning leads to changes in an interest group's strategy, such as when MacMillan Bloedel actively courted the media and the public and formed alliances with other timber companies, native groups, and labor unions after decades of operating in a rather insular fashion.[15]

The B.C. government, of course, was more accustomed to public attention and advocacy. But the globalization of the Clayoquot Sound conflict required it to expand its efforts by courting international public opinion and making alliances outside the province and the nation. Some of these efforts were very public, such as when Harcourt took a European tour in 1994 to reassure European industries, politicians, and the public that British Columbia now had "world class forest standards." Harcourt also corresponded privately with European and U.S. politicians, such as Vice President Al Gore, indicating in his letter to Gore that the Clinton administration's involvement in the Clayoquot Sound controversy (on the side of environmentalists) was neither necessary nor particularly valued (Harcourt 1993). As noted in the previous chapter, the Harcourt administration courted allies at home as well as abroad, particularly First Nations. For example, the 1994 "Interim Measures Agreement" between the provincial government and the Nuu-chah-nulth tribes gave natives some authority over forest management in Clayoquot Sound. Environmentalists considered the agreement "a shrewd political manoeuvre [*sic*] by the government to split the alliance between environmentalists and First Nations people in the region—by coming to terms with First Nations peoples, the industry undercut environmentalists who claimed to be representing the interests of aboriginals" (Hoberg 1996, 278). It is clear from these examples that both the B.C. government and the timber industry increasingly exploited the expansion of conflict by courting native leaders, workers, the media, foreign officials, and the like.

Conclusion

E. E. Schattschneider (1960, 2) believed that policy outcomes are largely shaped by the extent to which the public gets involved in a conflict. If Schattschneider is correct, then a key strategy in politics is controlling and managing the participation of other policy actors and the broader public in policy conflicts. This chapter has demonstrated the validity of Schattschneider's proposition by examining the strategies of advocacy groups as they attempted to expand and contain the participation of other advocacy groups and bystander publics. The analyses highlight the importance of creating alliances to increase the scope of conflict around an issue. In the case of Clayoquot Sound, local environmentalists successfully built regional, national, and then international alliances that eventually forced the B.C. government and the timber industry to make changes in their forest policies and practices.

The movement to protect Clayoquot Sound began like several other wilderness campaigns in British Columbia—that is, with a rather small group of local activists who focused on securing protection for their backyard. In time, however, Clayoquot Sound became a rallying point for the fragmented and diverse forest protection movement in British Columbia. The movement's tolerance for diversity helped to maintain the Clayoquot coalition, given that individual groups were able to preserve their distinctiveness while in alliance with others. International and transnational environmental organizations were drawn to the Clayoquot conflict for a variety of reasons. In addition to recognizing the symbolic importance of Clayoquot Sound, international groups hoped to broaden their forest campaigns and increase their legitimacy by focusing on rain forest destruction in an industrialized, Western country.

Greenpeace and others also saw an opportunity to use their specialized strategies and tactics in international political and economic venues.

The B.C. government and the timber industry attempted to control the expansion of the Clayoquot conflict, particularly as the campaign spread to Europe and the United States. They attacked the credibility of the individual groups and the movement as a whole in an attempt to decrease attention to their opponents' substantive claims and impede the growth of the anti–British Columbia campaigns abroad. At the same time, they courted their own allies, including foreign officials, the domestic media, and B.C. First Nations. The fact that the B.C. government and the timber industry had to devote so much time and resources to a public campaign suggests how successful the Clayoquot Sound coalition had been in expanding the scope of conflict.

Based on this case, we can offer a generalization about the dynamics of conflict expansion as it relates to participation. Established interests are initially reluctant to "go public" because of the risk that any exposure and public participation poses. They will first try to limit the role of anyone making new claims. As Schattschneider (1960, 36) noted, once a conflict enters the public arena, uncertainty is introduced—new actors are likely to participate and upset the current balance of power. Consequently, those interested in maintaining the status quo will work to restrict the role of the public in a dispute. When and if these strategies fail, they then engage in symbolic politics by denigrating the character of their opponents and challenging the right of new actors to participate. Eventually, even groups who initially tried to limit participation will recruit their own allies and court the public in order to counteract the increasing strength of their opponents. In short, advocacy groups switch to a strategy of "conflict management," which often includes recruiting the same allies and appealing to the same audiences as their opponents.

This case also illustrates the importance of understanding processes of alliance building and subsequent coalition dynamics. Alliances do not always naturally form because of shared belief systems and policy goals; advocacy groups must at times be convinced to work with others on particular campaigns. Some groups solicit allies (the "solicitors") because they need to carry on a campaign in a venue where they have little experience and few resources to compete. Others (the "receivers") will accept an invitation to join a conflict because they perceive organizational benefits to doing so and can play to their strengths by occupying a strategic niche. Rather than impede alliances, diversity of membership can encourage the growth and maintenance of coalitions by allowing individual groups a degree of autonomy and a distinct identity within a coalition.

A final lesson from the Clayoquot Sound case concerns the importance of small shifts in allegiance between competing coalitions. In the conflict over Clayoquot Sound, the switching allegiance of peripheral actors in the conflict led to significant political and policy changes. The retail customers of MacMillan Bloedel, such as Home Depot and the *New York Times*, were not part of the timber coalition in the way we traditionally think about alliances and coalitions. However, they had "supported" the timber coalition prior to the Clayoquot markets campaign by the very fact that they were customers of MacMillan Bloedel. While seemingly politically neutral, the power of these actors became evident when environmental activists convinced them to stop purchasing old-growth timber products.[16] Their defection shifted the behavior of the B.C. timber industry and the provincial government, who were concerned about the loss of markets for B.C. wood products. The lesson here is that even actors who are on the periphery of policy subsystems can affect the politics within it. The cooperation of peripheral actors with one set of advocacy groups, rather than another—or their defection from one to another—can have a critical effect on the politics surrounding a policy conflict.

Venue Shopping in an International Context

The previous chapter examined patterns of participation in the Clayoquot Sound case in order to understand why and how it attracted the participation of actors around the globe. Battles over who gets involved in an issue are important components of policy conflicts because the extent of audience participation changes the nature of the conflict and shapes policy outcomes. As participation increases, the balance of power among the original policy actors often shifts as segments of the public weigh in on one side or the other. In contrast, limited public participation tends to safeguard existing power relationships in the decision-making process.

Strategies aimed at expanding or restricting the scope of participation might be, as Schattschneider (1960) claimed, *the* key strategy in politics. As shown in the previous chapter, Clayoquot environmentalists actively sought outside allies after concluding that they could not fight and win the battle for forest protection on their own. The global network of activists and transnational environmental groups that eventually joined the conflict over Clayoquot Sound shifted the domestic balance of power in the B.C. forest policy subsystem. The once dominant industry-government alliance found itself, in the early to mid-1990s, facing a significantly larger and stronger set of opponents. Although the provincial government and timber industry first attempted to contain participation in the conflict, they eventually competed with environmental activists for the public's sympathy.

Baumgartner and Jones (1993, 36) argue that advocacy groups seeking policy change are not limited to simply engaging a wider public. Their strategies and tactics are more sophisticated and complex, involving efforts to shift decision-making authority over a policy issue to a more favorable policy venue. Indeed, Clayoquot environmentalists' decision to "go global" did not stem entirely from their desire to increase participation in the Clayoquot conflict. After all, the Canadian audience was presumably large enough that if the domestic public got involved, they would tip the scales in favor of environmentalists.[1] To fully understand why Clayoquot activists internationalized their campaign, we must consider the institutional constraints at the provincial and national levels in Canada. Environmental activists faced a closed, informal, and autonomous forest policy subsystem at the provincial level and limited alternate arenas at both the provincial and national level. These institutional constraints pushed the environmental coalition toward international venues and institutions with very different rules, norms, and procedures and allowed the environmental coalition to compete more equally and effectively with their opponents.

The key to understanding strategies of venue shopping entails recognizing that policy venues differ from one another on several dimensions. If all venues contained the same structure of bias, then advocacy groups would hardly benefit by shopping around for a different venue in which to press their claims. But because venues differ, with respect to their rules of access and participation, their decision-making procedures, their constituencies, and the incentives facing institutional actors, strategically minded advocacy groups will target a venue that offers the best advantage over their opponents. In a similar vein, competing advocacy groups will struggle to change (or protect) the rules governing decision-making processes in any particular venue so as to gain an advantage over their opponents. As Bosso (1987, 260) notes, "*Whose* game we play is as important, if not more, than the scope of that game in terms of the public role." Rules set the stage for the next round of conflict and thus become important battlegrounds for competing advocacy groups.

This chapter examines strategies of venue shifting in the conflict over land use and forest management practices in Clayoquot Sound. The following discussion highlights the different structures of bias in the various policy venues and the changing strategies of environmentalists as they attempted to shift policy arenas. I begin with a discussion of provincial venues and then focus on national and international arenas.

Provincial Politics and the B.C. Forest Policy Subsystem

The tight policy subsystem governing forest policy in British Columbia, described in chapter 2, started to break down in the 1980s as regional environmental conflicts in British Columbia increased the public salience of the forest issue. Opinion started to shift in favor of environmentalists as the public recognized a "forest problem" and started to question whether the experts in the Ministry of Forests and in industry were acting in the best interests of the public. One sign of the expansion of conflict is the migration of the forest issue into party politics. In the late 1980s, the Social Credit Party increasingly bore the brunt of environmentalists' criticism, and when the governing party collapsed in 1991, the NDP recognized an opportunity to regain control of the provincial government by exploiting the forest issue. The NDP staked out several environmental positions in its platform; one-third of the NDP platform was devoted to environmental and forestry reforms, although most of the proposals concerned procedural rather than substantive commitments (Harrison 1996a). The centerpiece of the party's environmental program, as suggested elsewhere, was the creation of multistakeholder advisory groups who were charged with developing land-use plans for the entire province. The NDP's main substantive commitment was to double the amount of protected areas in the province, from 6 percent to 12 percent (1 percent of the land area equals about one million hectares) and to enact forest legislation that gave more weight to ecological values.

Historically, the NDP has been more "green" than the opposition Liberal and Reform parties, reflecting its leftist orientation and constituency. Thus, when the NDP won the provincial election in 1991, environmentalists were hopeful that Premier Harcourt would live up to his green promises. Considering some of the substantive changes in the following years, it is clear that Harcourt and the NDP offered more policy concessions to environmentalists than their predecessors and made an attempt to expand public participation in land-use decision making. In fact, the procedural changes enacted by the NDP are perhaps more important, in the long run, than any substantive gains. Despite the failure of the Clayoquot Sound task forces and the CORE groups to come to an agreement, the experiments in multistakeholder bargaining recognized the legitimacy of environmental and First Nations participation in forest policymaking. Hoberg and Morawski (1997, 393) argue that such institutional changes were important precursors to substantive policy change: "While the revolution away from Cabinet-style government did not occur [as a result of CORE], CORE did provide an avenue for the institutional representation of environmental values, and for that reason, played a crucial role in regime transformation." One environmental activist put it succinctly by saying, "Once you've involved the public and communities in meaningful ways, it's hard to then say 'go home'" (quoted in Harrison 1996a, 296).

Some scholars have argued that the changes enacted by the Harcourt administration and the NDP moved environmentalists into the core of the forest policy regime (Hoberg 1996). However, environmental groups still faced a number of institutional barriers in the early 1990s and largely remained "proud outsiders" in the forest policy system. There were limits to how far Harcourt's government would go to reverse the many decades of favorable policy toward the timber industry because Harcourt had to answer to another constituency in addition to environmentalists—labor. Labor unions have traditionally been part of the NDP coalition, including timber unions like the International Woodworkers of America. Indeed, when the NDP came to power in 1991, labor was at the core of its constituency and had been the major source of funding for the party (Carroll and Ratner 2005). Not surprisingly, the International Woodworkers of America largely opposed environmentalists' calls for changes in forestry practices and were especially alarmed by their efforts to permanently remove watersheds and other large areas from the timber base.

The NDP's loyalty was torn between these two important constituents. After its 1993 decision on Clayoquot Sound, many environmentalists felt that the NDP had abandoned them and sided with the timber unions and industry. Several of the environmental activists interviewed for this study downplayed the significance of the 1991 elections and the subsequent change in administration. As Joe Foy of WCWC remarked, "Our choice structure is either a government which is beholden to the large timber companies or a government beholden to the large timber unions . . . our obstacles are the same—they are the government and the timber industry" (2000). Despite Foy's cynicism, the movement of the forest issue from the confines of the forest policy subsystem to the electoral arena, and the subsequent election of the NDP, had a significant influence on forest policy (see Cashore and others 2001).

Political-Economic Pressures in British Columbia

The election of the NDP in 1991 and their narrow reelection in 1996 provided opportunities for environmentalists and also presented continuing challenges to those wishing to restructure forest policy and policymaking in British Columbia. As Cashore and his colleagues (2001, 234) note, "The election of the NDP in 1991 transformed the government from one openly hostile to environmental initiatives in the forests to one dedicated to bringing about 'peace in the woods.' The NDP pursued a bold package of policy reforms designed to appeal to urban environmentalists as well as the party's more traditional supporters in the labour movement." But the Harcourt administration was constrained by the NDP's commitments to labor and by the substantial power of the forest industry. Put differently, the political economy of forestry in British Columbia limited the ability and willingness of the provincial government to accommodate environmentalists' demands, particularly in later years when the B.C. forest industry experienced a sharp economic downturn.

When the NDP was pursuing reforms in the early 1990s, the forest industry was enjoying high demand and prices for its products, due in part to the slowdown in timber production in the U.S. Pacific Northwest after the spotted owl litigation (Cashore and others 2001, 26). According to Cashore and his colleagues (2001), these favorable market conditions decreased the power of the industry; the government was less constrained in imposing new costly regulations on the industry when the market for B.C. wood products was strong. By 1996, the economic picture for the industry had reversed as foreign competition increased, the prices for pulp plummeted, and Asian markets for timber collapsed. Moreover, multinational timber companies were exploring alternate sources of timber, thereby increasing international competition in the timber products industry. As a result, the B.C. government felt pressure to keep its regulations "reasonable." An article in the 1999–2000 annual report by the Canadian forest service expressed such concerns: "The global wood market has been reshaped in the past two decades by the entry of new producers, especially from the Southern Hemisphere, that are growing wood fast and pricing it low. . . . [They] are developing new sources of hardwood and softwood that are increasing their market share and *posing a competitive threat to nations that produce wood more slowly and more expensively*" (Natural Resources Canada 1999–2000, 42–43; emphasis added). Under these circumstances, the NDP government under newly elected premier Glen Clark responded to industry's complaints about the high cost of the new forestry regulations (Cashore and others 2001, 83–84).

While the relative power of the forest industry shifted with changes in the business cycle, the forest industry in British Columbia throughout the 1990s enjoyed considerable structural advantages because of its economic contribution to the provincial economy. Table 5.1 indicates a slight downward trend in employment in the timber industry in the recent past, but even at its lowest, timber jobs accounted for at least one in eleven jobs in the province. The importance of timber to the overall B.C. economy is more evident in table 5.2, which shows the value of wood products exports and British Columbia's balance of trade during the same time period. Forestry exports account for nearly 60 percent of British Columbia's exports and account for the province's positive balance of trade.

In sum, the B.C. government, even under liberal "green" administrations, is constrained by the structural power of the timber industry. One indication of these constraints can be found in the so-called 6 percent solution devised by

TABLE 5.1 Employment Trends in the B.C. Forest Industry

	1994	*1995*	*1997*	*1998*
Direct jobs	98,000	107,000	102,000	97,000
Indirect jobs	89,000	91,000	79,000	78,000
As fraction of total employment	1 job in 9	1 job in 9	1 job in 10	1 job in 11

Source: Compiled from Natural Resources Canada, annual reports from 1994–95, 1995–96, 1997–98, and 1998–99.

B.C. Minister of Forests Andrew Petter during the development of implementation guidelines for the 1994 Forest Practices Code. The 6 percent solution limits the extent to which the Forest Practices Code can decrease the annual allowable cut in the province to 6 percent below existing levels. Such limits impose constraints on the power of the Ministry of Environment and environmental advocacy groups to realize their policy goal of biodiversity protection, which might require far greater decreases in timber production (Cashore and others 2001, 80). Another policy constraint is the forest tenure system described in chapter 2. Under tenure agreements, the provincial government is obligated to compensate private timber companies if they change the terms of a tenure agreement. If the government withdraws lands from a tree farm license belonging to MacMillan Bloedel, for example, it must compensate the company for lost revenues. Such policies can serve as barriers to park designations and wilderness set-asides, particularly under conditions of fiscal restraint.

In the end, environmental activists' *perceptions* about the economic and political power of the timber companies may have been more important than any so-called objective measures of industry power. Clayoquot activists assumed that there were strong economic and political ties between the timber industry and the B.C. government, pointing to certain notable events as evidence. For example, environmental activists made much of the fact that the B.C. government purchased $50 million of MacMillan Bloedel stocks in early 1993, increasing its share in the company from 1 to 4 percent and making

TABLE 5.2   Forest Products Exports, British Columbia

	1993	*1994*	*1997*	*1998*	*1999*
Value of exports ($ billions)	11.8	14.1	14.6	13.2	15.3
Balance of trade ($ billions)	11.1	13.5	13.5	12.1	14.1

Source: Compiled from Natural Resources Canada, annual reports from 1994–95, 1995–96, 1997–98, 1998–99, and 1999–2000.

it the single largest investor in MacMillan Bloedel. The timing of the purchase could not have been worse: it came just two months before the government was scheduled to announce its Clayoquot Sound Land Use Decision. Environmentalists claimed that the government's investment in MacMillan Bloedel prevented it from making a decision that might devalue MacMillan Bloedel stocks. And while the courts did not find a legal conflict of interest over the stock purchase, the incident raised questions about the supposed impartiality of the NDP administration.[2]

Environmental groups also used Premier Harcourt's trip to the European Union in early 1992 as evidence of a strong liaison between the provincial government and the timber industry. Harcourt's trip and subsequent $1.5 million campaign to promote B.C. wood products abroad was followed by a European tour by B.C. Minister of Forests Art Charbonneau and the executives from three forest companies. The purpose of this government-industry trip was to promote British Columbia's forestry practices in Europe and prevent a European boycott of B.C. wood. But the trips also revealed the provincial government's dependence on the timber industry and its willingness to promote it as the industry faced increasing criticism from foreign consumers. Events like these convinced Clayoquot environmental activists that the executive and electoral venues, while once somewhat promising venues for forestry reform, offered only limited prospects for policy change.

Institutional Biases at the Provincial Level: Lobbying and Litigation

Many Clayoquot environmental activists believed that the NDP, despite its promises to environmental constituents, was economically tied to the timber industry and politically beholden to the timber unions. Consequently, they lost faith in the Harcourt administration and in the possibility of resolving the Clayoquot conflict through government-sponsored task forces. The task forces created by the government did not satisfy Clayoquot environmental activists, many of whom resigned from them. Paul George of WCWC felt that the task forces were flawed from the outset because "they put a cap on the amount of forests that could be protected" and they allowed the companies to continue to log while the talks proceeded (2000). Both Valerie Langer of FOCS and Ian Gill of Ecotrust Canada hinted that timber representatives might have deliberately stalled negotiations so that they could continue to log while the groups were trying to reach consensus (Langer 2000b; Gill 2000).

Clayoquot activists also perceived obstacles in the legislative arena. In general, organized interests in Canada and in British Columbia do not enjoy the same level of access to the legislative process as do groups in the United States. This is due in large part to Canada's parliamentary form of government, which fuses the executive and legislative branches. The prime minister, provincial premiers, and cabinet members are all chosen from the majority party in the legislature. The majority party therefore dominates policymaking through the executive branch; individual members of Parliament are extremely disciplined along party lines and are much less entrepreneurial than their counterparts in the United States. The legislature, in short, plays little independent policymaking role, unlike in the United States where the legislature is separate and relatively autonomous from the executive. As a result, the Canadian (and B.C.) institutional structure "affords more limited access to nongovernmental actors, as third-party interest groups in Canada have found it difficult to influence these decisionmakers due to the strictures of cabinet dominance and party discipline at both levels of government" (VanNijnatten 1999, 270).

This is not to say that interest groups play no role in policymaking. But interest group lobbying in British Columbia is less visible and formalized than in the United States, taking place "behind closed doors" in the offices of cabinet ministers and legislative representatives (Kristianson 1996, 201). There are no rules that require public hearings on proposed pieces of legislation, nor are there any institutions that provide outside groups with regular access to legislators (Kristianson 1996, 209–10). Such a system favors those groups with existing ties to the government. Moreover, it rewards interest groups who can hire professional lobbyists—lobbyists stand a better chance of gaining access because they have learned how to manipulate the system and force their way in. The Council of Forest Industries and the B.C. Federation of Labour are two such organizations, representing the interests of the timber industry and timber workers respectively. Both of these groups have had long-standing ties to government and possess the necessary resources to lobby it effectively.

Many of the activists interviewed for this study envied U.S. interest groups for the amount of access they had to state legislatures and to Congress, making lobbying an effective campaign strategy in the United States. Valerie Langer pointed out that in British Columbia, they could not directly petition the provincial legislature to take up an issue: "We need to get some politician in one of the parties to put forward a bill and then it may never make it past that politician. You need a certain amount of 'buy in' by the government before we can even start debating a bill before the legislature" (2000b). None of the activists interviewed for this study named a B.C. legislator as a supporter, although a few considered member of Parliament Svend Robinson an ally (Robinson was arrested in Clayoquot Sound on the first day of protests during the summer of 1993).

While environmental groups in the United States have more opportunities in the legislative arena than their Canadian counterparts, their advantages are even more pronounced in the judicial arena. In British Columbia, courts generally do not play a significant nor active role in environmental policymaking. Regulatory styles in British Columbia are more collaborative and informal than in the United States, and the courts typically respect this by deferring to agencies. More importantly, there are very few laws that give citizens or interest groups the right to challenge agency decisions in the first place. For example, Canada does not have the equivalent of the U.S. National Environmental Policy Act (NEPA), which U.S. environmental activists have used to delay and sometimes halt government actions that could negatively affect the environment. Environmental laws in British Columbia also do not include citizen suit provisions, which give environmental groups automatic access to a court where they can challenge government or industry actions.

The substantive laws that B.C. environmentalists had to work with in the early 1990s were limited as well. At the time, Canada had no endangered species act, a law that U.S. environmental groups used to halt old-growth logging in the Pacific Northwest.[3] Moreover, prior to the enactment of the Forest Practices Code in 1994, British Columbia had no general laws governing forest planning or management. The most important forest law (from the perspective of those who wanted to protect forest ecosystems) in these years was a federal law governing fisheries. Sergio Paone of FOCS suggested that environmentalists needed more federal and provincial "sticks": "One of the reasons there has not been a lot of legal action is because we do not have an Endangered Species Act. . . . There has always been the federal Fisheries Act but the problem is that most of the prime, salmon habitat has already been logged so the issue of damaging large salmon streams is not really an issue anymore. Other than the Forest Practices Code, there has been very little in terms of real, strong laws" (1999).

Although MacMillan Bloedel had been convicted of more than twenty-three violations of the federal Fisheries Act as of November 1990, environmentalists claimed that the fines were too small to serve as a deterrent; between 1969 and 1990, the single largest fine MacMillan Bloedel was asked to pay was fifteen thousand dollars. Clayoquot activists also charged MacMillan Bloedel with noncompliance and claimed that the government turned a blind eye to violations. A press release by Greenpeace Canada notes that although a government audit of logging in Clayoquot Sound revealed extensive noncompliance by MacMillan Bloedel, officials nonetheless issued a road building permit to the company a week after the report was released. And in late 1993, Greenpeace and the Sierra Legal Defence Fund publicized a Ministry of Forests document that showed MacMillan Bloedel had not complied with fish and forestry guidelines in twenty-one of twenty-seven cut blocks logged in Clayoquot Sound.

Environmental groups contrasted the government's weak enforcement of MacMillan Bloedel's legal violations with its seemingly overzealous enforcement of the law against Clayoquot protesters. During the 1993 Clayoquot Sound blockades, MacMillan Bloedel had obtained numerous court injunctions to prohibit members of the public from physically impeding its logging operations. MacMillan Bloedel used these injunctions to initiate civil contempt proceedings against protesters. The courts, in turn, found in favor of MacMillan Bloedel and then upheld the legality of the injunctions when Greenpeace's lawyers tried to overturn them.[4] More importantly, the judiciary invited the attorney general of British Columbia to prosecute the protesters for *criminal* contempt, on the basis that the protesters' deliberate violation of the injunctions lessened societal respect for courts and the rule of law. With the involvement of British Columbia's attorney general, the conflict in the courts transformed from a private dispute between MacMillan Bloedel and individual protesters to a public dispute between the government and its citizens. From the environmentalists' perspective, judges had gone beyond their duty to uphold the law and had actively enlisted the support of the provincial government to increase the burden on protesters. They used this as evidence that the judiciary was on the side of industry and the government.

The final blow occurred during the mass trials of Clayoquot protesters during 1993 and 1994. Many activists thought that the jail sentences and fines issued by the various judges were excessive for what amounted to peaceful protests by "regular" citizens who had no previous criminal convictions. For example, several protesters received forty-five-day jail terms and fines ranging from a thousand dollars to twenty-five hundred. Protesters claimed that the court was violating their civil rights because it refused to try protesters individually and give all their "day in court." Similarly, the judges did not allow the convicted protesters to state their reasons for violating the injunction, depriving the activists of using the courts as a public protest forum. Not surprisingly, the courts contained the issue by narrowing the question to whether or not the convicted protesters had violated the injunction. B.C. Supreme Court Justice Bouck made it clear that he would not expand the debate any further: "Many defendants would like me to try the political question of whether government forestry policies are right or wrong. They would also like me to decide whether MacMillan Bloedel Ltd. follows proper forestry practices. But *those are not the legal issues the law says I must decide"* (Bouck, *MacMillan Bloedel Ltd. vs. Sheila Simpson* et al., 1993, 6; emphasis added). With little hope of using the courts to fundamentally change forestry practices in Clayoquot Sound or to advertise their grievances, environmental groups largely eschewed the judicial route to change.[5]

By the mid-1990s, the B.C. government was getting tougher on forest companies in order to prove to the public and international community that it was serious about changing forest policy and practices. In late 1993 the Harcourt administration announced it would enact new forestry rules. Among other things, the Forest Practices Code included Ministry of Environment officials in forest policy decision making; increased the fines associated with noncompliance of the law from two thousand to one million dollars per day; limited the size of clear-cuts; prohibited logging in riparian zones; and required a new level of planning at the watershed level. While the Forest Practices Code promised a stronger level of enforcement and greater inclusion of environmental concerns in forestry practices, Clayoquot environmental groups were skeptical. For one thing, the code was not scheduled to go into effect until 1995 and would not be fully implemented until 1997. And as noted previously, in 1997 the Sierra Legal Defence Fund examined implementation of the Forest Practices Code, concluding that clear-cutting was still the favored method of harvesting in British Columbia, that the size of the cuts had not decreased, and that special areas for biodiversity and wildlife had not been set aside as promised (Bryner 1999, 319).

Opportunities and Constraints at the Federal Level

The policy changes enacted by the B.C. government in the early and mid-1990s, while significant if looked at from a historical perspective, meant less to the activists who demanded complete protection for Clayoquot Sound. Indeed, as Clayoquot activists increased their demands and expectations, they were bound to be dissatisfied with what they saw as half-measures from the provincial government. Paul George of WCWC suggested that biases in the provincial government actually became more obvious as the conflict developed and environmentalists started gaining a foothold: "Once you start pushing the government, you find out it really isn't fair. You have to push, or you don't find these things out" (quoted in Bossin 2000). When B.C. Minister of Forests Dan Miller said that the government would not back down on its April 1993 decision—no matter how many protesters filled the jails—environmentalists understandably felt that they had reached a dead end. Consequently, they searched for policy venues beyond the provincial level, venues that might lead to more significant reforms and serious commitments from the timber industries, the NDP, and the Harcourt administration.

The next logical step would be to target national institutions that might go over the heads of provincial officials and force changes in B.C. forest policy and practices. In the United States, the dramatic changes in forestry policy in the late 1980s and early 1990s were due in part to nationalization of the old-growth logging issue. U.S. environmental groups moved conflict into national venues like the federal courts and Congress and solicited executive branch support during the Clinton administration. For Canadian environmentalists, however, the national arena provided few opportunities for venue shifting, and environmental groups made only intermittent and halfhearted attempts to enlist the support of federal institutions and officials.

The lack of opportunities at the national level is mainly due to the decentralized structure of power in the Canadian political system. The Canadian constitution limits the power of the federal government in the environmental policy arena. As F. L. Morton (1996, 41) explains, "Unlike its counterpart in the United States, Ottawa was not possessed of a broad and preemptive commerce power upon which it could confidently launch a new environmental regime." Historically, most environmental legislation has been enacted at the provincial level, such that when the federal government turned its attention to environmental issues in the late 1960s, provincial legislation already occupied the field (Morton 1996, 41). Provincial dominance is especially notable in the area of natural resources policy: Section 92 of the Constitution Act of 1982 gives provinces authority to manage and sell public lands under their ownership. In British Columbia, this gives the province jurisdiction over about 95 percent of the land.

In general, the decentralization of power in the forestry policy arena benefits the timber industry. Forest companies have long-standing ties and access to provincial institutions and their economic influence is enhanced at the provincial level. In the mid-1990s, the forest industry was the largest employer in the province and represented about 18 percent of the province's annual gross domestic product (Bryner 1999, 313). While the forest industry is important to the Canadian economy as well (accounting for about one in fifteen jobs in 1994), its economic dominance in British Columbia is more pronounced (Natural Resources Canada 1994–1995). Paehlke (2000, 172–73) argues more generally that "many of Canada's resource industries can bring maximum political pressure to bear at the provincial level. . . . In general, the relative power of multinational entities is maximized relative to smaller governmental units."

While Canada's constitutional structure limits the role of the federal government in environmental policy, it does not prevent federal officials and agencies from intervening altogether. For example, the Constitution gives the federal government jurisdiction over renewable resources and over environmental issues that extend across provincial borders (see Campbell and Thomas 2002). Moreover, the federal government retains residual powers to "make laws for the 'Peace, Order and good Government of Canada'" (Campbell and Thomas 2002, 224). This vague but rather expansive phrase was interpreted liberally in the 1988 Supreme Court of Canada case *The Queen v. Crown Zellerbach*, which gave the federal government jurisdiction over pollution discharges in provincial sea waters. The political ramifications of the decision, Morton claims, "were obvious: acceptance of this argument would not only establish a new federal environmental jurisdiction over both national and provincial sea waters but also confer a *prima facie legitimacy on federal regulation in almost any environmental policy area deemed to be of national concern*" (Morton 1996, 46; emphasis added).

Despite a growing constitutional and legislative basis for federal involvement in environmental policy, the national government has taken a rather limited view of its own powers in this area. Even when it can legitimately intervene in the natural resource policies of British Columbia, it is often hesitant to do so (Harrison 1996b). This general reluctance on the part of the federal government to expand its jurisdiction is tempered somewhat during periods of high public attention to an issue, when electoral incentives favor intervention and federal legislation (Harrison 1996b). For example, in 1988 the national government passed the Canadian Environmental Protection Act in response to heightened public concern over environmental problems (Campbell and Thomas 2002). But even when the federal government gets involved in environmental matters, it often has to consult with the provinces due to their primary jurisdiction over environmental issues or due to uncertainty about the limits of federal power. And as Karen Litfin (2000, 242) notes, "Because federal-provincial conferences operate by consensus, policy outcomes tend to gravitate toward the lowest common denominator."

Litfin (2000, 242) also points out that the Canadian government has shown more restraint in its dealings with the provinces in the last decade, largely because it wants to placate Quebec separatists: "Having survived Quebec's last independence referendum by a tiny margin, the federal government is trying to demonstrate its commitment to decentralization, with the environment being a lead policy area in that respect." Litfin's claim is evidenced by the 1998 "Harmonization Accord" signed by the federal government and the provinces. This accord gives provinces even more control over environmental policy-making and implementation; it was opposed by environmental groups who feared that it would further close the door to federal venues and remove any hope that the federal government would act as a watchdog over the provinces (Paehlke 2000, 173).

The Clayoquot Sound case bears out many of the general propositions about the role of the federal government in provincial affairs. Until 1993, the federal government seemed content to let British Columbia resolve the Clayoquot Sound controversy and determine the direction of future forest policy on its own. However, after the 1993 protests when public attention to Clayoquot Sound was at its highest point in both British Columbia and the nation, the federal government expressed some willingness to intervene in the conflict. Jean Chrétien and other prominent leaders in the Liberal Party promised to negotiate with British Columbia over the issue of turning Clayoquot Sound into a national park, when and if they gained control of the federal government. But after the Liberal Party won the national election in the fall of 1993, it started to backtrack from its promise. The government refused to compensate British Columbia for lost jobs and for Crown lands that were taken out of timber production, prompting then B.C. Minister of Environment Moe Sihota to charge, "The federal overtures are nothing more than a hoax" (quoted in Bohn 1993b, B1).

Environmental groups bear some responsibility for the federal government's failure to follow through with the national park idea. According to Ken Wu of WCWC, FOCS and other environmental groups did not want to endorse national park status for Clayoquot Sound because of opposition from First Nations. First Nations were wary of having their tribal lands turned into national parks that would be off-limits to any kind of resource use. The national park idea embraced a decidedly western notion of preservation, and FOCS—who already had uneasy relations with First Nations—did not want to sour them any further. Wu, however, thought that they missed an opportunity to move the conflict into a national venue: "We squandered a hell of an opportunity because some of the key players did not come behind the idea [of a national park]. Even though Chrétien made a promise, if the environmentalists don't get behind it, then he has the leeway to back out" (2000).

More generally, the Clayoquot coalition did not perceive many opportunities at the national level and did not spend a lot of energy trying to shift venues to national arenas. As Sergio Paone admitted, "We have hardly worked at all at the federal level. We primarily deal with the B.C. government—

occasionally we have sent letters to the federal government to intervene, but *when it comes to forestry their general response is, this is a provincial matter. . . .* They have made statements about Clayoquot Sound, but they don't do much. Chrétien made a statement that yes, he would try to find a resolution, but when he became prime minister, he said this is a provincial matter and I can't really do anything" (Paone 1999; emphasis added). What is notable about the Clayoquot Sound case is that provincial politicians made a greater effort to involve the federal government than did environmentalists. This contradicts the general proposition that provinces will try to maximize their authority over issues and fight off any attempts by the federal government to intervene (see Paehlke 2000, 172). While this may be true in the majority of cases, the Clayoquot case suggests that if a conflict proves intractable, provincial officials have an incentive to "hand off" the problem to other institutions. As the B.C. government found itself less and less able to control the Clayoquot issue, it welcomed the federal government's involvement, hoping it might help resolve the conflict for them.

International Institutions and Global Venues

The discussion thus far suggests that the majority of policy venues at the provincial level gave the timber industry an advantage over environmental interests. Taken together, the obstacles (both perceived and "real") at the provincial and national level prompted leaders of the Clayoquot Sound campaign to consider moving the conflict into international institutions and venues. In time, Clayoquot activists became convinced that economic globalization *required* political engagement at the international level. Thus, what started out as a case of venue shopping led to policy learning on the part of environmental activists, who understood the importance of enacting changes in the global marketplace for wood products.

Environmental groups involved in the international Clayoquot campaign targeted both political and economic venues at the international level. In general, the international venues targeted by environmental groups required different types of resources to effectively compete in them compared with venues at the provincial level. Environmental groups like Greenpeace and FOCS were able to capitalize on their strengths, such as their ability to frame issues, make symbolic appeals, and mobilize international public opinion. Put differently, power in international venues was tied less to political and material resources and more to cultural resources. This gave environmentalists some advantages over their opponents, who had relied on traditional political resources like lobbying and electoral influence when competing in venues at the provincial level.

The timing of the international campaign also favored environmental groups. Leaders of the Clayoquot campaign, whether by design or by luck, moved the conflict into international venues just when public support for their position was waning in British Columbia. An Angus Reid poll, conducted in late November 1993 after the summer of protest, showed that close to 59 percent of British Columbians supported the government's Clayoquot compromise (Baldrey 1993). The protest tactics were also starting to backfire with the B.C. public. An earlier poll of five hundred British Columbians, commissioned by MacMillan Bloedel, indicated that support for the Clayoquot compromise had *increased* from 53 to 63 percent since the blockades began. Environmental activist Paul George alluded to the public's lack of enthusiasm for protest tactics when he complained about the "law and order" beliefs of Canadians: "Canadians lose sight of what you are protesting if you are defying court orders because they are more concerned that you are breaking the law" (2000).

Clayoquot campaigners also shifted to international venues at about the same time that their opponents were intensifying their countercampaign at home. By 1993, timber companies and timber unions were becoming better organized and publicly active. In August, five thousand timber supporters gathered in Ucluelet for a two-day rally to show their support for the Clayoquot Sound Land Use Decision.[6] In addition, prologging grassroots "Share" groups were proliferating around the province, many of whom were backed by timber industry dollars (Hoberg 1996, 284). And finally, timber companies were increasingly cooperating with one another, consolidating their power through the Forest Alliance of British Columbia, which ran sophisticated public relations campaigns to counter environmentalists' message. The backlash against the Clayoquot movement was powerful but, as Langer explained, it did not derail the movement: "There was a big backlash in British Columbia and around Canada. However, by that time *we had moved our campaign into the marketplace and it really didn't affect us that much*. . . . We are willing to deal with that backlash in British Columbia because where we need to focus our attention is in the marketplace, and work on the demand for wood products" (Langer 2000a; emphasis added). As Langer suggests, the effectiveness of the countercampaign was blunted by the venue shifting strategies of environmentalists, who had moved the conflict to new arenas that were fairly immune to their opponents' tactics. The following sections look more closely at the advantages that environmentalists enjoyed at the international level.

Political Venues and Symbolic Politics

Environmental activists were the first to fully exploit opportunities at the international level, taking their opponents by surprise and forcing them to respond and react to environmental groups. As detailed in chapter 3, Clayoquot activists effectively defined the issue in the international arena, giving them an advantage over their opponents who were left trying to counter the criticisms of environmentalists in terms that did not favor their arguments. Clayoquot activists were also the first to court European and U.S. politicians, many of whom publicly condemned logging practices in Clayoquot Sound. And while Premier Harcourt regained some support during his numerous trips to Europe, the administration and the timber companies were forced to expend significant resources in a battlefield that was far less familiar to them, and thus more difficult to control. The government and industry watched nervously as Clayoquot demonstrations and protests materialized in cities as far away as Tokyo, Japan, and New Delhi, India. Meanwhile, city councils in the United States and elsewhere were debating resolutions regarding Clayoquot Sound and British Columbia's old-growth forests—thus bringing the conflict to forums or venues that were largely impenetrable to the B.C. government and the timber companies. Table 5.3 indicates the scope of the activism around Clayoquot Sound specifically and British Columbia's forest practices generally.

Environmental activists also used international laws, treaties, and norms to shame Canada into changing its forestry policies and practices. These international laws and treaties, while devoid of any real enforcement power, provided a rich array of symbols and arguments to environmental groups, often adding legitimacy to their claims (see Bernstein and Cashore 2000; Keck and Sikkink 1998). As noted elsewhere, Clayoquot campaigners argued that the continued clear-cutting of Clayoquot Sound defied the spirit and intent of the UN Convention on Biological Diversity that Canada had signed at the Earth Summit in 1992. Such appeals played on Canada's self-identification as a leader in environmental stewardship and were successful to the extent that Canada had concerns about its international "green" reputation (see Paehlke 2000, 162–63). As Keck and Sikkink (1998, 29) argue, countries "that aspire to belong to a normative community of nations" are most susceptible to this type of international pressure.

The reaction of provincial and federal politicians suggests that environmental groups were successful in their efforts to tarnish Canada's otherwise positive international image regarding its environmental practices. As

TABLE 5.3   International Clayoquot Protests and Campaigns

Cities that held at least one demonstration for the preservation of Clayoquot Sound	Cities with sustained campaigns	Cities, regions, and governments that passed or debated resolutions regarding Clayoquot Sound and British Columbia's old-growth forests[a]
Tokyo, Japan	London, England	San Francisco Region Board
New Delhi, India	Hamburg, Germany	of Councilors
Brasilia, Brazil	Vienna, Austria	European Parliament
Sydney, Australia	Amsterdam, The Netherlands	Marin County, California
Wellington, New Zealand	Tokyo, Japan	Oakland County, California
Edinburgh, Scotland	San Francisco, California	Contra Costa city council
London, England	New York, New York	Edinburgh city council
Oxford, England	Washington, D.C.	Nottingham city council
Vienna, Austria	Seattle, Washington	
Paris, France	Vancouver, Canada	
Hamburg, Germany	Tofino, Canada	
Rome, Italy		
Amsterdam, The Netherlands		
Jokmok, Sweden		
St. John's, Newfoundland		
New York, New York		
San Francisco, California		
Los Angeles, California		
Sacramento, California		
Denver, Colorado		
Seattle, Washington		
Bellingham, Washington		
Washington, D.C.		
Tofino, Canada		
Vancouver, Canada		
Victoria, Canada		
Edmonton, Canada		
Winnepeg, Canada		
Toronto, Canada		
Ottawa, Canada		
Halifax, Canada		

Source: Valerie Langer, "Index for Clayoquot World Map," Friends of Clayoquot Sound, Tofino, B.C.

[a]The resolutions passed in all of these governments except the European Parliament.

Maryjka Mychajilowycz of FOCS remarked, "They [the European Parliament] tried to pass some resolutions in Europe and that really unnerved the government because they wanted others to believe that we are international leaders in responsible forestry" (1999). Toward that end, the B.C. Ministry of Environment issued a report in 1996 outlining British Columbia's progress toward meeting its biodiversity commitments. The agency also attended the World Conservation Union's international conference that same year in order to promote its new approach to forestry and to improve British Columbia's international green image with respect to environmental practices (British Columbia Ministry of Environment 1996).

Politicizing the Global Marketplace

The international Clayoquot campaign began as an effort to increase global awareness of Clayoquot Sound and British Columbia's forest practices, but it soon developed into a sophisticated markets campaign aimed at changing forestry practices through direct economic pressure on forest companies. In other words, Clayoquot campaigners eventually bypassed traditional political venues and moved the conflict into the marketplace, politicizing what was allegedly an apolitical space. The struggle for power thus shifted from domestic political arenas to the global marketplace, and to customers of MacMillan Bloedel's wood products more specifically.

The incentive to switch to a market-based strategy was due to a combination of strategic considerations and policy learning on the part of Clayoquot campaigners. Many leaders of the movement suggested that the markets campaign was a "last ditch" effort to improve British Columbia's forest policy and practices. As Tamara Stark of Greenpeace Canada said, "The feeling was that if we could not affect government decisions or a company through the tactics that we had all pursued for decades, then we needed to be able to impact them financially. . . . In the absence of strong governments, in the absence of corporations choosing to pursue strong environmental initiatives, we really felt it was the only thing we could do. It was our last option" (Stark 2000). Stark went on to explain that many environmental groups had tried to find solutions through domestic political venues, such as CORE and other land-use processes, but with little success. Moreover, according to Stark, the "blockades did not work," making it clear to everyone that they would have to try something different.

Stark's explanation confirms the general proposition that advocacy groups try to move conflict into alternative venues when they run into obstacles and biases in existing ones. However, venue shifting may also result from policy learning on the part of advocacy groups. During the course of a campaign, advocacy groups might develop a better understanding of the nature of a policy problem and solutions to it (see May 1992). A new (or more complex) appreciation of the problem may encourage an advocacy group to move an issue into a venue that reflects this new understanding. Clayoquot activists, for instance, not only recognized the strategic advantages to taking the conflict directly to consumers but also felt that long-term changes in forestry practices would require changes in the global consumption of wood products. Valerie Langer offered this analysis of the efficacy of policy change in an era of economic globalization: "We are working in the context of globalization, so that policy initiatives that don't take that into account end up with people making decisions at a little table that *have absolutely no effect on the market-place*. So the pressures to log the area are just as great—if you get a moratorium for eighteen months, after those eighteen months they will go and log it. *I think people need to take into account globalization, and get involved at that level, rather than just work locally*" (Langer 2000b; emphases added).

The question remains how Clayoquot activists effectively mobilized the marketplace and forced a response from MacMillan Bloedel. What opportunities were available in this particular policy venue? First, it is important to note that British Columbia is a large exporter of wood products around the globe, making it possible to launch an international markets campaign. Bernstein and Cashore (2000, 77) argue that markets campaigns "require [economic] globalization to the degree that the target government or firms must be relatively dependent on the external market in which the boycotts are launched." As noted above, British Columbia is highly dependent on its timber exports. And two of the largest importers of British Columbia's wood products—the United States and Europe—have strong domestic environmental movements.[7] For these reasons, Clayoquot activists were confident that their efforts to politicize the U.S. and European markets would be successful, due in part to the high level of environmental awareness and organization in consumer countries.

The international markets campaign targeted retail customers of MacMillan Bloedel's products rather than individual consumers in order to conserve the organizational resources of the Coastal Rainforest Coalition (formerly known as the Clayoquot Rainforest Coalition); coalition members included Rainforest Action Network, Greenpeace, Natural Resources Defense Club, Coalition for Forests, Pacific Environment and Resource Center, and FOCS. A general boycott would have required alerting and then convincing a vast number of potential consumers to stop purchasing a wide variety of consumer products made from B.C. timber—for example, tissue paper, newspapers, and lumber. By targeting large retail customers, the Coastal Rainforest Coalition could have a similar effect on MacMillan Bloedel's profits without expending as many resources and without relying on the purchasing habits of millions of individuals. Toward this end, the coalition wrote letters to the purchasing and public relations managers of MacMillan Bloedel's retail customers, including Home Depot, Kinko's, the *New York Times*, and Pacific Bell Directories. The letters urged the companies to phase out their purchase of old-growth products within three to five years; if the companies did not respond favorably, the coalition threatened to stage protests outside corporate headquarters and retail outlets (Langer 2000a).

Several of these companies cancelled their contracts with MacMillan Bloedel or agreed to search for alternative suppliers. In the United Kingdom, Scott and Kimberly-Clark were the first to respond to the boycott threats, and several large European and U.S. customers followed their lead (see Stanbury and Vertinsky 1997). The companies worried that consumers might associate their products with clear-cuts and other environmentally destructive activities. And while some of the companies had had long-standing purchasing ties to MacMillan Bloedel, their "loyalty" was largely to stockholders. Indeed, the lack of rules or loyalties in the marketplace helped Clayoquot activists; as Valerie Langer explained, "These companies don't care where they buy [wood products], unless there is a good reason to switch. And what we needed to do was to give them a good reason and that is where things like direct action come in" (Langer 2000a).

In short, it was relatively easy for the Clayoquot coalition to politicize the marketplace, given that there were no "rules" governing the choices of MacMillan Bloedel's customers. Moreover, access to this venue was open and, indeed, plentiful. Because MacMillan Bloedel had many retail customers, Clayoquot activists had multiple targets, not all of which had to cooperate in order to make the campaign successful. Unlike the electoral arena, environmentalists did not need a majority of consumers to be on their side in order to be effective. As Warren Magnuson explains, the rules of the marketplace are much different than the rules in conventional political arenas: "Companies are often extremely sensitive to market behavior. When it comes to elections, you need at least a plurality. In contrast, you don't need all the consumers on your side to have an effect on the market. If you shift just five percent or less of the consumers, often the companies will respond because that may be their profit margin" (Magnuson, quoted in Bossin 2000). Valerie Langer admitted they did not get enough contracts cancelled to actually "bring MacMillan

Bloedel down" but claims that MacMillan Bloedel stopped their operations in Clayoquot Sound in response to the markets campaign and to international pressure more generally (2000). One environmental activist, commenting on the shift toward the marketplace, boldly stated, "The government is irrelevant; it is the marketplace. We give Home Depot 25,000 post cards. Home Depot responds" (quoted in Cashore and others 2001, 49).

The markets strategy persisted even after logging in Clayoquot Sound came to a virtual standstill at the end of the 1990s, when the rate of cut was about 2 percent of what it had been at its peak.[8] Environmental groups continued to use boycotts (or threaten them) in the conflict over the so-called Great Bear Rainforest in northern British Columbia. And in 1999, FOCS, Greenpeace Canada, and Sierra Club of British Columbia formed a "Markets Initiative" designed to encourage Canadian publishers to choose paper made from nonvirgin fibers. The coalition claims to have influenced the development of several new types of 100 percent recycled fibers and counts among its more notable victories the publication of a Harry Potter book on 100 percent ancient forest–free paper (Friends of Clayoquot Sound, "Markets Campaigns").

Forest advocacy groups have also been promoting forest certification as a way to create a market for sustainable forestry products. Forest certification programs grew in the 1990s as part of a shift toward more voluntary and market-based mechanisms in environmental policy. The Forest Stewardship Council (FSC), formed in 1993, is perhaps the best known certification program and the one with the greatest influence in British Columbia. The FSC's list of ten "sustainability" principles and criteria serves as a guide for certification programs around the world, and the FSC itself accredits organizations to ensure compliance (Cashore and others 2001, 88). Individual timber companies pursue certification on a voluntary basis; if their operations meet the certification requirements, they can label their products with the FSC logo.

In January 2003 the B.C. regional FSC body received preliminary accreditation from the Forest Stewardship Council International (Forest Stewardship Council n.d.). Several forest companies, including Weyerhauser (which has taken over MacMillan Bloedel's holdings in Clayoquot Sound) have pursued accreditation through the FSC (British Columbia Ministry of Forests n.d.). A rather dramatic sign of success of the certification movement in particular and the markets campaign more generally was when MacMillan Bloedel announced in 1998 that it would halt the practice of clear-cutting so as to comply with certification requirements. As quoted in Cashore and colleagues (2001, 88), MacMillan Bloedel President Tom Stephans explained his decision this way: "It [the decision to halt clear-cutting] reflects what our customers are telling us about the need for certified products, but equally important it reflects chang-ing social values and new knowledge about forest ecology." The environmental activism sparked by the Clayoquot Sound conflict, while not wholly respon-sible for the changes Stephans cites, played a large role in shifting not only the venues for politics and policy but also the values guiding them.

Conclusion

Venue shopping is an integral part of the policy process and at the heart of many political strategies. Advocacy groups or policymakers who want to change agendas and policy are often frustrated by biases within institu-tional venues where key decisions about a policy are made. One strategy for overcoming such biases is to shop for an alternative venue and attempt to move the conflict (and decision-making authority) to a new policy arena. As Baumgartner and Jones (1993, 34) put it, "Losers always have the option of trying to change the policy venue from, say, the national government to sub-national units, or from so-called iron triangles to election politics, and such efforts are a constant part of the policy process." Agenda and policy change can result from venue shifts when new understandings of issues are advanced in alternative venues, new and different actors participate in the conflict, and alternative institutional rules are invoked for decision making.

This chapter has demonstrated that Clayoquot environmentalists faced limited opportunities for advancing their cause at the provincial and national levels, prompting them to move the conflict over Clayoquot Sound into the international political arena and eventually into the international market-place. Keck and Sikkink (1998, 36) call this pattern of influence the "boo-merang" effect; domestic political actors reach out to international audiences and allies to pressure domestic decision makers. Unable to realize their policy goals in local, regional, or national venues, activists may target institutions further and further from the original site of conflict, with the hope that out-side pressure will "boomerang" back home. Keck and Sikkink (1998, 204), in considering what types of issues become targets for transnational organizing, argue that "issues involving bodily harm to vulnerable individuals, and legal equality of opportunity" appear most prominently. The particular values and belief systems associated with these issue characteristics transcend cultural and political boundaries and thus become ripe for transnational organizing.

The Clayoquot Sound case belies the "bodily harm" thesis advanced by Keck and Sikkink and illustrates the potential for other issues to become a target for transnational organizing. As these last chapters on the Clayoquot

Sound case illustrate, environmental groups successfully framed the issue of forest destruction in Clayoquot Sound in ways that resonated with international actors and audiences, facilitating the movement of the issue to international arenas. The globalization of the issue, in turn, helped to shift the terms of the forest debate away from what environmentalists saw as a limited (mainly economic) view of forestry. The expansion of the conflict effectively distanced and minimized the importance of the economic arguments put forth by the industry (and to an extent the B.C. government), reinforcing an ecologically based definition of the "forest problem." Put differently, the change in issue definition and change in venue supported one another, leading to a "positive feedback" process. Baumgartner and Jones (1993, 37) describe the dynamics of such a process: "Where the rhetoric begins to change, venue changes become more likely. Where venue changes occur, rhetorical changes are facilitated. With each change in venue comes an increased attention to a new image, leading to further changes in venue, as more and more groups within the political system become aware of the question. Thus a slight change in either can build on itself, amplifying over time and leading eventually to important changes in policy outcomes."

While a positive feedback process might lead to relatively rapid agenda and policy change, often the build-up to change takes years and even decades. In the Clayoquot Sound case, environmental groups first solicited traditional policy venues at the provincial level. Only after a decade and a half of encountering roadblocks at the domestic level did FOCS turn its attention to international arenas. This suggests that venue shopping is not always the highly rational process sometimes portrayed in the literature. That is, advocacy groups might not be fully aware of the various opportunities and constraints present in different policy venues. Sometimes they must "get their hands dirty" and try their luck in various arenas before discovering one where they hold an advantage over their opponents. Moreover, internal organizational concerns can limit the extent to which advocacy groups take advantage of opportunities in alternative venues. Clayoquot environmental groups, for example, refrained from pursuing an opportunity to involve the federal government of Canada for fear of alienating First Nations allies.

The turn to international venues was by no means inevitable: By some standards, the Clayoquot activists had been successful before they "went global." Not only did the Harcourt administration set aside one-third of the sound for protection, but he also initiated comprehensive land management processes that promised a greater degree of public involvement in forest policymaking. In some ways it was the limited success of Clayoquot environmentalists at home that prompted them to move the conflict to the international arena. Their victories at the provincial level raised expectations and pushed FOCS in particular to intensify its demands for change. As scholars of social movements note, success often enhances the motivation of activists, particularly if the successes are only partial (Ganz 2000; Meyer and Staggenborg 1996). At the same time, environmental activists gradually learned more about the causes of forest depletion and the needed solutions to it, leading to a further embrace of international arenas, particularly that of the global marketplace. The success of B.C. environmentalists in using the marketplace is best seen in the government's 2006 announcement to protect an additional 3.3 million acres in the Great Bear Rainforest. While environmental groups involved in the Great Bear campaign used traditional political methods such as lobbying and civic action, and even participated in government-sponsored land-use forums, they point to the international markets campaign as putting the needed pressure on industry to negotiate an agreement (ForestEthics 2006; Wu 2006).

Another indication of success in the marketplace is the growing popularity of forest certification programs. As Cashore and his colleagues argue (2001, 90–91), the effect on the B.C. forest policy sector could be dramatic: "It is too early to tell what sort of impact certification will have on BC forest practices, but it does have the potential to create a revolution in the governance of forest products, as private standard-setting bodies may become more important in driving forest practices than are government regulators. . . . At its core, the new regime would reflect a dramatic combination of a shift in the strategy of environmental groups to emphasize international markets and the emergence of powerful environmental sentiments among BC forest product consumers."

The case of Clayoquot Sound reminds us of the potential for relatively contained policy conflicts to dramatically expand in their scope, leading to a cascade of agenda and policy change. Over the years of the Clayoquot conflict, the forestry issue in British Columbia was redefined in ways that emphasized the environmental costs of deforestation, new actors from around the globe took an interest in Canada's forest practices, new patterns of participation took hold, and new institutional venues for policy change were activated. Environmental activists played an important role in initiating such changes by their innovative strategies and dogged determination. The case study of the Quincy Library Group in the next four chapters also highlights the innovative strategies of advocacy groups, but in this case, the goal and result of this innovation was to contain the scope of the conflict.

Part II

The Containment of Conflict in Northern California

6

U.S. Forest Policy and the Birth
of the Quincy Library Group

Forest policy and politics in the Sierra Nevada mountain range in California, home to nine national forests covering about nine million acres of public land, followed a similar historical path to that of other regions in the western United States. For the first part of the twentieth century, conflict over the use of forest resources was relatively contained as the forest service took a largely custodial approach to forest management (Schrepfer 1997). But this consensus broke down in the 1960s in response to an enormous increase in timber production in national forests after World War II coupled with the rise of the environmental movement. In the 1990s, the conflict over old-growth logging in the Pacific Northwest marked the high point of public controversy over the forest service's management practices. Not surprisingly, this conflict reverberated in the Sierra Nevada region as critics also questioned the forest service's conservation strategy for the California spotted owl. The Quincy Library Group (QLG) formed in the midst of these larger debates and growing controversy over public lands management. It hoped to avert an escalation of conflict and bring peace to one region of the Sierra Nevada, and for some time, it looked like the small group might succeed.

The first part of this chapter provides a historical overview of the U.S. forest policy subsystem prior to the formation of the QLG. The discussion focuses on the institutional arrangements underpinning the U.S. forest policy subsystem and examines challenges to the subsystem by environmental advocacy groups starting in the 1960s. Attention is given to the U.S. forest policy system generally and to developments in the Sierra Nevada in particular. This discussion sets the stage for an in-depth examination of the QLG in the next three chapters. A brief overview of the QLG at the end of this chapter provides an introduction to the case.

The Origins of U.S. Forest Policy

Until the late nineteenth century, the logging of forests in the United States—from the spruce trees of New England, to the white pines of the Midwest, to the Douglas firs on the west coast—proceeded at a rapid pace. The vast nation seemed to contain an unlimited supply of timber, and the few voices who urged restraint were largely drowned out by the "cut and run" philosophy and practices of the mid-nineteenth century.[1] In the Sierra Nevada region, a logging industry developed to support mining activities and to supply housing material and fuel to the camps that grew up around the mines. The forests of the Sierra Nevada also supplied timber for the Central Pacific railroad, which was built to settle the west and facilitate transcontinental trade (Beesley 1996, 6). The precise extent of logging in the Sierra Nevada and its effects on the environment during this period are not known, but an 1886 report by the California State Forestry Board claimed that one-third of the timber had been "consumed and destroyed" (Beesley 1996, 6).

Between 1871 and 1897, Congress considered more than two hundred bills relating to forests in the west, signifying growing concern over the lack of regulation over forest resources. Two pieces of legislation—the Forest Reserve Act of 1891 and the Organic Act of 1897—made it past legislative hurdles. The first law authorized the president to "set apart trust reserves where, to preserve timber, he shall deem it advisable," thereby initiating a policy of public ownership of forested lands. The Organic Act provided guidance as to the purpose of the forest reserves, perhaps the most important being to "furnish a continuous supply of timber" (Cooper 1998, 912). These early laws signified a shift away from the disposal of public lands to public retention. Today, public land in the United States amounts to about 28 percent of the total land base. More than 50 percent of publicly owned land is in the western part of the country, reflecting the relatively late entry of the federal government into the "land grab" game.[2]

The early twentieth century witnessed the growth of conservationism and a new era in forest policy. The U.S. Forest Service (USFS), established in 1905 under the leadership of Gifford Pinchot, embraced principles of scientific management to administer the national forests for long-term use. While the forest service would later be criticized for being in the business of timber production, prior to the 1940s it largely played a custodial role. Beesley (1996, 11) notes that forest service officials were engaged in "establishing accurate boundaries, preventing timber theft and trespass, suppressing fires, managing special use activities such as mining and grazing, building ranger facilities, preparing and supervising timber sales, and building campgrounds." He claims the USFS practiced "multiple use" during this era, even though the phrase itself was not used. Annually, the forest service only cut about one billion board feet on its 190 million acres, evidence that timber production was not the overriding duty of the forest service even if the agency embraced timber production as its primary mission (Burnett and Davis 2002, 205).

In the Sierra Nevada, much of the demand for timber was being supplied by private entities, so pressure on the national forests for timber was low and the practice of multiple use relatively easy to maintain (Beesley 1996, 12). In the pre–World War II era, forest service practices and policy were relatively uncontroversial and the service often worked in cooperation with conservation groups even if relations were sometimes strained. Susan Schrepfer (1997) describes how the forest service developed a relationship with the Sierra Club, one of the first conservation groups in the United States whose original focus was on land and forest preservation in the Sierra Nevada region. According to Schrepfer (1997, 129), the forest service saw political advantages to establishing a clientele relationship with the club and received "general support from the organization during the 1940s and early 1950s." This cooperative relationship transformed into a more adversarial one, however, as the forest service shifted away from its custodial role toward a policy of aggressive timber production.

The U.S. Forest Policy Subsystem

The forest service's almost singular orientation toward timber production began after World War II when the demand for timber from national forests increased dramatically. The pressure was due to both a decreased supply of timber from private lands (often due to overcutting and poor management practices) and a greater demand for wood fueled by the postwar housing boom. By 1968, logging on national forests had doubled from prewar levels to 12.8 billion board feet (Cooper 1998, 914), while the percentage of the nation's timber supply coming from the national forests also doubled, from 5 to 10 percent.[3] The Sierra Nevada forests, while not as affected as those in the

Pacific Northwest, were logged more intensely to meet the needs of a growing population in California (Beesley 1996, 18).

Conservation groups, along with some individuals in the forest service and other government agencies, were alarmed at the acceleration of logging on national forests. The Wilderness Society and Sierra Club, for example, questioned the forest service's preference for timber production over other uses of the national forests and began to break with their former ally. Despite their growing criticism of the agency's policies, Hoberg (1997, 49) argues that conservation groups were largely peripheral players in the forest policy subsystem during this period. Conservation groups stood outside the policy subsystem (also dubbed an "iron triangle") inhabited by the forest service, timber companies, and relevant appropriations and authorizing committees (and subcommittees) in Congress.

A number of institutional factors supported the forest policy subsystem, delaying agency and congressional response to the criticisms and demands of conservation groups. Some of these factors date back to the founding of the forest service and to its statutory requirements. The forest service was founded with a clear mission to manage public forests for sustainable timber production. It was staffed by professionals who not only believed in the mission but also used technical, scientific terms that often excluded those who could not speak their professional language (see Clary 1986). And while the forest service cultivated relationships with conservation groups in the earlier part of the century, the agency also developed close ties to the timber industry. Private timber companies relied on the forest service for access to national forestland after it became clear that private lands could not keep up with the nation's demand for timber. The forest service, in turn, relied on the companies to "get the wood out" so it could fulfill its organizational mission and meet congressional mandates.

Congress is also responsible for cultivating and maintaining the closed forest policy subsystem. Congressional representatives had an electoral incentive to support timber production on the national forests. An early twentieth-century law mandated that 25 percent of the revenues from sales on national forests go directly into the treasuries of bordering counties, ostensibly to make up for the loss of taxable property in the county. In 1976, an even more generous formula for local revenue sharing was enacted with the passage of the Payments in Lieu of Taxes Act. These policies ensured widespread rural support for increased timber sales on local national forests and predisposed legislators to favor timber production because of the revenue it brought to their districts. Moreover, as Burnett and Davis (2002, 205) point out, the extraction of timber from national forests created jobs in rural congressional districts: "For legislators representing forested areas, timber sales to lumber, paper, and related industry were favored as a source of jobs for their constituents."

Congress created further incentives for the forest service to maintain a high level of timber production when it passed legislation in 1930 allowing the agency to keep a portion of its timber sales receipts for reforestation purposes. This served as a financial incentive to increase production because the agency's budget was tied to the annual volume of timber sold on its lands. In 1976, Congress granted the agency more discretion in how to spend these funds—it did not have to use the revenue just for reforestation purposes—with the understanding that the agency would reach mandated timber harvest levels (Burnett and Davis 2002). In 1990, the funds from timber sales receipts amounted to $629 million.

One of the more notable aspects of the forest policy subsystem (up until at least the 1970s) was the local orientation of the forest service and of forest policy more generally. Regional USFS offices enjoyed a great deal of discretion and autonomy and were understandably oriented toward local concerns and needs. As Rothman (1997, 110) describes it, "Many factors helped create this local emphasis. The division of management of the agency into regions, its policies of recruitment and promotion from within, its early emphasis on enforcement of federal rules and regulations, and the lonely nature of the life of early foresters—to say nothing of political necessity—all contributed to a decentralized hierarchy that responded to the needs of ranchers, farmers, and timber concerns." Foresters at the local level often implemented policy in a parochial fashion, unaware of how their decisions might affect the national interest in the forests (Rothman 1997).

Beginning in the 1950s and 1960s, however, several local and state-based conservation groups in the Sierra Nevada mounted a challenge to both the USFS and the National Park Service over local issues such as uncontrolled growth in the Tahoe Basin and road expansion within Yosemite National Park (Beesley 1996, 21). Regional forest officials, who had once counted on strong local support for their policies and practices, were faced with growing criticism. Forest service officials often balked at the criticism, as Bolle (1997, 166) explains: "On the local level, some of the protest was directed to Forest Service officials, but it did not find sympathetic ears. In fact, it met with outrage, or at least bureaucratic unhappiness. Most forest officials were deeply committed to the timber mission. They considered the criticism uninformed and totally unfair. They ignored it and tended to withdraw from the public and close off the corridors of communication." But as local political campaigns and protests grew, they combined with larger critiques of administrative policy and practices, making them difficult to ignore. The nationalization of forest policy had begun.

Breaking the Iron Triangle: The Nationalization of Forest Policy

The post–World War II U.S. forest policy subsystem described above bears some similarities to the structure of the B.C. forest system during the same time period. Each system privileged timber production over other uses of the forests. In addition, both the B.C. Ministry of Forests and the USFS maintained close ties to timber companies but were largely autonomous from public scrutiny. And finally, policies and rules were enacted so as to protect and maintain the closed policy subsystem. However, the resemblance between the two subsystems started to fade in the 1960s as U.S. forest practices were subjected to increasing public scrutiny, congressional inquiries, and procedural changes.[4] Participants in the forest policy subsystem, like their counterparts in British Columbia, tried to hold onto their power in the face of these challenges. They succeeded for some time, but changes were afoot that would eventually dislodge the iron triangle.

One of these broad changes was a general trend in the U.S. political system toward what Hoberg (1992) calls "pluralist legalism." Pluralist legalism was a critique of existing administrative and regulatory practices as well as a prescription for how to proceed in the future. According to Hoberg, pluralist legalism was a reaction to three sets of criticisms. First, there was a growing feeling that private interests had captured many regulatory agencies and thus were not attentive to the larger public interest. Second, many thought that Congress made such relationships possible through its willingness to grant a high degree of discretion to government agencies. And finally, critics claimed that professional arrogance on the part of some agencies combined with their discretionary power made it nearly impossible for the public to effectively participate in agency decision making.

The proposed solutions to these "crises," not surprisingly, centered on formalizing administrative procedures, encouraging Congress to write more detailed statutes in order to minimize agency discretion, and creating new opportunities for public participation. Many of these proposals were enacted in the 1970s through amendments to the Administrative Procedures Act, by enactment of the Freedom of Information Act, with the passage of NEPA, and through numerous substantive laws that mandated greater public participation and granted citizens the right to sue agencies for statutory noncompliance.

The most important development for environmentalists, however, concerned a shift in the judicial branch. Prior to the 1970s, courts largely deferred to the "better" judgment of government agencies, making it very difficult for environmental groups or anyone else who was unhappy with agency decisions or practices to challenge them in court. However, the judiciary started to take a harder and closer look at agency decision making in the 1970s, asserting its power in new policy arenas and over a wider range of political questions. In 1975, for example, the Supreme Court ruled that the forest service had been breaking the law for more than seventy years by failing to abide by the standards set out in the 1897 Organic Act. This victory emboldened environmentalists, who now had access to a powerful, alternative venue—the courts.

New Forest Policies, New Opportunities

The litigation strategy pursued by forest activists in the 1980s depended on several procedural and substantive environmental laws passed by Congress in the 1960s and 1970s. The Multiple-Use Sustained Yield Act of 1960 directed the forest service to manage forest resources for multiple uses, the first time that the USFS was directed to respond to pluralistic, public values. However, the act left so much discretion to the forest service that it was a poor vehicle for environmental groups to challenge agency decisions in court (see Cawley and Freemuth 1997). The 1976 National Forest Management Act (NFMA) changed this; it decreased the forest service's discretion by including more specific procedural and substantive guidelines. For example, NFMA required the forest service to develop land resource management plans for all national forests and to consult with the public in the development, review, and revision of the plans. The substantive components of the law, while vague and still allowing for agency discretion, have provided the basis for many environmental lawsuits including the famous spotted owl litigation. The forest service itself turned one of the vague biodiversity requirements of NFMA into an action-forcing standard, mandating that the agency maintain viable populations of fish and wildlife in each forest planning area (Hoberg 1997, 52).

NEPA, passed five years earlier by Congress, added another layer of process to forest planning and thus opened up many avenues for citizen participation and litigation. NEPA required all government agencies to undergo an environmental impact review process when their activities had a significant effect on the environment and provided the public with valuable information about agency decision-making processes published in environmental impact statements (EISs). Citizens can challenge EISs in court on the basis that an agency failed to consider all the possible alternatives to its proposed action, that the environmental assessment was not supported by sound scientific evidence, or that an agency failed to go through an EIS process altogether. While the public participation requirements of NEPA are still evolving through case law, a 1992 case suggests that government agencies not only have a responsibility to solicit public input, but they should also consider public comments on EISs in making their final decision (see U.S. Office of Technology Assessment 1992, 79).

Another avenue for citizen participation and redress involves the administrative appeals process. The forest service is not required to provide its own venue for citizen appeals of its decisions, but it has maintained one in various forms since the beginning of the twentieth century. According to a 1992 report by the Office of Technology Assessment, the current administrative appeals system is fairly informal.[5] Nevertheless, environmental groups (and timber interests) have used the appeals process to challenge forest plans and specific projects within a plan. The number of appeals more than doubled during the 1980s, from 584 in 1983 to 1,298 in 1988 (U.S. Office of Technology Assessment 1992, 96). In 1989, Gericke and Sullivan (1994) surveyed ninety-six national forests that had completed a final land resource management plan and found that citizens' groups had filed an impressive 811 appeals challenging the plans (574 of which were subsequently resolved). And in 1991, the forest service faced ninety-six lawsuits (the next stage after administrative appeals), the majority of which concerned timber sales on public lands (Hoberg 1997, 53).

These numbers suggest that environmental groups have taken advantage of both administrative and formal legal avenues to challenge forest service policy and practices. It is important to note that along with these formal institutional changes, a number of informal changes in the forest service have made it (over time) more accessible to environmental interest groups and more amenable to their views on ecosystem management. Largely because of the new substantive requirements in NFMA, the forest service had to hire wildlife biologists, hydrologists, fisheries specialists, archaeologists, and soil scientists. William Dietrich (1992, 98–99) argues that these new employees are more "liberal, worldly, and wildlife-oriented than their predecessors." Dave Peters, project manager for the Plumas National Forest in northern California in 2001, confirmed that these internal changes have opened up the forest service to new ideas: "The idea of having anything other than a forester or maybe an engineer in the line positions was unheard of years ago. . . . But that has changed dramatically, as foresters are certainly not in the majority in terms of professionals. . . . As leadership changed, particularly with Chief Dombeck [chief of the forest service from 1997 to 2001] who is a fisheries biologist himself, people started believing that things had changed in the Forest Service" (Peters 2001).

The changes in forest policy described above did not lead to immediate changes in forestry practices, however. In the 1980s, the level of timber harvest on national forests increased dramatically under the Reagan administration, reaching a record level of more than 12.5 billion board feet in 1987. Environmental groups became increasingly active on forest issues around this time, in response to the recalcitrance of the forest service and the Reagan administration. In 1987, the Sierra Club Legal Defense Fund launched a series of lawsuits aimed at protecting old-growth forests, leading to several court injunctions that virtually halted logging in many Pacific Northwest forests. Timber interests, recognizing that their environmental opponents had won in the judicial arena and were making inroads into the administrative arena, switched their attention to Congress. The northwest delegation to Congress responded to the lawsuits by exempting existing timber sales from the court injunctions via an appropriations bill rider. Environmental groups fought back in their preferred venue—the courts—and once again, the courts found in their favor, striking down significant parts of the rider.

While the litigation in the late 1980s and early 1990s only applied to forests in the Pacific Northwest, its effects were felt in the Sierra Nevada. The California spotted owl, whose habitat includes parts of the Sierra Nevada, is closely related to its northern cousin. This fact left the forest service vulnerable to the same claims made in the Pacific Northwest, namely that their policies for protecting the California spotted owl were inadequate. When the NRDC challenged a series of timber sales in the Tahoe National Forest in 1991, the forest service took note. In an attempt to avoid litigation, the agency worked in cooperation with the state of California to assess the viability of the California spotted owl. This process produced what has been called the CASPO report (the California Spotted Owl report), setting the stage for further restrictions on old-growth logging. It is in this context that the QLG formed.

The Forging of Consensus by the QLG

The northern region of the Sierra Nevada mountain range in California is home to the Lassen, Plumas, and Tahoe national forests. The three national forests encompass about 3.5 million acres, making the USFS the predominant land manager in the region. The town of Quincy itself is surrounded by the Plumas National Forest. The Plumas and nearby Lassen national forests are relatively dry, fire-adapted forests that have been logged for the commercial timber market since the beginning of the twentieth century. While timber jobs have historically been an important part of the local economy, from 1985 to 1995 employment in the timber industry fell about 40 percent while employment in the service sector increased by roughly the same amount. The job losses in the timber sector were typically blamed on environmentalists, setting the stage for a conflict between the "usual suspects"—the timber industry, workers, and various local business owners versus environmentalists.

In the mid-1980s, the first signs of conflict between the timber industry and regional environmentalists surfaced. The Friends of Plumas Wilderness (FPW), a local environmental group, was working with the Sierra Club, the Wilderness Society, and the NRDC to halt logging in surrounding roadless areas and old-growth forests. During this same time, the forest service was preparing a draft management plan for the Plumas National Forest as mandated by NFMA. In 1986, FPW presented their "Conservationist Alternative" to the Plumas National Forest Plan. Their alternative called for selective logging, old-growth set-asides, and timber harvests of 247 million board feet. The timber industry vehemently opposed FPW's plan, and the forest service subsequently rejected it.[6] In the next two years, the forest service allowed record timber harvests in the area: In 1987 the industry logged 587 million board feet in the Lassen, Plumas, and Tahoe national forests. In 1988, timber harvest topped out at 640 million board feet.

But the tide began to turn in favor of environmentalists in the early 1990s. By this time, court injunctions had virtually halted logging in the Pacific Northwest in order to protect northern spotted owl habitat along the Washington and Oregon coasts. In addition, antilogging groups had successfully nationalized the forest issue by using the federal courts and appealing to a national constituency, one that increasingly demanded more attention to ecological values in the management of U.S. national forests (Hoberg 1997). Closer to home, local and regional environmentalists were using NFMA and NEPA to delay and periodically block timber sales in the Sierra Nevada mountain range, with quite a bit of success. In 1992, when California state authorities released the CASPO report, it was clear that current policy and practices were inadequate to protect the owl and prevent it from being listed under the Endangered Species Act. More restrictions, it seemed, were inevitable.

Not surprisingly, tensions between timber workers and local environmentalists in Quincy and the surrounding communities flared. As mills threatened to close, local environmentalists were asking for even more wilderness set-asides. Tom Nelson, director of timberlands for Sierra Pacific Industries (owner of the largest sawmill in the area), was acutely aware of the industry's vulnerable position. In the fall of 1992 he admitted to environmental attorney Michael Jackson that Jackson had won. Nelson and Jackson agreed to meet with local county supervisor Bill Coates, who had called for an informal meeting among the three men to discuss a possible compromise. Out of these humble beginnings the QLG was formed. The three men subsequently drafted the Quincy Library Group Community Stability Proposal, a management plan for 2.5 million acres in the Plumas, Lassen, and parts of the Tahoe national forests.

The QLG's plan was based on the 1986 FPW conservation alternative, the alternative forest plan that industry had rejected six years earlier. The QLG proposal purportedly struck a compromise between ecological and economic goals: On the preservationist side, it set aside about a half million acres of roadless areas, limited clear-cut logging to three acres, and provided for buffer zones around aquatic ecosystems. In order to supply the local mills with timber, the QLG plan allowed group and individual tree selection on about 1.5 million acres, although the actual harvest per year would be closer to nine thousand acres. Later, the QLG added a significant fire management strategy that called for the construction of fuel breaks ("defensible fuel profile zones") on about sixty thousand acres per year as a way to decrease the spread of catastrophic wildfires.

As news about the proposal spread through the small town, Jackson, Coates, and Nelson decided to "go public." On July 10, 1993, at a town meeting that attracted about 250 people in the region, they asked people to sign on to the plan (the vote was estimated to be 245–5 in favor). After the meeting, the core group grew to about forty members, and they fanned out to the nearby towns of Susanville, Sierraville, Chester, and Greenville to do community outreach and build wider regional support for the plan. Notably absent from these meetings were the local employees of the forest service, who were purposefully excluded because of QLG members' suspicion of the forest service.

Eventually, though, the QLG had to involve the local forest service office because it had the authority to implement the QLG's plan. But a reportedly cool reception by the local USFS representatives sent QLG members to greener pastures. In early 1994, QLG went above the heads of the regional forest office and met with USFS Chief Jack Ward Thomas and Jim Lyons, undersecretary for natural resources and environment, in Washington, D.C. Over the next several years, the QLG cultivated its relationships with these officials in hopes of finding an administrative solution. The forest service, however, was slow in altering existing management plans in order to accommodate the

QLG proposal, leading the QLG to go over the head of the forest service and appeal directly to the Clinton administration and top officials in the Department of Agriculture ("The Quincy Library Group" 2001, 11).

In November 1995, Secretary of Agriculture Dan Glickman announced that the agency would provide $4.7 million to fund parts of the Quincy Library Group Community Stability Proposal. Most of these funds were to go toward fuels management activities, including the removal of overstocked timber and the creation of defensible fuel profile zones designed to prevent the spread of forest fires. In explaining his decision to fund part of the QLG plan, Secretary Glickman praised the QLG for its innovative process: "This is a California experiment to see if we can talk to each other about natural resources instead of killing each other. . . . The value is in the process. That's what we're investing in here" (quoted in "The Quincy Library Group" 2001, 11).

Secretary Glickman's gestures toward the QLG were welcomed but did not satisfy the group. The QLG wanted its entire proposal to be adopted; eventually, QLG leaders concluded that the administrative route was a dead end and turned to Congress instead. When the QLG had first visited Washington in 1994, it had met with more than one hundred members of Congress, forging close ties to Representative Wally Herger (R-CA) and Senator Dianne Feinstein (D-CA). In 1997, these efforts paid off: Representative Herger introduced a bill (HR 858) based on the QLG proposal. After HR 8588 passed overwhelmingly in the House Resources Committee, representatives debated it on the floor, where it was amended and then passed by an almost unanimous vote of 459–1. The bill did not do as well in the Senate, where Senator Barbara Boxer (D-CA) blocked debate on the proposal due to concerns that the plan did not adequately protect the environment. However, QLG sponsors found a way around the Senate when in October 1998 they attached the bill as a rider to a federal appropriations bill. President Clinton signed the bill later in the month and the Herger-Feinstein Quincy Library Group Forest Recovery and Economic Stability Act became law. The law authorizes $98.8 million to fund a five-year pilot project for implementing the recommendations of the QLG and directs the forest service to consider amending land-use plans for the Plumas, Lassen, and Tahoe national forests to accommodate QLG projects in the future (Davis and King n.d.).

The QLG was not without critics: Some individuals and organized groups had opposed the QLG and its plan from the beginning. Most of this opposition came from environmentalists at the local, regional, and national levels who were concerned with the substance of the plan as well as the precedent it might set in terms of local management of national forests. Local opponents, such as John Preschutti and Neil Dion, had tried rather unsuccessfully to get the attention and support of the national environmental organizations early on; to their chagrin, the national groups waited until the plan was being debated on the floor of the House to wage a serious opposition campaign. According to Dion, their efforts to expand conflict and increase attention and participation were "too little and too late" (2001). The QLG, despite appealing to federal institutions and attracting national opposition, successfully managed the conflict over forests in their region and relocalized it.

The next three chapters examine in detail how the QLG kept conflict contained and explain why their strategies were successful.

7

Retreating to the Local

Issue Containment in Northern California

The battle over old-growth forests in the United States captured public attention throughout the 1980s and into the 1990s as the bitter fight over the ancient forests in the states of Washington and Oregon raged in and outside the courtroom. While the Pacific Northwest was the epicenter of the conflict in the United States, northern California was also experiencing its share of "timber wars." The bitter rhetoric and occasional violence that characterized the conflict in the Pacific Northwest were less intense in the small logging towns of the northern Sierra Nevada but were not entirely absent either. In the town of Quincy, tensions between local environmentalists and timber industry workers sometimes flared. Quincy environmental attorney Michael Jackson, for example, recalls days when logging trucks would drive back and forth in front of his office, honking their horns to protest his environmental activism (2001).

In November 1992, in the midst of the conflict, three former adversaries in the Quincy area—representing logging interests, environmentalists, and local officials—sat down with one another to find a way to end the timber wars. After several months of negotiations, the group presented its forest management plan to surrounding communities in northern California, a plan that called for the local management of about 2.5 million acres of federal forestland. The proposal sought to balance environmental concerns with economic ones by designating some sensitive lands as off limits to logging while allowing significant thinning and selective cutting in other areas to ensure an adequate supply of timber to the local saw mills. The QLG, as the group of collaborators came to be known, searched for a way to get the forest service to accept and implement its plan. Meanwhile, community tensions had subsided, former adversaries were treating one another civilly, and some local residents were beginning to believe in a "win-win" solution to the timber conflict after all.

In short, it was clear that the conflict in the northern Sierras, while not over, had altered significantly. The QLG had done what seemed impossible—it had contained a conflict that showed every sign of spiraling out of control. The group had also shifted the terms of the forest debate in the region, effectively reinserting the discourse of the local into what had become a national issue. In fact, the nationalization of the forest issue was a key component of environmentalists' strategy during the conflict over logging in the Pacific Northwest. Policy success for environmental groups in that conflict had hinged on including a wider public in the debate so as to shift the balance of power away from regional timber interests and their allies in Congress. As George Hoberg (1997, 60) notes, the changes wrought in the U.S. forest policy subsystem in the 1990s "would not have been possible if the [forest] issue continued to be constructed in regional terms, as forest policy has traditionally been."

Given national attention to the old-growth forest issue, how did the QLG reframe the debate as a local problem that required a local solution? How did the group contain the issue in the face of attempts by national environmental groups to expand it? This chapter investigates the problem definition strategies of various parties involved in the Quincy case with an eye toward understanding how the Quincy coalition redefined the debate over national forests in their region. In the case of Clayoquot Sound, we saw how environmentalists successfully *expanded* the issue of logging from a local issue to a global one, to the point where Clayoquot Sound became linked to the problem of biodiversity and the fate of the world's rain forests. In the case of the Quincy group, by contrast, the conflict over logging was *relocalized* so that the issues, rather than broadening and becoming more conflict-ridden, became narrower and contained.

The QLG used two sets of issue definition strategies to defuse conflict and to garner support for its forest management plan. First, it restricted conflict in a contentious policy subsystem by subsuming more emotional issues associated with the management of national forests—issues such as the spotted owl, levels of timber harvest, and the preservation of old growth—under the less controversial and more technical issue of forest fires and the broader (but rather vague) issue of "forest health." Because the problem of forest fires is easily constructed as a local problem, the fire focus supported the Quincy coalition's call for more local involvement in national forest management.

And a focus on forest health, or in this case a lack of health, justified the otherwise controversial logging components of the QLG plan.

A second strategy for containing conflict involved focusing on the QLG's decision-making process, a process widely viewed as a solution to the so-called resource wars in the west. The Quincy group and its supporters tapped into positive, culturally salient images associated with local collaborative processes, sometimes referred to as "grassroots ecosystem management" (Weber 2000). The allure of the cooperative and community-oriented rhetoric proved difficult for opponents to combat and impossible for Congress to resist. As long as the discussion was focused on the QLG decision-making process, proponents of the QLG plan were at an advantage and opponents were fighting an uphill battle to expand conflict and shift the debate to more substantive (and controversial) issues.

The reframing of the forest debate served important purposes: It helped to create and maintain the QLG itself, and it proved instrumental in securing the support of Congress for the QLG legislation. Both the QLG and its proposed legislation were potentially controversial. First, the problem of old-growth forests was considered by much of the public to be a national problem. The Quincy group plan, though, called for increased local control over national forest management. QLG members and supporters necessarily invoked arguments and rhetoric that national environmental groups had been fighting for decades—namely, the argument that local (typically rural) communities have more of a stake in the fate of federal forests than urban and national interests. Second, the Quincy plan included a significant increase in logging at a time when regional and national environmental groups were calling for decreases and moratoriums on logging in national forests. Forest activists, with the support of significant portions of the American public, were demanding large wilderness set-asides and complete protection for old-growth forests in Oregon and Washington. The QLG legislation, however, would double the amount of logging and intensively manage major portions of the Lassen, Plumas, and Tahoe national forests.

This chapter examines how Quincy proponents were able to win support for a plan that defected from the preservationist ideal. The first section offers a short theoretical discussion about strategies for defusing conflict. Next, I look at how the Quincy plan and its authorization of more logging in particular was framed as a *solution* to the catastrophic forest fires that had been burning in the Sierra Nevada in the 1980s and 1990s. The chapter then examines how the QLG's decision-making *process* helped to mask the substantive criticisms by opponents to the QLG plan. Finally, I consider the alternative interpretive packages offered by QLG opponents who tried to expand conflict around the QLG plan, and explain why they failed in their efforts.

Defusing Conflict

The story of the QLG and how they contained conflict differs from typical studies of issue containment, many of which examine how small groups of policymakers prevent conflict by tightly controlling access to and debate within the policy process (see, for example, Bosso 1987). Because conflict was already present in the forest policy subsystem at the time the QLG formed, the Quincy coalition had to defuse rather than prevent conflict. As suggested above, the politics and rhetoric surrounding forest management were contentious in the early 1990s; the days when the forest service could manage the national forests in consultation with timber interests, and with relatively little public critique or oversight, were long over. Indeed, conflict had been developing for decades within the policy subsystem. Environmental groups had successfully challenged forest service land management plans in the courts, and in the early 1990s they won an important victory in the court of public opinion as the issue gained national prominence. In short, the issue of logging on national forests had broken out of its earlier boundaries where forest management was seen as a technical issue best left to the experts and forests were valued principally as a source of timber (Hoberg 1997).

The Quincy group therefore faced considerable challenges. It is more difficult to contain a conflict once it has developed than prevent conflict from erupting in the first place. As Schattschneider (1960, 15) argued, "The best point at which to manage conflict is before it starts. Once a conflict starts it is not easy to control because it is difficult to be exclusive about a fight." Conflict implies the presence of competing issue definitions, and these competing definitions make it hard for any one group to control the direction of policy. Conflict injects uncertainty and volatility into the policy process, as different groups assert competing causal stories about a problem and advocate for their policy solutions (Stone 1988). To defuse conflict after it has developed, these competing policy images must be overcome or diminished.

The issue definition strategies of groups who want to recontain conflict differ from those employed by groups trying to prevent attention and conflict in the first place. The strategy of denying the existence of a problem is not available once conflict has erupted. For example, the QLG could not ignore the problem of the California spotted owl, particularly given the attention to its cousin, the northern spotted owl.[1] Rather than deny a problem, advocacy groups who want to contain conflict must try to diminish the perceived importance of a problem by reassuring the public that it is being addressed, or by minimizing its scope and significance (Cobb and Ross 1997; Rochefort and Cobb 1994; Cobb and Elder 1972). But even these strategies can fail if a problem is highly visible and competing advocacy groups are rehearsed in effective issue expansion tactics.

If conflict around an issue expands, what strategies can groups pursue to recontain it? One issue definition strategy involves shifting attention to the least controversial elements of a policy issue. As Baumgartner and Jones (1993) suggest, policymakers and the media rarely reflect on all aspects of an issue simultaneously; rather, different components of an issue are considered separately. Some of these components are particularly divisive along partisan and ideological lines or tap into deeply held cultural values. Pollack, Lilie, and Vittes (1993, 30) call these issues "easy" in that they are "familiar, ends-oriented and symbolic," allowing everyday citizens to have strong opinions even if they are not attentive to the details of the policy debate. Other elements of an issue may engender a level of consensus among competing groups or involve such highly technical matters that a majority of the public pays little attention to the debate. Groups and individuals who are trying to restrict conflict will focus on the less controversial aspects of an issue. Put differently, strategically minded advocacy groups will redefine an issue in a way that promotes consensus. Their opponents, on the other hand, will try to redirect attention to the more divisive aspects of an issue so as to expand conflict.

The multifaceted nature of policy problems allows advocacy groups to focus on different aspects of an issue depending on which are most salient to their members, politicians, or the public. For example, the "forest problem" includes the problem of timber harvest levels and methods, road-building and its effects, the preservation of roadless areas and old growth forests, the status of forest-dependent species, the frequency and severity of forest fires, the quality of water resources in the forests, and the status of timber-dependent jobs. As the focus shifts from one dimension to another, different interests will be advantaged or disadvantaged, and different publics mobilized or demobilized. For example, when the forest problem is defined primarily in terms of fire risk, fire experts are empowered. Environmentalists calling for zero harvesting on public lands are disadvantaged because their no-cut position appears to defy some fire experts who insist that thinning the forest is essential for preventing catastrophic fires.

The question arises whether the QLG's rhetoric about forest fires and forest health merely reflected objective facts about the Sierra Nevada forests.

Certainly, the claims made by the Quincy coalition about fuel loads, forest fires, and disease-ridden forests have some factual basis: As Best (1989, 247) notes, "Calling a statement a claim does not discredit it." But for the purposes of this study, knowledge about the objective state of the forests is less important than analyzing the content and viability of various claims being made about them. In other words, I want to understand why some claims are more prevalent and successful than others without denying that objective components of an issue may place limits on (or provide opportunities for) the kind of claims that can be made (Best 1989).[2] As Pollack, Lilie, and Vittes (1993, 32) argue, "Any given issue has objective aspects that place limits—narrow or broad—on the subjective claims that can be made about it." The relevant questions are why claims emerge, why some claims are more robust than others, and what kind of policies result when certain claims win out over others. The next section explores the QLG's claims about forest fires and forest health and explains their effect on the forest conflict in northern California.

Issue Containment in Northern California: Forest Fires, Forest Health, and Spotted Owls

Environmental activist Linda Blum celebrated a significant, if temporary, victory in 1990 when the USFS agreed to suspend logging plans on three northern California forests where the California spotted owl nested. Linda Blum and Michael Jackson, a Quincy attorney and fellow environmental activist, had filed two lawsuits opposing the timber sales; after several appeals they finally won. But just three months after the forest service's decision to halt logging, a wild fire consumed major portions of the Sequoia forests. For Linda, it was an ironic victory. They had succeeded in preserving California spotted owl habitat only to see it damaged in a fire and subsequently logged for salvage timber (Blum 2001).[3]

Forest fires are a natural and common component of the Sierra Nevada ecosystem. The forests have adapted to these fires over the course of many centuries; species that survive fires (or thrive in it, such as lodge pole pines) dominate the forests. However, most experts agree that the risk of fire has increased in the last century due to at least three human-caused factors. First, for most of the twentieth century, the USFS implemented a fire suppression policy, spending millions of dollars to prevent fires in national forests through its "Smokey Bear" campaigns and the like (Busenberg 2004). In the Sierra Nevada, these policies have resulted in a build-up of highly flammable understory and brush, debris that would have been removed by natural fires had they been allowed to burn. Second, timber harvesting programs that took the largest (and most valuable) trees while leaving the fast-burning smaller ones have also been cited as causes of large-scale forest fires. Finally, some experts and environmentalists claim that clear-cutting spreads forest fires because the practice leaves highly flammable slash in place of more fire-resistant large trees.

Whatever the cause of the fires, the Quincy coalition agreed that forest fires were a major problem facing the community. For local residents, fire threatened their private property and personal safety. For loggers, fire was both an economic and safety issue. And for local environmentalists, fire threatened the very forests and species they were working to preserve. Moreover, forest fires could not be controlled using conventional tools in the environmentalists' tool chest. As Linda Blum put it, "[Fire] was the one factor that I could not nail down politically. If push came to shove, I could help file a lawsuit to stop someone from doing something bad, or I could try a public relations campaign to push for a change in the law. But I could not do anything about it when fires broke out" (Blum 2001).

Despite local concern about forest fires, fuels management was not initially part of the 1993 Quincy Library Group Community Stability Proposal. By 1995, however, fire reduction had become an important, even central, issue to the group and its supporters. According to Louis Blumberg, an outspoken critic of the QLG, the group "stole" the fire issue away from a regional coalition that had secured federal funding for fuels reduction in the Sierra Nevada. The Quincy group learned that the fire issue had "political cache" and had the potential to bring in federal money because it "was an area where there was agreement between environmentalists and industry, and politicians will always gravitate toward an area where they see compromise and agreement" (Blumberg 2001). Other critics of the QLG echoed Blumberg's arguments: Neil Dion, a local opponent of the group, claimed that the QLG piggybacked on the issue after forest fires became a "hot" topic that almost everyone agreed on (2001). Quincy group members, not surprisingly, explain it differently. According to Jackson, the QLG had been concerned about fire from the beginning yet were "too humble" in 1993 to suggest a solution. Two years later, they adopted the fuel reduction recommendations of a joint Congressional–Forest Service study of the Sierra Nevada forests, the Sierra Nevada Ecosystem Project (SNEP) report (2001).

The QLG's use of forest fires as a way to reframe the forest problem might have been less of a conscious strategy than its critics suggest. Nevertheless, QLG members acknowledge the significance of fire as a unifying issue to the group. One of the cofounders of the group, Plumas county supervisor Bill Coates (n.d.), explains what brought the diverse interests together: "We strongly agreed that national planning wasn't working and that the forty-year-old concepts of the 'Smokey the Bear' campaign needed to be replaced with a 'healthy forests, healthy streams' campaign that seeks to restore forests to pre-settlement conditions." QLG member Frank Stewart also acknowledged the importance of the fire issue to the group: "It is the reality of catastrophic forest fires and the devastation that they wreak on the communities and the environment," he claimed before a Senate subcommittee, "that feeds the passion of our commitment to this effort" (U.S. Congress, Senate, "Hearing on S. 1028," 1997).

A number of events kept the issue of fire on the Quincy coalition's agenda and the public's agenda. The 1994 Cottonwood fire in the Sierras near Quincy, a fire that burned 47,800 acres, described as "a holocaust" by Linda Blum and "completely fuels related," suggested that a more aggressive fuels management program was needed (Blum 2001). As the Quincy group approached various agency officials and congressional representatives with its plan in the mid-1990s, fires continued to burn in California and in other areas in the western United States. In 1996, for example, 860,000 acres of forest were consumed in California (6.7 million acres burned nationally), following a record season just two years earlier that resulted in more than 550,000 acres of forest fires.

In sum, the threat of forest fires united the fledgling group, generated local support for the QLG plan, and bolstered congressional support for the 1997 Quincy Library Group Forest Recovery and Economic Stability Act. The forest fire issue contained conflict around the forest issue locally by giving former adversaries an issue to agree on and by making further negotiations around more controversial issues possible. More importantly, perhaps, it helped the QLG sell its solution to key allies in Congress. Several members of Congress initially resisted supporting a bill that increased logging in the Sierra Nevada. In general, legislators had to take into account the fact that public attitudes toward the national forests were increasingly preservationist in nature. Public opinion surveys showed that a majority of the public valued the forests more for their ecological assets than their economic potential. Western legislators in particular faced cross-cutting pressures from extractive industries on the one hand, and middle and upper income urban voters on the other, due to several demographic and economic changes in the west.[4]

The fire frame, however, shifted the terms of debate in two key ways, opening a window of opportunity for supporters of the QLG plan, including those in Congress. First, forest fires were blamed for the ecological degradation of the national forests and the decline of the California spotted owl. Blame was shifted from logging to forest fires, so that the key trade-off was not "owls versus jobs" but "owls versus fires." This reframing of the famous (or infamous) trade-off between timber jobs and spotted owls significantly decreased and defused conflict over the Quincy plan. A second effect of the fire frame was that it relocalized the forest issue. Because fires affect local communities more than distant locales, the focus on fires helped QLG supporters argue for more local control in national forest management.

Redefining the Debate: Owls versus Fires

The QLG formed just two years after U.S. District Court Judge William Dwyer halted all forest service timber sales on old-growth forests until the agency developed a plan to protect the northern spotted owl. This 1991 decision and similar rulings in subsequent lawsuits meant that logging in many timber-dependent communities in the Pacific Northwest ground to a halt. The conflict that ensued was intense and laden with powerful symbols and images. Pictures of the spotted owl (most famously on the cover of *Time* magazine on June 25, 1990), clear-cuts, and intact ancient rain forests graced national newspapers and magazines, inviting the public to sympathize with the preservationist cause. On the other hand, images of out-of-work loggers and depressed logging towns served as a reminder of the human costs of preservation policies. Taken together, these images were highly emotional, political, and value-laden. They were the visual equivalent of the "jobs versus owls" rhetoric that simplified the choice before the public; they also invited public controversy because of the stark trade-off between human needs and environmental preservation implied in the discourse.[5]

In order to decrease the level of conflict in the Sierra Nevada region, the Quincy coalition had to defuse the polarizing images and rhetoric that characterized conflict in the Pacific Northwest. This was accomplished in part through the substitution of forest fires as the threat to owls, rather than logging and timber sales on national forestlands. Clearly, the survival of the California spotted owl was already an issue, a problem that could not be ignored or easily minimized.[6] The task before the Quincy coalition was to address the spotted owl issue and yet reduce conflict in the process. By focusing on forest fires as the primary threat to the owl's survival, they effectively raised an alternative causal story to the owl's decline and the ecological state of the forests generally.

In several statements by QLG members and supporters, fire became the biggest threat to the owl and its habitat rather than logging. Consider, for example, the following statement from a letter the QLG sent to the forest service: "Success in dealing with the owl issue has correctly been said to depend largely on *reducing the probability of high intensity wildfire* and increasing the amount of habitat" (Quincy Library Group 1998; emphasis added). Bill Coates, in an interview with a reporter, put it this way: "The environmentalists talk about danger to spotted owls—well, I know two places where they don't exist. One is a 60,000 acre wildfire burn. The other is a burn that covers 40,000 acres" (quoted in Martin 1999, A15). Michael Jackson, one of the founders of the QLG, confessed that his former views about the owl—namely, that loggers were the biggest threat to its survival—were wrong. Today, he is convinced that fire is more dangerous to the owl than the logger's chainsaw (Jackson 2001).

Members of Congress largely accepted this causal story. Representative Helen Chenoweth, a strong supporter of the QLG bill in the House, argued that forest fires were the dominant threat to wildlife: "It just does not take a rocket scientist to realize that when you have uncontrollable fires in the forests, it destroys the wildlife, the little critters and the big critters."[7] What is most notable about the statements is how logging disappears as a source of the owl's decline, the health of the forests, or even as a contributor to the fire problem. Representative Don Young (R-AK), for example, openly exonerates the logging industry for any role it might play in degrading forest habitats: "Yes, our national forests are in terrible, deplorable shape, *not because they were logged*, but because this administration and, yes, other administrations decided that every area could live naturally" (emphasis added).[8] Stories that identified "mismanagement" as a cause of the forest problem also served to shift attention away from logging. Mismanagement was a code word for flawed fuels management policies that could be blamed on unnamed political actors, such as the USFS, Congress, or the president.

Republican members of Congress were not the only ones who blamed fires for creating ecological problems in the national forests. For example, Representative Charles Stenholm, a Democrat from Texas, endorsed the QLG bill, claiming, "Catastrophic wildfire is a chief threat to the ecological integrity of the forest system," without mentioning any other threats, such as clearcut logging.[9] Senator Dianne Feinstein (D-CA), a key ally of the QLG, also acknowledged the centrality of forest fires to the QLG and its plan: "Their [the QLG's] overriding concern was that a catastrophic fire could destroy both the natural environment, wildlife and old-growth trees, and the potential for jobs and economic stability in their community" (U.S. Congress, Senate, "Hearing on S. 1028," 1997).

Overall, during congressional floor debate on the 1997 Quincy Library Group Forest Recovery and Economic Stability Act, logging or excessive timber harvest was mentioned only three times as degrading the ecology of the

Sierra Nevada. Forest fires, on the other hand, were mentioned thirteen times as a general problem and eight times as a cause of forest "sickness" specifically. As seen in table 7.1, causal stories that shifted the blame away from loggers and onto something else dominated the congressional debate. Interestingly, the individuals who named logging as a problem were all initially opposed to the QLG legislation, while those who mentioned forest fires as the problem were uniformly supportive of the bill.[10]

Forest fires and fuels mismanagement were also a big concern during a 1997 hearing on the QLG bill in the House Subcommittee on Forest and Forest Health (see U.S. Congress, House, "Hearing on H.R. 858," 1997). Witnesses and representatives cited forest fires as a general problem facing the national forests (or the Sierra Nevada specifically) nineteen times, while the QLG bill was constructed as a solution to the fire problem another eighteen times. In short, the fire "crisis" displaced other crises in the woods, such as clear-cuts and the damage they inflict on terrestrial and aquatic habitat.

The technical nature of the fire discussion helped the Quincy coalition defuse the forest conflict by shifting the rhetoric from more emotional, value-laden debates to detailed discussions about the nature of the fire problem and solutions to it. In addition, the fire issue relocalized the debate over national forests. Proponents of the Quincy plan constructed the fire problem as a local issue because it is the neighboring population that suffers most directly from forest fires. Consider, for example, the statement of Representative Young

TABLE 7.1   Causal Stories in Congressional Floor Debate on the QLG Bill

Cause of forest problem[a]	Number of mentions[b]	Percentage by pro-QLG speakers[c]
Fires	8	100
Mismanagement	4	100
Logging	3	0
Drought, Insects	2	100
Population Growth	1	0

Source: Compiled by the author from *Congressional Record* 143 (July 9, 1997): H4924–44.

[a]Each statement that identified a problem with the forests and explained what caused the problem was counted.

[b]Every causal statement was counted, regardless of whether the speakers had made similar statements earlier in their speeches.

[c]Supporters were those members of Congress who expressed their support for the QLG bill during the floor debate on July 9, 1997.

(R-AK) during debate over the QLG bill: "Listen to those that are directly affected. *Yes, this is a national forest, but there are people that live in, around, and with the national forest that every day they wake up, they are faced with a problem of mismanagement under this administration.* . . . They are managing it today [like] a bunch of aliens who have no concept about the potential of the fire damage, no concept of the homes that are lost" (emphasis added).[11]

In sum, the fire frame helped to decrease conflict over the QLG proposal. Many environmentalists agreed that forest fires were a problem, as did timber workers and timber companies. Consequently, when the focus of the debate was on fires and the Quincy group's fuels reduction program, the debate between the two most contentious groups in the forest policy arena—the timber industry and environmentalists—was subdued. As shown later in the chapter, environmental opponents attempted to question both the extent of the fire problem and the QLG's solution to catastrophic fires, but the ensuing discussion was rather technical in nature and thus did not expand the issue significantly. The Quincy coalition argued that the fire components of their plan would restore the forests to "pre-settlement" conditions—to the "open, fire-resistant state European settlers found when they first arrived" (Coates, quoted in Little 1997, A6). The symbolic framing of their solution as "restorative" and "natural" further helped to legitimize the QLG plan.

Reimagining the Forests: Images of Forest "Sickness" and Health

The theme of restoration and naturalness was contrasted to the current state of Sierra Nevada forests, which were characterized as "sick" and "unhealthy." Images of sick forests were prominent in the Quincy coalition's statements and literature. These images effectively undermined one of the most potent symbols that environmentalists used to expand the forest issue and to increase attention to the problems in U.S. national forests—namely, the image of relatively intact and grand forests. Images of old-growth forests are the symbolic equivalent of large charismatic mammals like the whale and elephant, animal species that have elicited widespread public support for preservationist policies. As Louis Blumberg (formerly of the Wilderness Society) admitted, the area covered by the Quincy plan lacked some "charisma"; as he put it, "The notion of two million acres of national forest land spread out over seven counties that includes the good, the bad, and the ugly, you know it is hard to garner a lot of focus," even though the area contains significant stands of old growth (2001).

In the Clayoquot Sound case, environmental groups used images of intact rain forests to secure support for their preservation goals. The images and associated rhetoric proved very successful in eliciting sympathy from other environmental organizations, segments of the Canadian public, and the broader international community. Clayoquot Sound, and British Columbia's rain forests more generally, were advertised as the largest remaining temperate rain forests in the world—exquisite forest ecosystems that were relatively untouched by humans. Human interference in these forests, except for purposes of recreation or spiritual practice, was constructed as threatening and unhealthy for the forests. The activists' rhetoric tapped into what Lowe and Morrison (1984, 79) identify as a dramatic metatheme in environmental discourse, one of "unspoiled nature" against human-caused pollution or interference.

The images and rhetoric during the QLG debate were notably different. The Sierra Nevada forests were not portrayed as pristine, holistic ecosystems that should be revered, but rather as sick and dying—prone to wildfires, insect infestations, rot, and an assortment of diseases. The image of the Sierras as a broken ecosystem helped to build support for the Quincy forest plan, which called for extensive thinning and management of the forests. Images of sick and unhealthy forests surfaced in the QLG's literature, in testimony and floor debate over the QLG bill, and in the media's coverage of the QLG. For example, in a House subcommittee hearing on the QLG bill, there were eight different references to sick, dying, or unnatural forests (U.S. Congress, House, "Hearing on H.R. 858," 1997). Similarly, during the debate on the QLG bill on the House floor, representatives frequently referred to a forest and ecosystem "health crisis." Representative John Doolittle (R-CA) described the extent of the crisis: "Our forests are really in deplorable condition. My colleagues can see and anyone who flies over the Sierra Nevadas can see just what a terrible state they are in, how years of drought and insect infestation have killed in some cases more than one-third of all the standing trees. . . . We have had some devastating forest fires. And the prognosis is, unless we manage these forests, we are going to have fires on even greater scale than we have seen so far."[12]

Representative Helen Chenoweth echoed these sentiments when she told a reporter that the entire nation's forests are "dying and rotting" because of forest service policies (quoted in "Timber Wars in Congress" 1998, A22). David Bischel, president of the California Forestry Association, endorsed the QLG plan by saying that it "uses the best science available to restore health to our national forests that are overstocked with *dead and dying* trees [which are] vulnerable to *disease, insect infestation and catastrophic wildfire*" (Bischel 1998). Finally, in a feature article on the QLG in a regional newsmagazine, pictures of "crowded and dying" trees were contrasted with a "healthy, park-like forest" that had been selectively logged fifteen years earlier (Christensen 1996).[13]

A study of congressional hearings on timber harvesting policies by Burnett and Davis (2002) suggests that the rhetoric of "forest health" was not limited to the debate over the QLG bill. From the 1960s through the 1980s, the protimber coalition's consistent message to Congress was that the forest service must maintain high levels of timber production. However, the authors found a different rhetoric in the 1990s: "In recent years, testimony has been increasingly directed toward maintaining community stability or enhancing forest health, positions that convey the impression of concerns for both resources and people" (Burnett and Davis 2002, 220). The QLG forest management plan fit neatly into industry's new discourse; it was sold as a way to both enhance community stability and improve the health of the forests.

Proponents of the QLG plan took advantage of the opportunity created by the less-than-healthy state of the Sierra Nevada forests. But their construction of the forests was not the only possible (or plausible) issue definition. The forests could have been described as fragile rather than sick, which changes the tone of the rhetoric. In fact, some opponents of the QLG offered more positive images of the Sierra Nevada forests in an effort to rally support for preservationist policies. For example, environmental activist and QLG opponent Alexander Cockburn offered images of the Sierra Nevada forests more akin to those in the Clayoquot Sound conflict: "At stake is some of the *last intact* forest in the Sierra. These *beautiful stretches* of Douglas fir, the *last prime forest habitat* in California, are falling victim to that most deadly of all procedures, the consensus process, from which principled opponents of environmental destruction are by definition excluded" (Cockburn 1997, B9; emphases added). Cockburn's description of the Sierras as "intact" and "beautiful" was notably absent from the congressional hearings and debate on the QLG bill and only made a rare appearance in the QLG literature.

Cockburn's critique of the QLG's consensus process was also a minor note in the overall symphony of congressional discourse. As detailed in the next section, the overwhelming praise for the QLG process secured congressional support for the group's forest management plan and muted the voices of QLG opponents.

Conflict Containment in Congress: The QLG Process and the End of the "Timber Wars"

When the QLG asked Congress to write its forest management plan for the Lassen, Plumas, and Tahoe national forests into law, members of the group knew it could be politically risky. Consideration of the Quincy bill in Congress would give QLG opponents an important opportunity to increase publicity around the plan, shift the definition of the issue, and otherwise expand conflict. In his study of French policymaking, Baumgartner (1989) found that a parliamentary debate was the best way to expand an issue and thus the greatest threat to those who wanted to keep a conflict contained: "For those who wish to keep an issue restricted to specialists," he writes, "the results of a lively parliamentary debate can be disastrous" (Baumgartner 1989, 184). Moreover, in turning to Congress, the QLG threatened its identity as a local, collaborative group that was untainted by special interest politicking inside the beltway.

How did the Quincy coalition manage the issue when it emerged in a national venue? A key strategy for limiting debate and thus containing the issue was to keep the focus on the QLG *process*, a process that was almost uniformly praised by legislators. A related tactic involved constructing the QLG itself as a solution to the "timber wars." This construction of the issue redefined the conflict in the forest policy subsystem such that *conflict itself* became the central problem that needed to be resolved, rather than the substantive concerns of environmental opponents.

Praising the Process: Issue Management in the QLG Debate

The QLG developed against a backdrop of criticism aimed at the U.S. federal regulatory system. Since at least the administration of Ronald Reagan, support for centralized, command-and-control regulation had been waning. Of course, these critiques were not new to free-market conservatives and libertarians, but even liberals in the 1990s (most notably the Clinton administration) jumped on the devolution and deregulation bandwagon as part of President Clinton's "reinventing government" program. In time, both conservatives and liberals were advocating decentralization and cooperative regulatory approaches, particularly in the environmental policy arena. Not surprisingly, local collaborative decision-making groups became increasingly popular as alternatives to seemingly endless adversarial legalism and bureaucratic stalemate (Glasbergen 1998; Weber 2000).

As noted, the QLG proposal was potentially quite controversial because it increased logging in national forests, its fire management strategy was relatively untested, and it was exempt from certain federal environmental laws (as originally written). These substantive issues could have overwhelmed the debate in Congress and significantly changed the definition of the issue and direction of the conflict. Opponents to the QLG bill successfully raised these concerns, but they failed to expand the issue appreciably. Rather, proponents effectively shifted attention away from emotional issues such as the spotted owl, old-growth logging, and roadless areas and replaced it with attention to the QLG process. The focus on process disarmed opponents, who were hard pressed to combat its overwhelmingly positive characterization.

In the debate over the QLG bill on the floor of the House, members referred to the Quincy group's collaborative process forty-eight times. As seen in table 7.2, the majority of these references were positive. A much smaller number of individuals expressed some reservations about the QLG process while still praising it overall; only three statements were explicitly negative.

Representative Porter Goss's (R-FL) praise for the QLG process was typical: "This bill presents a long overdue cooperative, locally driven approach to protect our precious resources and our jobs and well-being. *It is a fresh approach to land management. I applaud it. It is one that empowers local folks to make decisions and find solutions that work for them*" (emphasis added).[14] Representative Vic Fazio (D-CA) was even more straightforward about the need to "validate the process that these local community activists have so long and thoroughly engaged in."[15] In an earlier hearing he made the same point: "It is our *obligation* at the Federal level to preserve this spirit of cooperation" (U.S. Congress, House, "Hearing on H.R. 858," 1997, 7; emphasis added). Sam Farr, a Democrat from California with high ratings from the League of Conservation Voters, accepted an amended version of the QLG bill, saying, "It is essentially a bottom-up process . . . both sides of the issue, environmentalists and non-environmentalists, have come to consensus."[16] Even legislators who

TABLE 7.2   References to the QLG Process in Congressional Floor Debate

Tone of comment[a]	Number of references[b]	Percentage by QLG supporters[c]
Positive	39	97
Positive with reservations	6	0
Negative	3	0
	Total = 48	

Source: Compiled by the author from *Congressional Record* 143 (July 9, 1997): H4924–44.

[a]Tone was assessed based on whether the statement expressed support for local decision-making processes, or conversely, critiqued the process or aspects of it.

[b]Every time a speaker referenced the QLG process it was counted, regardless of whether the speaker had made similar statements earlier in his or her speech.

[c]Supporters were those members of Congress who expressed their support for the QLG bill during the floor debate on July 9, 1997. Nonsupporters were those who expressed reservations or outright opposition to the bill.

disagreed with the substance of the QLG bill were eager to show their support for the QLG process—as Representative Bruce Vento (D-MN) reiterated, "I want to make it clear that I am not critical of the Quincy Library process."[17]

Conflict within Congress over the QLG bill was effectively contained because partisan differences were not activated when the focus was on the QLG's decision-making process. In fact, supporters of the QLG forest management plan liked to point out that President Clinton had urged communities to resolve forest conflicts through consensus-based processes during the 1993 Forest Summit. As QLG member Bill Coates said in his testimony before the House Subcommittee on Forests and Forest Health: "We have brought you a gift. . . . It is an agreement. It is an agreement that President Clinton asked us to come up with in Portland [Oregon]. He told us to get out of the courtrooms and get into the meeting rooms and find a way to cooperate and get along with each other and do some listening as well as some talking" (U.S. Congress, House, "Hearing on H.R. 858," 1997, 30). Representative Chenoweth (R-ID) later reminded her colleagues that the QLG "heeded the President's call to leave the courtroom and meet at the conference table."[18] In short, the veneration of local participation and place-based solutions transcended the partisan divide. Everyone, it seemed, was eager to show support for republican virtues of self-governance.[19]

The Quincy coalition, in addition to taking advantage of a growing disillusionment with command and control regulation, capitalized on a broader cultural movement centered on bringing more civility to political discourse. Civility proponents have lamented adversarial interest group politics, particularly when name calling replaces informed and intelligent political discussion. Many politicians and pundits have taken up these themes and consider "naming and blaming" contests important public problems in themselves. These critics say that the lack of civility in present-day politics produces at best a less informed and more cynical citizenry; at its worst, policy stalemate and even violence can result.[20]

In the debate over the Quincy bill, the forest problem was redefined so that the *ongoing conflict between environmental groups and the timber industry became an important problem in itself*. Legislators echoed newspaper headlines that spoke ominously of the "timber wars" in the western United States. Representative Wally Herger (R-CA), for example, praised the QLG as a "new way of doing business on environmental issues," after "more than fifteen years [in which] environmentalists and members of the forest products industry have waged war over managing western forests."[21] Senator Dianne Feinstein (D-CA) also referenced the timber wars, calling the House approval of the QLG bill a "real victory of local communities like Quincy which seek to avoid the polarizing and often paralyzing battles that have characterized forest management issues for the last decade."[22]

War, of course (while perhaps seen as necessary), is rarely constructed in positive terms. Instead, we look forward to the day it will end and life returns to normalcy. The Quincy process was thus championed for bringing peace to one region of the western front. According to Neil Dion, Congress and the media could not resist the "great myth" that there was a "big war [in Quincy] and then the QLG sat down and brought peace" (2001). Indeed, Quincy group members were lauded for their role as ambassadors of reconciliation, while opponents were chastised for their stubborn insistence on prolonging the conflict. As the next chapter shows, these negative characterizations of QLG opponents served to delegitimize their critique of the QLG's forest management plan.

In sum, the QLG process and plan were constructed as a *solution* to a number of ecological and political problems, including forest fires, forest health, the survival of the California spotted owl, the timber wars, and a general decay in the state of political discourse surrounding natural resource conflicts. In some ways, this could be seen as a case of issue expansion, because the QLG became linked to numerous issues. However, because the QLG and its plan were described as solutions to these problems, both engendered a level of consensus that limited the expansion of conflict. Opponents to the QLG thus fought an uphill battle to try to redefine the issue and transform the image of the QLG process. It is to their efforts that we now turn.

Expanding the Issue: Opponents' Strategies and Tactics

From its beginnings, the QLG faced skeptics and critics, some of whom quietly doubted the group's ability to succeed, and others who publicly opposed the QLG forest management plan and the group's decision-making process. The main opponents were local, regional, and national environmental groups who objected to parts of the Quincy plan and expressed concern that the process excluded national interests. These critics attempted to expand the conflict so as to block passage of the QLG legislation in Congress and to slow the potential tide of local, collaborative groups inspired by the Quincy group's success. Opponents to the QLG engaged in issue redefinition and expansion tactics so as to undermine the QLG forest plan and to prevent its serious consideration by Congress.

Quincy group opponents faced considerable challenges. First, as long as the QLG forest plan was defined primarily as an effective fire management tool, they were at a disadvantage. As argued above, the focus on forest fires served to justify the QLG plan: all parties acknowledged that forest fires were an important problem. Moreover, the fire discussion shifted the discourse toward more technical matters and away from the emotional (and thus expansive) rhetoric that characterized the larger national debate over forest management. The second challenge was related to the first: In order to redirect attention to the more controversial aspects of the QLG bill (such as the amount of logging it authorized), opponents would have to crack the overwhelmingly positive image of the QLG process. As Louis Blumberg lamented, "The politicians have not been willing to take off the fancy wrapper and look inside [the QLG plan]." He went on to admit that the QLG was hard to combat "because it's sugar coated with this local consensus and collaboration theme" (quoted in Sonner 1997, 8A).

In spite of these challenges, QLG opponents tried to redefine the debate over both the substance of the QLG plan and the process by which it was created. They used two tactics. First, they attempted to raise alarm over the substance of the Quincy Library Group Community Stability Proposal by suggesting it was simply a logging plan masquerading as a fire reduction program, and a poor one at that. Second, opponents also took aim at the idea of local collaborative decision making, arguing that the management of national forests was a national issue, not a local one.

A Logging Program under Disguise? Raising Alarm over the QLG

The utility of the "fire frame" stemmed in part from the fact that many environmental groups acknowledged the fire threat and supported efforts to reduce it through better fuels management. The California Ancient Forest Alliance, an environmental coalition that predated the QLG, had been working for several years to reduce the fuel load in California's national forests. The 1992 CASPO report and the 1995 SNEP report both concluded that fire suppression policies in the Sierra Nevada had increased the likelihood that fires would destroy spotted owl habitat. Environmental groups largely supported these documents, including their call for better fuels management. In other words, a consensus around the idea that forest fires were a threat to forests and the California spotted owl made denial of the fire problem a weak strategy for opponents to pursue. Denial was also risky because much of the public (particularly in the western United States) had either directly experienced fires or seen images of them in the media. Whether the incidence or severity of the fires was in fact greater than in the past mattered little to this audience, whose perceptions were shaped by more immediate focusing events (see Birkland 1997; Kingdon 1995).[23]

However, there was much less agreement on how to best reduce the fire threat, and QLG opponents capitalized on this uncertainty to expand conflict over the Quincy forest plan. One tactic was simply to question the effectiveness of the fire reduction components of the QLG plan. According to many critics, the QLG fire strategy was unscientific and untested—based on "back of the envelope calculations" by people who had no expertise in the field (Don Erman, quoted in "The Quincy Compromise" 1998, A22). In her testimony before a Senate subcommittee, Debbie Sease, legislative director of the Sierra Club, went further and condemned the entire QLG bill as "a vast experiment with inadequate scientific justification" (U.S. Congress, Senate, "Hearing on S. 1028," 1997). Criticism eventually settled on the fuel break component of the QLG fire reduction program (the defensible fuel profile zones). The Quincy plan mandated the construction of quarter-mile fuel breaks on forty thousand to sixty thousand acres of forest a year. These breaks were designed to reduce crown fires by removing small trees and brush that carry fire into the forest canopy. In addition, the zones would allegedly slow the spread of fire by reducing fuels along forest valleys and mountain ridges.

In press releases, position papers, and testimony before Congress, QLG opponents raised questions about the wisdom, workability, and true purpose of the defensible fuel profile zones.[24] For example, Felice Pace, director of the Klamath Forest Alliance, told a Senate committee, "The QLG's fuel-break idea . . . is a disaster . . . in the past fuel-breaks have most often exacerbated rather than quelled wildfire" (U.S. Congress, Senate, "Hearing on S. 1028," 1997). Opponents argued that the fuel breaks might actually increase, not decrease, the fire risk. An editorial in the *San Francisco Chronicle* also raised this possibility: "The 'fire break' approach is highly questionable. Scientific studies have shown that aggressive logging can actually increase the risk of wildfire by leaving highly flammable slash in its aftermath, and allowing the growth of dense brush to replace the more fire-resistant trees" ("Sierra Logging Bill Needs Major Revisions" 1997, A22).

Some opponents did not question the effectiveness of the fuel breaks as much as they questioned their "real" reason for being in the QLG plan. Many environmentalists suggested that the fuel breaks were simply a way for the timber industry to increase logging without generating lawsuits. They portrayed the Quincy plan in general and the fuels management program in particular as a "logging program [sold] under the guise of fuel reduction" (Blumberg 2001). Overall, QLG opponents tried to shift the debate from the rather technical language of fuels management toward the more emotional and polarizing issues of timber harvesting and habitat degradation due to logging. Alexander Cockburn's (1997, B9) criticism was typical: "The Quincy plan is nothing more than an excuse for companies . . . to log more than 70,000 acres a year of Douglas fir with scant legal constraint. The excuse comes in the following guise: a need to carve a network of firebreaks. . . . These 'firebreaks' are no less than 440 acres across, clear-cut avenues that will fragment some of the last contiguous habitat in California." Here Cockburn skillfully relabels the fuel breaks "clear-cuts." Representative George Miller (D-CA), one of the early opponents of the QLG bill, also brought up the controversial issue of clear-cutting in an attempt to expand the scope of the debate: "These mountains and these forests are important to millions of Californians, and we will not delegate the right to destroy those forests to a handful of people who have decided that cutting trees is the only way that we can protect this forest. We can have clear-cuts under this legislation."[25] And in a rather direct attempt to refocus the debate toward logging, Steve Holmer from the Western Ancient Forest Campaign reminded forest activists in bold terms, "Logging is the problem not the solution" (Holmer 1998).[26]

Another tactic opponents used to expand conflict and reframe the image of the QLG plan was to compare the QLG bill to the infamous "timber salvage rider." The 1995 salvage rider was tremendously unpopular among environmentalists and their allies because it increased logging on national forests under the aegis of promoting forest health. Moreover, like the original QLG bill, the activities authorized by the salvage rider were not subject to federal environmental laws.[27] If the QLG bill could be sold as another salvage rider, its image as a beneficial fire management program would be tarnished. Representative Miller (D-CA) reminded his colleagues about the controversy surrounding the salvage rider: "This legislation, in fact, contains the very same timber salvage rider that got this Congress into so much trouble with the American public when they saw that the cutting of trees took precedence over every other multiple use in the forest."[28] Native Forest Council Director Tim Hermach issued this warning to his environmental colleagues: "We are in trouble. Big trouble. This thing [the QLG bill] could make the Salvage Rider look like a Sunday picnic" (quoted in Mazza 1997).[29]

Overall, environmental opponents were successful in raising questions about key substantive components of the QLG plan. However, they did not successfully redefine the problem in key policy arenas: Congress, for instance, largely accepted the issue definition presented by QLG members. This was due in part to the technical nature of the topics under question. Debating the merits and demerits of a fuel break system might inspire some committed and knowledgeable activists to get involved, but it was unlikely to draw in the larger public. Moreover, the general lack of scientific certainty on this question paradoxically lent a measure of credibility *and doubt* to both sides in the debate.[30] Consequently, once the QLG plan was constructed as a fire reduction program, it was difficult to dislodge this particular issue definition by challenging the factual basis of the QLG coalition's claims.

It was even more difficult for opponents to reconstruct the positive image of the QLG process. Louis Blumberg complained that the only reason the QLG succeeded was because it was sold "under the guise of local collaboration" (2001). The next chapter shows how environmental opponents challenged the QLG's claims of consensus by noting that some local citizens opposed the plan. Here we consider how opponents tried to counter the discourse (and veneration) of the local by reframing the issue as a national one.

Whose Forests Are They? Redrawing Boundaries in the Quincy Case

Forest activists in the United States won an important victory when the issue of logging in national forests gradually gained recognition as a national problem. In many ways, this reframing of the issue was not a policy change as we typically understand it—no laws were passed, no regulations were enacted, no funds were allocated. But as George Hoberg (1997) notes, the concrete changes in forest policy that occurred in the 1990s would not have been possible if the public considered the ancient forest issue to be of regional concern only. The environmentalists' success in expanding the issue nationally led to other policy victories because it attracted a wider set of actors, people who perceived a stake in the ancient forests of the American West and who were willing to weigh in on the side of preservationists.

It is not surprising, then, that some forest activists saw a threat in the QLG. The QLG plan mandated an unusual level of local involvement in national forest management and would require arguments to justify that change. The rhetoric of the local threatened to reinject itself into the forest policy debate. And this rhetoric—whether it referenced local knowledge, local participation, or the like—had taken on a benign, even virtuous meaning. "Local control" (dubbed local "involvement" by the QLG members) did not necessarily conjure up images of local industries strong-arming federal resource management agencies, as it might have in the past.

Environmental opponents attempted to expand the boundaries around the QLG issue by reminding politicians and the public that the Lassen, Plumas, and Tahoe forests were *national* forests that belonged to all Americans. They suggested that the problem (whether it be fire, forest health, or the spotted owl) was not merely a local one because the forests themselves were publicly owned. Environmental organizations found an ally in Representative Maurice Hinchey (D-NY): "It [the QLG bill] has been characterized as a local initiative on a local forest, but the fact of the matter is . . . it involves about 2,500,000 acres, two and a half national forests. . . . *This is a lot more than a local activity affecting a local region*" (U.S. Congress, House, "Hearing on H.R. 858," 1997, 17; emphasis added). Michael McCloskey (1999) of the Sierra Club put it this way: "The very name of these forests reminds us that we all own them; they belong to all of the citizens of this nation, not just to those who live nearby."

Opponents to the Quincy plan also tried to expand conflict and increase visibility by warning that Quincy-style management could be "coming to a national forest near you." They argued that the significance of the Quincy plan extended beyond the 2.5 million acres covered in the legislation—if the bill passed, it would have a spillover effect on other national forests. In an e-mail message to environmental activists, the John Muir Project of Earth Island Institute issued this warning: "QLG is a scam written by and for the timber industry, and while it directly affects only forests in the Sierra Nevada mountains, it's a Trojan Horse designed to open the door to similar bills for *all* national forests. If this one goes through, MORE WILL DEFINITELY FOLLOW! Your national forests will be next!" (John Muir Project of Earth Island Institute 1997; emphases in original). The above is an example of what Cobb and Elder (1972) call arguing for "temporal relevance." Groups trying to expand the scope of an issue will define it as having consequences for future generations, or spillover effects to individuals and groups beyond those immediately affected. These could be defined as positive effects if the goal is to gain support for a program. Conversely, an advocacy group would emphasize negative consequences if it wanted to prevent a program from moving forward, which was the case with opponents to the QLG plan.

Members of the QLG coalition responded to the spillover argument by reassuring members of Congress and others that the bill authorized only a "pilot project," an experiment that would be carefully monitored for its effectiveness before it was tried elsewhere. Tom Nelson, a QLG member and employee of Sierra Pacific Industries, responded to his opponents before a Senate subcommittee in this way: "While we have been criticized by some urban-based environmental groups as being 'too large in scope,' . . . [w]e see it as a *very modest program* that makes good sense" (U.S. Congress, Senate,

"Hearing on S. 1028," 1997; emphasis added). Representative Helen Cheno-weth (R-ID), responding to the comparison between the QLG bill and the salvage rider, said: "This *pilot project, and let me reemphasize it is a pilot project*, is designed to reduce the risk of catastrophic fire and to prevent the need for salvage riders in the future because we will be taking care of the salvage in this particular area" (emphasis added).[31] As it turns out, Nelson and Chenoweth's reassurances might have been unnecessary. Many representatives looked forward to the day when QLG-style management would be adopted in their state's forests. After all, local collaborative decision-making processes were gaining widespread popularity as an alternative to defunct, and decidedly unpopular, command-and-control regulatory schemes.

Opponents to the QLG plan waged an uphill battle against the positive norms of consensus and cooperation associated with the QLG process. Supporters of the QLG were just as enthralled with *how* the plan came into being as they were with the substance of it, if not more so. Symbols and themes of self-reliance, collaboration, and teamwork permeated the discourse over the QLG, making it popular with a Congress and public fed up with adversarial interest group politics. One opponent to the QLG, Michael McCloskey, took direct aim at the idea that conflict is inherently unwelcome in politics: "It is troubling that such processes [place-based collaboration] *tend to de-legitimize conflict* as a way of dealing with issues and of mobilizing support. It is psychologically difficult to simultaneously negotiate and publicly attack bad proposals from the other side. This tends to be seen as acting in bad faith. Too much time spent in stakeholder processes may result in demobilizing and disarming our side" (McCloskey 1996; emphasis added).

McCloskey's position—namely, embracing conflict as a method of resolving disputes—did not elicit a lot of support among key audiences. In general, opponents to the QLG used more situational, or what Cobb and Elder (1972) call "lower-order," symbols while proponents used "higher-order" symbols in their issue definition campaign. Higher-order symbols appeal to enduring, deep-seated American values, such as freedom from government, individualism, and private property rights, to name just a few. Lower-order symbols are more context-specific, do not appeal to as wide a range of audiences, and may not evoke as intense a response as do higher-order symbols. The environmental opposition, while trying to raise alarm by labeling the QLG process as undemocratic, relied somewhat more on arguments that made distinctions between "good" versus "dangerous" collaboration. Such distinctions might have been lost on a public and Congress susceptible to appeals based on republican virtues, small government, and local self-reliance.

Environmental opponents, however, did not fail entirely in their efforts to expand the conflict around the QLG. Louis Blumberg readily admitted that he and his colleagues did not "win" this battle—after all, the QLG bill passed Congress with a vote of 429–1. However, he believed the opponents were successful to the extent that they "were able to educate many people—well, certainly those that followed it [the QLG] closely—that it was controversial, that there was local, regional, and national environmental opposition to it, and that it was not a good example of local based, true collaboration" (Blumberg 2001). At least twenty environmental groups, including the Sierra Club, the Wilderness Society, and the NRDC, actively opposed the QLG bill when it was being debated in the House of Representatives in 1997 (Clifford 1997). Once the QLG bill became law, several more joined the anti-QLG coalition. However, Blumberg's caveat—that the "people who followed the QLG closely" opposed it—suggests that environmentalists were only moderately successful in increasing public attention to the QLG. As Blumberg said somewhat disappointedly, "Environmentalists have found that it [the QLG issue] is seen as a regional issue" (2001).

Conclusion

Local stakeholder groups are occupying an increasingly popular position in natural resource politics. Academics, politicians, bureaucratic officials, and foundations have all praised their collaborative, consensus-based approach to resolving intractable policy disputes. But few have asked how local stakeholder groups are able to sell their management plans to key policy actors and the wider public. After all, local stakeholder groups are not without critics—and their opponents (often national environmental groups) are sophisticated political strategists in their own right.

This chapter has examined how one local stakeholder group, the QLG, was able to decrease conflict over its forest management plan and sell it to key policy actors. The QLG coalition defused and localized conflict by subsuming more controversial forest management issues under less controversial ones. The "crisis" of forest fires displaced other crises in the national forests and served to justify the Quincy plan by providing a rationale for an increase in timber production. The QLG also used broad, resonant symbols and themes associated with its decision-making process, a process widely touted as a solution to environmental policy conflicts. This solution-oriented frame helped to contain conflict around the QLG plan and reframe the debate over logging in the Plumas, Lassen, and parts of the Tahoe national forests.

This case suggests that there are at least two types of issue containment strategies. The first involves defining issues so as to preempt conflict and policy participation. In tight policy subsystems, a small group of policy actors attempts to define issues in ways that produce either apathy or support from other policymakers and the public. Issue containment under these circumstances can be relatively straightforward if no competing definitions of a policy issue exist.

A second type of issue containment occurs when there are already multiple contending images of issues, or in Baumgartner and Jones's (1993, 8) words, when policy debates take place in the "wake of crumbling public images." During such times, it is neither practical nor possible to ignore the competing issue definitions promoted by opposing groups. Advocacy groups who want to contain issues do so in a more challenging political context than actors working within a contained policy subsystem. The difficulty lies in acknowledging the multiplicity of issue images while also promoting one's own version as the most accurate or helpful for guiding policy. The analysis in this chapter suggests that one way of negotiating this difficult terrain is to subsume more contentious components of the problem under less controversial ones.

Three additional conclusions can be drawn about issue definition strategies when we compare the QLG case to the Clayoquot Sound case. First, like the Clayoquot case, the QLG points to the importance of timing and audience when crafting issue definition strategies. Advocacy groups must adapt their messages to the political context of the moment in order to wage successful issue definition campaigns. Those who fail to do so risk being dismissed and may even alienate certain policymakers and segments of the public. As Linder (1995, 225; emphases added) notes, "Once attention shifts from whose argument it is, to which argument is better, *context generally becomes a crucial arbiter of advantage.* Some discourses may be more easily apprehended, other may evoke widely held values, and still others may capture inchoate sentiments, and so on. *Timing, however, may have more to do with which one prevails.*"

In the QLG case, opponents of the plan successfully raised alarm in the forest activist community by warning that the QLG's preference for local control could spread elsewhere. This strategy, however, was less effective in Congress and among the general public, due in part to the fact that American political culture has long romanticized the virtues of local self-government. To counter this belief is no small task. In contrast, the Quincy library coalition made symbolic appeals based on enduring American values—such as fear of big government, distrust of bureaucracy, and, as noted, a veneration of local self-control. Their rhetoric was all the more appealing given that it coincided with a national political trend toward decentralization and devolution.

A second and related conclusion we can draw from the cases is that benefits accrue to those actors who initially define an issue in a way that resonates with particular institutional or public audiences. In other words, it is important to "get there first"—to be the first to define an issue as it begins to generate conflict and at the moment when it moves to another policy venue (see Pierson 2000). Stories, once crafted and presented to the public, can be difficult to displace, as Roe (1994, 2) makes clear: "Stories commonly used in describing and analyzing policy issues are a force in themselves. . . . These stories often resist change or modification even in the presence of contradictory empirical data, because they continue to underwrite and stabilize the assumptions for decision-making in the face of high uncertainty, complexity, and polarization." The QLG effectively created a positive image of itself and its forest management plan from the start, making it difficult to dislodge these images when opponents began to mobilize against the QLG plan. Similarly, in the Clayoquot Sound case, environmental groups presented their images and rhetoric to European audiences before the provincial government and the industry offered counterimages and claims.

A final observation concerns the relationship between strategies of issue definition and processes of policy change. Most studies of agenda setting and policy change assume that issue *containment* strategies predominate in the struggle to deny certain issues a place on the agenda. However, groups might also *expand* issues as a way of forestalling agenda and policy change. Environmental opponents attempted to expand conflict around the QLG forest plan so as to prevent Congress from enacting the legislation, but they were ultimately unsuccessful in doing so.

It must be kept in mind that problem definition strategies are often used as a means to another end—namely, as a way to control participation in a conflict. From an advocacy group's perspective, success in defining an issue may be the most powerful way of expanding or limiting the participation of outside players. The next chapter looks more closely at these patterns of participation with an eye toward understanding the success of the QLG as it tried to manage and control the involvement of other actors.

Allies, Opponents, and Audiences

Containing Participation in the Quincy Library Group

In 1997, when the U.S. House of Representatives was debating the Quincy Library Group Forest Recovery and Economic Stability Act, 140 environmental groups signed a letter to Congress expressing opposition to the legislation. But the House passed the bill over the objections of the environmental lobby, and passed it overwhelmingly—only one member of Congress, a Republican, voted against the legislation. How could this formidable display of strength and unity from the environmental community be ineffective in securing the votes of long-time allies like Representative George Miller and Senator Dianne Feinstein, not to mention other conservation-minded Democrats? The last chapter suggested that the success of the QLG was due in part to its framing of the issue. Specifically, the QLG coalition narrowed the debate over forest management and practices by focusing on technical issues like forest fires, and they capitalized on the popularity of their local, collaborative decision-making process in order to defuse criticism around the QLG forest plan.

The issue definition strategies only tell part of the story, however. The Quincy coalition also successfully managed participation in the conflict, staying "under the radar screen" of potential opponents long enough that an effective and unified countercampaign never fully developed. Notwithstanding the letter mentioned above, much of the environmental community was late in entering the conflict and their participation was rather minimal—of the 140 groups who signed the letter of protest to Congress, only a handful actively opposed the QLG. Moreover, supporters of the QLG summarily dismissed these occasional bursts of opposition as the grumblings of an out-of-touch, Washington, D.C.–based environmental movement intent on promoting the "conflict industry."

The QLG coalition successfully turned existing alignments in the forest conflict inside out (albeit only in their region). They replaced the dominant conflict—that of environmentalists against loggers and the timber industry—with a conflict constructed as a battle between local citizens and national environmentalists and bureaucrats. This chapter examines how the realignment was fashioned and the effect it had on patterns of participation. The discussion shows that managing the participation of supporters, potential allies, and audiences is a complicated process. One of the more sophisticated strategies for managing participation involves shifting the lines of cleavage among current and potential players, or what Schattschneider (1960, 60) refers to as the "displacement of conflicts." Successful conflict displacement requires the subordination or downplaying of an old conflict and the advertising or exploitation of a new one, a process wherein "friends become enemies and enemies become friends in a general reshuffle of relations" (Schattschneider 1960, 63). This reshuffling of alliances changes the dynamics of the policy subsystem: It creates new winners and losers, a different power structure, and alters the very meaning of a conflict.

The forging of a national environmental movement in the 1960s and 1970s and the recent trend toward local, consensus-based resource management serve as more general examples of conflict displacement. When the environmental movement in the United States successfully nationalized environmental policies and politics in the 1970s, the dominant political cleavage was generally between the national environmental lobby and the industry lobby. The environmental movement represented a "community of interest," one held together by a shared ideology and common policy goals. The recent trend toward local, consensus-based resource management suggests a potential breakdown in this community of interest and the emergence of "communities of place." The move toward place-based management encourages people to identify with a geographic place rather than with any particular ideological movement. In other words, the traditional cleavage between environmentalists and industry is being replaced in some cases by divisions based on geography. Shifting the lines of cleavage in this manner may allow a reframing of policy problems and encourage different policy solutions.

This chapter explores the participation management strategies of individuals and groups involved in the QLG conflict. The QLG coalition used a combination of conflict displacement and conflict containment strategies to manage participation in the QLG conflict. Their success was largely due to their ability to shift the lines of cleavage among existing players, a strategy that disarmed potential opponents long enough that an effective counter-campaign could not be waged. The discussion proceeds chronologically, with the first section explaining how the original members of the QLG formed an alliance and the effect this had on local political alignments. The next section looks at the activities of the QLG from 1993 to 1997, focusing on the strategies it used to build support for its plan and manage the participation of opponents and "outsiders." The final section considers how the QLG and their supporters in Congress successfully contained conflict around the QLG forest management plan, even as it attracted increasing national attention and criticism.

Turning Enemies into Friends: Forming the QLG Alliance

Residents of the town of Quincy differ in their assessment of how intense the "timber wars" were in the northern Sierra Nevada in the 1980s and early 1990s. Neil Dion, an opponent to the QLG, denies that there was a "big war" between environmentalists and timber supporters, despite the fact that someone once spray-painted an antienvironmental slogan on the outside of his house (2001). Others attest to a great deal of tension in Quincy and the surrounding communities, particularly as timber harvests dropped in the early 1990s. According to John Sheehan, director of the Plumas Corporation (a county development agency) and member of the QLG, "There really was in Quincy . . . a dichotomy between environmentalists and the logging community. It was unpleasant. There were people you didn't talk to on the street" (2001). Environmental activist Michael Jackson admits that the conflict was more severe in Pacific Northwest logging towns but also recalls how truckers used to drive by his office with large logs, taunting him with the sight of more fallen trees (2001).

While the precise level of tension between environmentalists and timber supporters in Quincy is difficult to gauge, there is no doubt that a cleavage existed between environmentalists who were appealing forest timber sales and the timber companies and workers who wanted to increase the cut. The question is why some of these environmental activists made an alliance with representatives from Sierra Pacific Industries and local county officials who were publicly aligned with the timber industry. The creation of the QLG is all the more puzzling for the fact that in the early 1990s, local environmentalists were succeeding in many of their lawsuits. FPW, the only organized local environmental group, had successfully appealed timber sales using NFMA and NEPA. As shown in figure 8.1, the rate of cut on the nearby Lassen, Plumas, and Tahoe national forests declined in the early 1990s due in part to these appeals and lawsuits.

FPW had been receiving help with their appeals from the Sierra Club, the Wilderness Society, and the NRDC since at least 1986, when the groups jointly filed a "conservation alternative" to the Plumas National Forest Plan. Linda Blum, a Quincy environmentalist who worked with Jackson, said they had had a "long-standing relationship with the Sierra Club, the Sierra Club Legal Defense Fund, and NRDC. We cooperated on forest planning, forest appeals, and the training of local activists" (2001). Their work paid off when the lawsuits prompted the state and federal government to conduct a scientific study on the status of the California spotted owl and its habitat in the early 1990s.

The fact that the California spotted owl technical team (the team responsible for assessing the viability of the California spotted owl) would almost certainly recommend further logging restrictions is a key to understanding why Bill Coates, Plumas county supervisor, approached Michael Jackson in 1992 and asked for his cooperation in developing a mutually acceptable forest plan for the region. As an elected official in a timber-dependent county, Coates wanted the county to retain as many forestry jobs as possible. The community was dependent not only on the jobs, but also on the revenue coming from

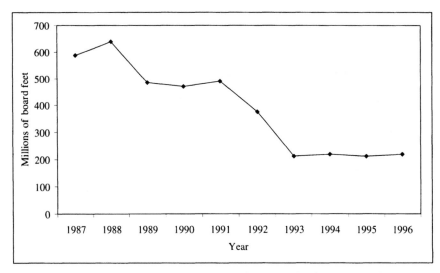

FIGURE 8.1   Timber Harvest in the Lassen, Plumas, and Tahoe National Forests, 1987–96

Source: Stone 1996.

timber sales on national forests; one quarter of the revenues went directly to the county school districts, and they were an important source of funding given the relatively low tax base in the area. Because of these dependencies, the local community was likely to develop a plan that was more sensitive to economic constraints than any decision coming from the forest service—or worse, from a federal judge.

The forthcoming CASPO report and the threat of more logging restrictions also help to explain why Tom Nelson of Sierra Pacific Industries agreed to meet with Coates and Jackson. If the three men agreed to adopt the FPW's 1986 conservationist alternative, Sierra Pacific Industries would get some timber out of the forests through an extensive thinning program outlined in the original proposal. In fact, any plan would help to stabilize timber supply, or at least alleviate some of the uncertainty generated by the changing political landscape. In a document outlining Sierra Pacific's objectives with regard to its participation in the QLG, the company claims it "requires an adequate, sustainable, and reliable source of National Forest logs for sale in order to continue our investments in our Quincy, Susanville, and Loyalton sawmills" (Quincy Library Group 1993). More importantly, the timber industry wanted to avoid a listing of the California spotted owl as an endangered species, knowing that such a listing could shut down logging in much of the Sierras.

Michael Jackson and Linda Blum, the two most visible environmentalists participating in the QLG, faced more favorable political opportunities but worried that the forest service would drag its feet in implementing the CASPO restrictions. Indeed, many of the QLG members were discouraged by the actions or inactions of the forest service. This fact alone helps to explain the formation of the QLG—the forest service became a target for the community's frustration. As Wondolleck and Yaffee (2000, 77–78; emphasis added) explain: "The sense of a shared problem [on the part of QLG members] was expanded by shared perceptions of the Forest Service as a significant source of the problem. . . . In many ways, the different interests in Quincy had little to lose to attempt a collaborative solution, but the *perception of the Forest Service as a common enemy* helped provide a starting point to their discussions." The various QLG members' grievances with the forest service were not identical, but these differences became less important than their overriding unhappiness with the agency.

Supporters of the QLG explain its formation in somewhat different terms. In this story, former enemies in the logging wars came together because they shared a common interest in preserving their community and the surrounding natural environment. Quincy participants realized that adversarial politics was leading them down a dead-end street of never-ending suits and countersuits, resulting in political stalemate and increasing animosity in the community. Consequently, they heeded President Clinton's advice during the Forest Summit by abandoning the courtrooms and heading to the Quincy library to search for a "win-win" solution. Jackson, for example, voiced concern about the survival of both the local community and the forests, saying his goal was "not to destroy these people or the owl. I found I could do both." He chastised the "urban environmental movement" for its apparent lack of concern for the loggers: "They see it as a holy war against a culture that is already gone" (Jackson 2001).

In sum, several factors help to explain the formation of the QLG alliance. The core participants joined for a variety of reasons and were motivated by self-interest, pragmatic politics, and community concern. What is interesting, however, is that the "community concern" explanation for the formation of the QLG is the one most often repeated in the popular press and in many academic articles. Professor Mark Sagoff (1999, 166) explains the formation of the group this way: "Everyone involved in the community around Quincy had come to his or her wit's end, and no one outside the community offered much hope or help," and, "Many of these people knew each other and deeply regretted the social animosity that had torn the community apart." A closer examination reveals that Sagoff's analysis is not entirely accurate. Not everyone in the community felt that they had arrived at an impasse and it was time to compromise. Neil Dion, a member of FPW, was opposed to the QLG plan from the start because he thought local environmentalists "did not have to make a deal [with the timber industry] because we already had a better deal to begin with, and that was CASPO" (2001). Louis Blumberg of the Wilderness Society also thought local environmentalists were "selling out" for no good reason. Environmentalists, he claims, could have easily protected the areas set aside in the QLG forest plan without giving the timber industry anything in exchange (2001).

Another member of the FPW, John Preschutti, joined the QLG with the understanding that the QLG plan was simply a short-term "deal" with the timber industry wherein "we were going to get something and give something up" (2001). Preschutti was dismayed (and subsequently quit the group) when the QLG plan was promoted as "God's plan that would solve all the problems in the forests" rather than a short-term compromise that would see them through until the CASPO guidelines came out.

Effect on the Community

These different local perspectives on the QLG suggest that the Quincy alliance did not end conflict in the community. Rather, the new alliance broke up existing local political alignments, shifting the lines of cleavage in the local forest policy arena. As Marston (1997b) notes about collaborative groups more generally: "Some of these are true consensus groups. . . . But others divide as much as they unite by destroying old relationships as they strive to create new ones." The formation of the QLG fragmented the local environmental organization, Friends of Plumas Wilderness. Even before the formation of the QLG, FPW was a small, loose-knit organization that could count on only six to ten people to show up at any given meeting. A handful of these members shifted their attention to the QLG after FPW members Jackson and Blum met with the group. Their absence, combined with the precarious state of the organization to begin with, meant that FPW folded as an organization soon after the QLG formed (Dion 2001). Dion and Preschutti were left filing timber sale appeals and actively opposing the QLG without any organizational affiliation.

According to Dion, other local residents opposed the QLG, but most of the community "didn't know what the hell was going on. . . . All people heard was that Jackson, Coates, and Nelson had made an agreement and they were all happy, so it must be good. In terms of selling it [the QLG plan], it was not difficult to do. Very few people knew what the Quincy Library Group was all about" (2001). The next section considers how the community participated in the conflict, and how the QLG managed this participation.

Promoting Consensus and Controlling Participation

When the QLG bill was being debated on the floor of the House, Representative Ken Calvert (R-CA) reassured his colleagues, "The Quincy Library Group was not created in a vacuum," and claimed that the "national urban environmental organizations" were aware of and involved in the QLG since its inception.[1] Calvert's suggestion that the QLG was open not only to local participants but also to national interests was not shared by Ron Stewart, who was at the time the regional forester for the USFS in the Pacific Southwest region in California. Asked to evaluate the proper role of local stakeholders in forest planning processes in general, and the QLG in particular, Stewart said this: "Our democracy has not been real supportive of deals cut behind closed doors, which is what was going on with the QLG. Some locals were not allowed at the table and did not feel that their views were represented" (2001).

Was the QLG experiment simply another example of backroom politics, cleverly disguised and packaged as grassroots democracy? Or was participation in the QLG broad and inclusive? The following discussion suggests that participation in the QLG was carefully controlled so that participation of "outsiders" was largely discouraged, and certain interests were excluded altogether. Participation in the QLG was neither open nor entirely closed but rather strategically managed so as to protect the integrity of the QLG plan and maintain a positive image of the QLG itself.

Expanding to the Community

For their first three meetings, the founders of the QLG met in secret, in the privacy of Michael Jackson's law office. But word of the meetings shortly spread in the small town, requiring the then nascent group to meet in the local library, where curious townspeople could listen to the discussions. (The media was excluded from these early meetings.) As their Community Stability Proposal began to take shape, QLG members sought the support of local organizations like FPW, the Plumas Corporation, and even regional environmental groups like the California Ancient Forest Alliance. Some of the individuals in these groups, along with nonaffiliated citizens, joined the QLG during the first few months of meetings. After nearly seven months of meetings, the group presented their plan to the public in a town meeting that attracted close to 250 people. Shortly thereafter, they reached out to the surrounding communities of Susanville, Sierraville, Chester, and Greenville. These towns were located near the three national forests covered by the QLG plan (the Plumas and Lassen national forests, and the Sierraville Ranger District of the Tahoe National Forest).

Participation in the QLG clearly expanded during the first year of its existence, growing from an initial group of three to about forty core members in the first few months. Once the QLG "went public," more than 175 people regularly participated in the group, according to cofounder Bill Coates (Coates n.d.). Membership was granted after an individual attended just three meetings, so many of the participants became official members of the QLG. Coates claims, "Everybody had a voice in the process—an opportunity to bring their concerns to the table—and eventually, all parties were able to agree on a plan to preserve their community, while agreeing to disagree on other issues" (Coates n.d.). Agreement among the participants (and community support generally) was facilitated by the fact the QLG proposal was vague. As Ron Stewart noted, "When you start to get specific, agreements fall apart. As long as you stay fuzzy, and everybody can interpret it the way they want, everyone feels comfortable" (2001).

The numbers cited by Coates suggest that participation in the QLG was not as restricted as some of its critics suggest. However, the number of participants does not fully capture the extent or quality of participation in the

QLG. First, the 250 individuals attending the first public meeting were asked to approve or disapprove of the QLG plan as written. Their role was simply to rubber-stamp the proposal rather than provide input or suggest changes to the forest management plan. John Preschutti claims that the QLG was never open, that "you had to buy into the whole thing and sign the pledge" (2001). He noted that the original Community Stability Proposal included a phrase that referenced the community's dependence on timber, "So when you sign you are saying we are timber dependent. Right there you are closing off something. If you keep it to that, it stifles things from the beginning" (Preschutti 2001).

In fact, several individuals claimed that from the start, the QLG forest plan was presented to them as a "done deal." Louis Blumberg, assistant regional director of the Wilderness Society at the time, recalls the first meeting he had with Michael Jackson: "I met with Jackson in 1992 with a coalition of environmentalists. Jackson said, 'Here is the deal—I negotiated on behalf of the environmentalists and I think it is a good deal and I want you to accept it.' *It was a done deal at that time.* He presented it to environmentalists statewide as a done deal, so there was no opportunity for input after that. No effort was made to take input from the California Ancient Forest Alliance" (Blumberg 2001; emphasis added). Ron Stewart, the regional forester for the forest service, agreed with Blumberg. Stewart was intrigued with the QLG because they represented, in his mind, several different interests in the community. But his admiration for the QLG did not extend to the manner in which they conducted themselves during meetings with the forest service. According to Stewart, they "had an agenda, they had their minds made up, they knew what they wanted to do and they were sort of throwing it into our laps" (2001). Even Jackson himself admits, "After the plan was written, there was not much opportunity to change it" (2001).

In addition to limiting the role of QLG members, particularly those who arrived after the plan was crafted, the QLG excluded some groups altogether. Forest service officials were not invited to the initial discussions and only participated as observers in subsequent meetings. As Timothy Duane (1997, 790) notes, many QLG members thought that the forest service was part of the problem, and therefore could not be part of the solution. According to Stewart, the QLG "did not think the forest service would help them, that they would have to help themselves. Their attitude was that they needed to do it alone" (2001). Jackson justified the exclusion of the forest service, somewhat paradoxically, by saying that the agency "represent[s] you [the general American public] as much as they represent us [the local community]" (quoted in Duane 1997, 790).

National and state environmental organizations also did not participate in the QLG. However, they were not deliberately excluded as was the forest service. National and state environmental groups could not—or chose not—to send representatives to the meetings, which not only were lengthy (many lasting three hours or more) but also were far from the urban centers where the groups maintained offices. The larger national organizations, such as the Wilderness Society and the NRDC, did not have local chapters in or even near these rural areas. Local environmentalists speculated that national environmental leaders might have thought the QLG "wasn't going anywhere" and did not "fully realize what was happening" and therefore did not initially get involved (Preschutti 2001; Dion 2001). Other critics suggested that individuals and groups had no incentive to participate because the substantive components of the QLG plan had already been adopted (Blumberg 2001).[2]

In short, the minimal participation by state and national environmental groups at this stage in the conflict was due to a combination of factors. The groups' strategic calculations and organizational structures must be considered along with the particular form of participation required by the QLG. In addition, participation was affected by individual perceptions about the openness of the QLG to outside input. Some critics, like Blumberg, suggested that "anyone who disagreed [with the QLG] locally was shunned and discouraged from coming, was demonized and made to feel unwelcome. They discouraged anyone from participating who disagreed with them" (2001). Erin Noel, a local environmentalist who went to several QLG meetings, also spoke of the cool reception she received: "At meetings most of my written comments were disregarded. My questions were met with a very hostile reaction from Michael Jackson. He told me, 'Raising questions is not OK'" (quoted in Marston 1997a).[2]

State and national environmental groups, while they did not regularly attend QLG meetings, did not completely ignore the QLG either. Beginning in 1994, some environmental organizations started to correspond with the QLG, expressing cautious support for the QLG's desire to solve problems locally while simultaneously raising concerns about the substantive components of the QLG plan. It is not entirely clear whether and to what degree these groups supported QLG. In at least two cases, the QLG apparently exaggerated the extent to which outside environmental organizations endorsed the Quincy forest plan. Steve Evans, from Friends of the River (a statewide river conservation group), suggested that the QLG inappropriately included his name on the Community Stability Proposal as someone who endorsed the proposal. Evans wrote a memo to Michael Jackson in August 1993 clarifying his position on the QLG: "At this time, I must state unequivocally that I cannot endorse the Quincy Library Group proposal as currently written, although I strongly endorse the ongoing discussions. *I never authorized use of my name on the original document in the first place*" (Evans 1993; emphasis added).

The NRDC also accused the QLG of misrepresenting its position to public officials. The NRDC argued that the QLG made "erroneous statements" about the NRDC's position: "These statements [about our alleged endorsement of the QLG plan] were reported to us independently by Forest Service, Congressional, and White House staff, *after* we contacted QLG members about their apparent misrepresentation of our position. Because, as the group understands, we have not endorsed the proposal yet, we felt it was important to set the record straight" (Edelson, Blumberg, and Waid 1994). The QLG stood to benefit if key policymakers thought there was widespread support for its plan. Naming other environmental groups as supporters, even if that support was tentative at best, was clearly in its interest.[3]

More generally, one strategy for controlling a conflict is to practice the "politics of consensus." Advocacy groups who want to contain conflict will try to minimize conflict and the appearance of it. Such strategies are effective as long as potential opponents are unorganized or unable to express their disagreement to the public and elites. Of course, some advocacy groups might refrain from taking a position on a policy proposal altogether, thereby allowing proponents to move ahead without a lot of resistance. This seemed to be the case with state and national environmental groups in the early years of the QLG. Over time, though, the QLG faced increasing resistance from outside environmental groups and from some forest service officials. But opposition to the QLG only served to unite its members to an even greater degree.

Presenting a United Front

The Quincy Library Group began as an experiment in local consensus-based decision making, but gradually it became something of an institution in and of itself. Opponents of the QLG referred to this pejoratively as the "Quincy cult," suggesting that the identities of the core members shifted over time such that loyalty to the QLG became more important than their individual commitments to the interests they were representing. The QLG case confirms Schattschneider's (1960) observation that sometimes unity is the price of victory. In any alliance, there will be points of disagreement, but eventually members of the alliance need to decide which battle is most important to them. Over time, the QLG decided that its battle with "outsiders" was the more significant one. As one observer notes, "They [the QLG] saw themselves as an entity united against the world, it seems" (quoted in Marston 1997c).

However, the unity of the Quincy coalition was tested on several occasions. One came after the Republicans gained control of Congress in 1994 and subsequently tried to increase logging in the national forests. Some of the areas slated for logging were designated as off-limits in the Quincy Library Group Community Stability Proposal. Rather than bid on the timber sales, Sierra Pacific Industries and Collins Pine (another local timber company) opposed a plan that called for logging around sensitive salmon habitat. A similar issue arose in 1995 after the forest service announced it would take bids on a salvage timber sale in the Lassen National Forest. Logging companies refused to bid when they were told that the QLG plan had set aside the area for preservation. Tom Nelson explained their restraint by saying, "A deal is a deal" (quoted in G. Smith 1996, A3). According to Jackson, they took a "beating" from the national timber companies over these events, but "it welded us together—we became the town team" (2001). Ron Stewart admitted that the QLG kept a "pretty united front and they did it very smartly—they had the timber industry talk about the environment and the environmentalists talk about the timber industry" (2001).

The QLG's identity as the "town team" was enhanced by an antiurban orientation in the community. Duane (1997, 789) argues, "Much of the community's shared sense of identity . . . derived from a belief that imperialist patterns of capitalist investment and exploitation had made the region a mere colony of urban interests." As QLG members increasingly identified with their "community of place" they identified less with, and arguably fought less for, their "communities of interest."[4] In interviews, local environmental representatives Jackson and Blum did not refer to themselves as "environmentalists," reserving that term for their former allies such as the NRDC and the Wilderness Society. Both Jackson and Blum dismissed such groups as "urban elitists" who were less interested in protecting the forests and more interested in maintaining their power over environmental policymaking.

Leaders in the Wilderness Society and NRDC were understandably alarmed by such rhetoric, and increasingly felt that Jackson, Blum, and Mike Yost (a forestry professor at the local college) did not represent the interests of the larger environmental community. As the conflict developed, the QLG stopped trying to court state and national environmental organizations altogether. Jackson, who used to work with the "urban environmentalists," later claimed that they were interfering with the QLG effort and suggested in a not very subtle fashion that their participation was not welcomed (Duane 1997, 791). For outsiders, the QLG's increasing cohesion made participation less feasible and less attractive, compounding the problem. In short, if the QLG was inclusive to begin with, such was not the case as conflict around the plan grew.

The next section examines this phase of the conflict, marked by the QLG's decision to ask Congress to write its forest management plan into law.

Managing Conflict in the National Arena

When members of the QLG appealed to Congress, they took a significant political risk; soliciting the support of a national political institution would give their opponents an opportunity to expand conflict and transform the positive image of the QLG. Going to Congress could also potentially open the doors to broader participation, particularly by national environmental groups who kept offices in Washington, D.C., and were well versed in congressional politics. The next chapter examines the reasons why the QLG shifted venues even though they feared their opponents might, in Jackson's words, "crush them" at the national level. The current discussion considers how the QLG's Congressional supporters delegitimized opponents by characterizing them as national environmental elites who were wedded to outmoded forms of politics. The participation of opponents at this stage in the conflict was not so much prevented as dismissed.

Characterization Contests in Congress

If the QLG developed against a backdrop of criticism aimed at the federal regulatory system, it also benefited from the increasingly popular belief that the mainstream environmental movement was inattentive to "Main Street." Critics on both the left and the right have suggested that the U.S. environmental movement has strayed from its grassroots origins. It is commonly thought that the "Big 10" environmental organizations have largely abandoned the difficult job of grassroots mobilization and have turned their attention instead to congressional meeting rooms and federal courtrooms. These critics also argue that the "insider" status of the Sierra Club, NRDC, the Wilderness Society, and other large organizations has removed them from the concerns of their members, not to mention average Americans whose environmental problems are rooted in where they live and work (Dowie 1995; see also Shaiko 1999).

In the congressional debate over the QLG bill, supporters used these common critiques of the U.S. environmental movement to delegitimize environmental opponents. Representative Don Young's (R-AK) dismissal of the environmental movement as ignorant and out-of-touch is representative and also reflects his personal disdain for national environmental groups who have long opposed drilling in the Arctic National Wildlife Refuge: "Yes, the national environmentalists oppose it. You know why? Because they lose their control, and this is what this is all about, control. The environmental so-called community around Washington, D.C., *it knows nothing about the environment.* Let's start listening to the local people. Let us start listening to those that live there" (emphasis added).[5] Young constructs the local citizens of Quincy as knowledgeable and reasonable—not "bent on conflict" like the national environmental lobby. Opponents to the Quincy bill were "obstructionists" who were fighting the QLG because they depended on conflict (and enemies) in order to maintain members and secure funding. Representative Doolittle (R-CA) echoed many of these themes when the QLG bill was debated on the floor of the House: "The QLG represents remarkable consensus amongst local residents, local timber experts, local businessmen, local environmentalists, all local people who have produced this consensus to properly manage the forests. The only group opposed to this legislation is the *arrogant, left wing, taxpayer subsidized environmental lobby,* because if we have consensus to manage our forests at the local level, they might not be necessary" (emphasis added).[6]

Members of Congress were not alone in engaging in these characterization contests. QLG members used similar rhetoric when they testified during House and Senate hearings. For example, Bill Coates responded to Louis Blumberg's negative testimony by saying, "He gets paid for conflict and I, like some of you folks, get paid to make things work" (U.S. Congress, House, "Hearing on H.R. 858," 1997, 40). Representative Helen Chenoweth (R-ID) later referenced Coates's remark, saying that she was very concerned about the "conflict industry" being promoted by environmentalists (U.S. Congress, House, "Hearing on H.R. 858," 1997, 41).

Congress eagerly praised the QLG's consensus-based process, one that eschewed conflict as a means of settling difficult natural resource issues. The national environmental groups were held up as the mirror image of the QLG's approach. They were characterized as historical artifacts, made up of individuals and groups who did not realize, or refused to embrace, this new era of environmentalism. As Jackson said in his testimony before a Senate subcommittee, "Our opponents offer nothing to you but the same. The status quo of endless fighting, divisiveness, and hatred" (U.S. Congress, Senate, "Hearing on S. 1028," 1997).

Supporters of the QLG also marginalized opponents by calling them "fringe," "wingnuts," and "eco-thugs." For example, Representative Young argued, "Only the groups on the *very fringe* oppose the bill and they have no rational basis to do so. We tried to get them to the table, but they refused.

There are groups that will never be satisfied. That is the way they make their living" (emphasis added).[7] It is difficult to reconcile Young's image of the opponents as "very fringe" with the idea (implicit in other statements and testimony) that they were established, national environmental organizations who were at the center of the environmental movement.

The success of the QLG coalition in Congress depended in part on their ability to construct the conflict as one between local, grassroots groups and national, Washington, D.C.–based organizations. The positive image of the QLG—as local, consensus-based, and representative of all interests—depended on ignoring or discounting the opposition of local and regional grassroots environmental groups. The next section looks more closely at how the QLG coalition successfully framed the conflict as one between local interests and national organizations.

Framing Participation: Locals versus Nationals

National environmental groups who opposed the Herger-Feinstein Quincy Library Group Forest Recovery and Economic Stability Act tried hard to prevent the battle from being characterized as one between local interests on the one hand and national environmental groups on the other. One strategy for combating this image was to raise the profile of local and state opponents of the QLG. The Wilderness Society, for example, paid for Neil Dion to testify before the Senate Subcommittee on Forests and Public Land Management when it held hearings on the QLG bill. Louis Blumberg of the Wilderness Society wanted to publicly ally his group with Dion and other local opponents; such an alliance would increase the legitimacy of the campaign by showing that disagreement was more widespread than Congress imagined.[8] In his testimony before the Senate, Dion claimed there was broad opposition to the QLG: "Because of the unwillingness and inability of the QLG to address the legitimate concerns of key stakeholders, their bill is opposed by *every environmental group that works on forest protection issues in the state of California*, including grassroots groups throughout the Sierra Nevada, as well as local environmentalists from the affected area" (U.S. Congress, Senate, "Hearing on S. 1028," 1997; emphasis added). Dion also criticized the extent and quality of participation in the group by claiming that the QLG forest compromise was "reached by three individuals who then recruited a dozen or more associates to support it" (U.S. Congress, Senate, "Hearing on S. 1028," 1997).

Despite Dion's testimony and that of Felice Pace from the Klamath Forest Alliance (a California environmental group opposed to the QLG plan), Congress seemed to largely accept the QLG's image of the conflict. As Blumberg remarked, it was "difficult if not impossible" to overcome the "locals versus nationals" frame (2001). The media's coverage of the QLG did not help the environmental coalition in their efforts to reframe the conflict. Both Neil Dion and John Preschutti (the two most active local opponents to the QLG) gave hours of interviews to journalists from the *Sacramento Bee*, the *San Francisco Chronicle*, *High Country News*, and *Smithsonian* magazine, but their critiques of the QLG were largely missing in the published articles. Said Dion, "They [the media] did not want to hear that it is all just a tiny group of people who have made this decision and sold it to the community. . . . They don't want to hear from a local environmentalist who does not agree because that does not fit the story" (2001).

An examination of the news coverage of the QLG in major national and regional newspapers lends support to Dion's claim. Very little coverage of the QLG appeared outside of specialized newsmagazines like the *High Country News*, which focuses on natural resource issues in the western United States. As shown in figure 8.2, only twelve noneditorial news stories on the QLG appeared in major U.S. newpapers from 1993 to 2000.[9] Of the twelve news stories on the QLG, only one identifies local opposition by quoting Dion and Erin Noel. Several articles reference a generic "opposition" and a few mention California environmental groups who opposed the QLG, but the articles quote national environmental spokespeople from the Audubon Society and Wilderness Society. Many of the editorials and opinion columns do not mention state or local opponents at all, adopting the "grassroots versus nationals" frame promoted by the QLG coalition. Finally, three of the articles (two news stories, one opinion column) effectively deny that any opposition exists by focusing only on how the QLG united previously warring factions in the timber wars.

The lack of coverage of the QLG points to weaknesses in the opponents' campaign—namely, their seeming inability to attract the attention and enlist the participation of the general public. (They were effective, however, in expanding the issue to the environmental community and specialized audiences such as academics and environmental policy experts.) The following discussion explains why QLG opponents failed to significantly expand conflict and participation.

"Too Little and Too Late": The Failed Attempt to Expand Conflict and Participation

The strategies of the QLG coalition, while effective, do not fully account for their success in containing conflict and limiting participation. In general,

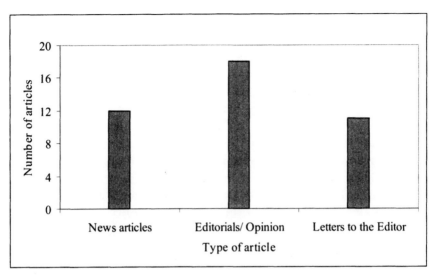

FIGURE 8.2   Coverage of the QLG in Major U.S. Newspapers, 1993–2000

Source: Compiled by the author from LexisNexis Academic Universe. Search words were "Quincy Library Group" and "Quincy Library."

it is difficult to understand why some actors succeed in the policy process without considering the actions, or nonactions, of their opponents. In this case, it means understanding the behavior of local, state, and national environmental groups who opposed the legislation based on the QLG plan. These organizations had considerable resources as well as political contacts in the Clinton administration. But their efforts, to put it simply, were too little and too late. As John Preschutti complained, "The national [environmental organizations] did not get on the ball early enough. . . . Everything was rear guard, too late—we were overrun trying to fight the little battles because we may not have been prepared well enough for the initial battle" (2001). By the time major environmental groups launched a national campaign against the QLG legislation, the QLG had secured the support of key allies in Congress and in the administration. More importantly, the QLG coalition had successfully defined the issue in terms that favored them and disadvantaged their opponents.

To understand why environmental opponents delayed their campaign, we must consider the political context in which the QLG developed. As noted in the last chapter, during the 1990s local collaborative approaches to resolving natural resource conflicts were becoming increasingly popular as alternatives to centralized, command-and-control regulation. The forest service and other government agencies had been experimenting with, and in some cases sponsoring, local stakeholder groups since at least the late 1980s. Everyone from academics to agency officials heralded the growth in local stakeholder groups as the precursor of a new environmentalism, one that was grassroots, community-based, and democratic (Sagoff 1999, 164–65). The mainstream environmental movement was well aware of the growing popularity of collaborative stakeholder groups; some organizations publicly supported the idea while others joined collaborative groups themselves. In this context, it is not surprising that national environmental groups were hesitant to publicly oppose the QLG and its forest management plan. Neil Dion claimed that the national groups were wary of criticizing the QLG "because they didn't want to look like the bad guys, didn't want to shoot themselves in the foot" (2001).

Some of the early letters to the QLG from state and national environmental groups reveal their halting support for the QLG. A group of California grassroots environmental groups wrote the QLG in early 1994 seeking clarification on a number of substantive and procedural issues related to its proposal. The letter (signed by Erin Noel, who later spoke out against the QLG) concluded with a statement of support for the QLG's initiative: "Your proposal is a bold attempt to move the current polarization of efforts in the Sierra into a rational and community solution to ongoing resource extraction issues. We are very interested in developing solutions and respect your pioneering efforts to do so" (Noel and others 1994). The Wilderness Society, Sierra Club, and NRDC also expressed support for the QLG process in a letter to Jackson dated March 31, 1994: "In general, we support collaborative approaches to addressing forest management problems and would like to support such an approach in the northern Sierra Nevada" (Yassa, Blumberg, and Waid 1994).

Another factor working against a unified and early opposition to the QLG from national environmental groups involved internal organizational politics. Put simply, national offices did not want to oppose their local and state chapters, some of whom had already endorsed the QLG. Such a move would give the impression that the national leaders did not trust their members and that the leaders in Washington "knew better" than the grassroots activists. Ron Stewart commented on the reluctance of some national environmental groups to get involved this way: "The nationals did not want to get in a fight with the local people. . . . It does not do them well to oppose their local chapters—it does not stir up camaraderie" (2001). Some environmental organizations, like the Audubon Society, had stated policies that prevented their national office from opposing the policy positions of local and state chapters. Interestingly, the Audubon Society eventually split with their local chapter over the QLG issue, the first time that this occurred in the history of the organization. Such a decision, we can assume, was not easy for Audubon leaders and it clearly did not sit well with the locals. The Plumas Audubon Society in Quincy wrote a letter to the national office, asking, "How can a local chapter of Audubon remain viable when the National office abandons, sabotages or undermines local efforts to improve conservation on the local scene?" (quoted in Sagoff 1999, 171).

In time, cautious support from the environmental community turned to outright opposition to the QLG; leaders in the Wilderness Society and Sierra Club even warned their supporters about the dangers of local collaborative groups more generally (see McCloskey 1996; Callahan 1997). But the countercampaign came too late in the case of the QLG. National environmental groups hesitated too long and this prevented them from forming a strong and early alliance with local opponents like Dion and Preschutti, individuals who could have lent legitimacy to the anti-QLG campaign. Neither Dion nor Preschutti had been entirely happy with his alliance with these groups in the past, charging them with being "too political" and abandoning grassroots groups like FPW when it was politically expedient to do so (Dion 2001; Preschutti 2001). They were similarly disappointed by the fact that the national groups waited until Congress was debating the QLG bill to launch a significant countercampaign.

The anti-QLG campaign also had a hard time finding allies in the Clinton administration and in Congress, in part because QLG members had secured the support of key allies long before the national environmental groups approached them. For example, in February 1994, forty-three members of the QLG met with USFS Chief Jack Ward Thomas and with Jim Lyons, undersecretary for natural resources and environment, to promote their Community Stability Proposal. They also met with every senator and representative from California and approached other members of Congress who sat on natural resources committees (Davis and King n.d.). Not long thereafter, Secretary Lyons, Senator Barbara Boxer (D-CA), and Senator Dianne Feinstein (D-CA) made public statements in favor of the QLG.

Senator Boxer later withdrew her support for the QLG bill in response to the growing opposition from regional and national environmental groups. But there were very few defectors overall, even though not everyone in the Clinton administration was supportive. In an interview with *High Country News* given after his retirement, Jack Ward Thomas spoke disapprovingly of the QLG, admitting he "disliked almost everything about the Quincy Library

Group, especially the fact that Sierra Pacific Industry was involved" (Marston 1997b). Official opposition was rarely voiced at the time, however. Indeed, regional forester Ron Stewart claimed that once Lyons and other administration officials had publicly voiced their enthusiasm for the QLG, "That kind of committed everybody to making it work, even though there were some fears that a lot of similar bills would follow this one" (2001).

The anti-QLG campaign was thus left with very few public allies beyond environmental organizations themselves. As noted in the last chapter, their efforts to expand the conflict to a broader public involved reframing the issue as a national one. Environmental opponents argued that the forests of the northern Sierra Nevada should concern all Americans because they belonged to the entire nation, not just one small community. A related strategy involved questioning the right of a "few well-placed individuals" to determine policy on a national forest. Both Dion and Blumberg referred to the QLG as a "special interest group" in their testimony before Congress, attempting to tarnish Congress's sanguine image of the group. In fact, Dion tried to frame the issue more generally as a case of special treatment for a minority interest: "Since every American has a stake in the management of our public lands, public participation in the management of National Forests should be as broad as possible. By coming to Washington and seeking *special* legislation and *special* funding, and by demanding *special* consideration from local Forest Service officials, the QLG is seeking to block the only avenue we all have to participate equally in the decision-making process" (U.S. Congress, Senate, "Hearing on S. 1028," 1997; emphases added). Dion charged that the select group of charismatic political "movers" who created the QLG did not represent the local community or the interests of the public at large. The QLG, opponents argued, was exclusionary, scheming, and fraudulent—certainly not an appropriate "poster child" for the local stakeholder movement.

In sum, opponents to the QLG engaged in characterization contests but with considerably less success than the QLG coalition. The image of the QLG as a local, consensus-based group survived the assaults of environmental opponents, emerging from the national political arena relatively unscathed. Even representatives from Sierra Pacific Industries, the largest mill operator in the region, were successfully constructed as "local," despite the fact that Sierra Pacific is the largest forest products company in the state of California, whose loyalty to local communities is uncertain at best.[10] The QLG's success in maintaining its positive image was due in part to the rather negative image of its opponents, whose complaints (and characterizations) were effectively dismissed and delegitimized. Moreover, QLG opponents were relatively late in launching their campaign, giving the QLG coalition time to secure key allies and frame the debate in terms that favored them.

Conclusion

> Despite pulling out every stop to kill the Quincy Library bill, environ-
> mentalists couldn't persuade one member of Congress to vote their way.
> Why were environmentalists so hysterical over an innocuous forest bill
> that few people had ever heard of? And if the bill was really "twice as
> bad as the salvage sale rider," why were environmentalists unable to do
> anything about it (O'Toole 1998, G1)?

Participation in forest policy conflicts in the United States has grown dramatically in the last several decades. Decisions about timber harvest levels, methods of harvesting, and the preservation of old growth and roadless areas rarely take place outside of the watchful eyes of forest activist groups and often attract widespread public attention. In the late 1980s, environmental activists successfully nationalized the issue of old-growth forest protection, setting the stage for extensive public awareness around (and participation in) national forest management issues. Given this, the success of the Quincy Library coalition in managing participation in the conflict over their forest plan is significant.

The QLG used a combination of strategies for controlling participation in the QLG itself. First, it overtly excluded the forest service on the grounds that the agency was part of the problem and had been ineffective in settling these issues in the past. The QLG suggested that environmentalists and the logging industry had more in common with one another than the forest ser-vice—or anyone else—had led them to believe. Simply stated, the forest ser-vice became a common enemy around which QLG members rallied. Second, the QLG, perhaps inadvertently, discouraged the participation of community members and groups who disagreed with its proposal. This was particularly evident when the QLG became a more cohesive, self-identified group—when individuals within the group began to associate more with their "community of place" and less with their "community of interest." Over time, the QLG became less tolerant of outside environmental groups who expressed concerns about the QLG plan and process. In March 1999, the QLG voted to close meetings of the committee that was established to monitor implementation of the QLG pilot project. Then in November 2001 the QLG suspended public meetings but continued to meet in private—proof, according to critics, of its exclusionary nature. As Erin Noel, attorney for the Sierra Nevada Forest Protection Campaign, said about the 1999 decision to hold closed meetings, "Until now, the Quincy Library Group has walked a thin line between public forum and special-interest group. This is a strong step toward special interests" (quoted in Little 1999).

When the QLG took its case to Congress, a move that threatened to expand participation in the conflict, the QLG coalition successfully managed conflict by negatively characterizing opponents, characterizations that many members of Congress were more than willing to accept. Like Clayoquot environmentalists, who took advantage of broader trends internationally, the QLG's timing—whether deliberate or by chance—was propitious. The QLG was able to capitalize on a general disillusionment with centralized, command-and-control regulation (whereas Clayoquot environmentalists capitalized on the Canadian government's commitment to the UN Convention on Biological Diversity). In addition, the QLG took advantage of public disenchantment with the mainstream national environmental movement, a movement that is increasingly seen as overly tied to Washington, D.C., neglectful of its grassroots constituents, and tied to outmoded ideas. The construction of QLG opponents as historical artifacts has an interesting parallel in the Clayoquot Sound controversy. In the Clayoquot case, though, the *timber industry* was labeled a relic of history, while environmental groups constructed themselves as the standard-bearers of new values and updated approaches to both politics and policy.

The most important strategy of the QLG coalition revolved around shifting the lines of cleavage in the forest policy system. The QLG effectively subordinated the dominant conflict in forestry politics (between the timber industry and environmentalists) while exploiting conflict between grassroots groups and national environmental organizations. This shift in alignments largely disarmed opponents, who were wary of being labeled as critics of local collaborative processes. National environmental organizations delayed their anti-QLG campaign for this reason, a delay that weakened the campaign and gave the QLG time to cultivate key allies and frame the conflict as one between locals and nationals.

This chapter has shown that the "local versus national" construction was not entirely accurate; there were many local and regional individuals and organizations who opposed the QLG. Leaders in the NRDC anticipated that this would be a problem as early as 1994 and urged the QLG to stop such characterizations in a letter to the group: "We are already hearing from some local activists that this is an issue of the 'grassroots' versus the 'nationals.' However, that tired rhetoric is simply inaccurate. There are plenty of 'grassroots' folks who have expressed significant concerns about the Quincy Library Group proposal. It may benefit someone's political agenda to paint the nationals as the 'bad guys' but that characterization is both unfair and destructive to our shared long-range goals" (Edelson, Blumberg, and Waid 1994). As it turns out, the "locals versus nationals" frame grew in popularity over the next few years as the QLG forest plan was debated in Congress and elsewhere. Congress's adoption of this frame helps to explain why environmental opponents to the QLG failed when they fought the proposed Quincy Library Group Forest Recovery and Economic Stability Act. Their complaints were dismissed as the grumblings of a power-hungry, national environmental movement who did not want to see a local group tread on its territory.

In the Clayoquot Sound case, timber interests and the provincial government attempted a similar strategy. They too focused on large environmental organizations, in this case international groups like Greenpeace, and tried to delegitimize the forest advocacy movement by saying it was led by meddling "outsiders." In effect, the provincial government tried to rally Canadians toward the government's position by appealing to their sense of patriotism and commitment to sovereignty. Their frame implicitly pitted outsiders against Canadians. But this strategy failed, in part because the forest advocacy movement in British Columbia was well established and well regarded by much of the public.

The story of how the QLG successfully managed participation provides general lessons about advocacy group politics. Recent theories of policy change argue that the lineup of allies and opponents around an issue is fairly constant over time (Sabatier and Jenkins-Smith 1993, 1999). The Advocacy Coalition Framework argues that a policy subsystem typically divides into two or more camps, each of which is held together by deep core beliefs that define a person's "underlying personal philosophy" (Sabatier and Jenkins-Smith 1993, 30). But by focusing on coalition stability we might overlook cases in which an advocacy group successfully repositions the fault lines within a policy subsystem. Breaking or reshuffling alliances can be thought of as the flip side of building them: Dividing opponents is the primary goal, not attracting allies. These cases might be rare, but they are nonetheless important because they suggest a potentially effective way of creating agenda and policy change.

The case of the QLG shows how change follows from the breakdown of alliances and the repositioning of coalitions. When two environmental activists defected from the local environmental organization in Quincy to join their former adversaries, the politics surrounding forestry in the region shifted dramatically. The QLG could plausibly claim to represent divergent interests in the community and gained legitimacy with the public and policymakers as a result. The logic was that if the strange bedfellows who made up the QLG could agree to a compromise solution, then their proposal must be reasonable. The reaction of members of Congress (many of whom extolled the virtues of the QLG much more emphatically and more often than they praised the merits of the proposal itself) to the QLG proposal illustrates that this logic was at work.

Coalitions of strange bedfellows, or "coalitions of convenience" as they are sometimes called, might be difficult to form and to maintain but they can be effective political actors. In highly polarized policy subsystems, any disruption can change the public meaning of a conflict and the behavior of other political actors. In the Clayoquot Sound case, similar dynamics were at work when environmental groups allied with First Nations. Members of FOCS admitted that their alliance with First Nations was largely a coalition of convenience. Nevertheless, it was an effective one. As discussed in chapter 4, the early alliance between environmental groups and First Nations captured the imagination of the sympathetic public in Vancouver, British Columbia, and beyond. The alliance also solidified the connection between forest preservation issues and human rights issues, greatly expanding the scope of the Clayoquot issue.

Further research is needed to understand how the lines of cleavage in policy subsystems are sometimes disrupted and what effect such changes have on the politics that follows. Similarly, much work remains to be done on the phenomena of coalitions of strange bedfellows. Zafonte and Sabatier (2004, 100), in their study of advocacy coalitions in the automotive pollution control subsystem, found a relatively high degree of stability in the coalitions over time rather than "shifting, short-term coalitions of convenience." The authors criticize case studies for their tendency to examine "interesting" behavior (e.g., the exceptions to the rule) rather than general patterns. Nevertheless, if coalitions of convenience have an unusual effect on policy change then the exceptions are worth studying. We might ask whether such coalitions tend to form around certain kinds of issues. Moreover, are they largely fleeting, or do they sometimes persist beyond the issue that brought them together? Do they carry more legitimacy with the public and policymakers? One danger is that policymakers will assume that any policy recommendations coming from such coalitions represent reasonable compromises, without critically examining the policy itself. In a world of polarized interest groups and partisan gridlock, policymakers may be more than willing to settle for outward signs of consensus rather than true political compromises.

Lawsuits, Libraries, and Legislatures

The Quincy Library Group and Venue Shopping

The preceding chapter illustrated how the QLG successfully contained participation in the conflict over its forest management plan. To members and supporters of the QLG, however, the idea that they had contained participation was absurd; members of the QLG note that the core group consisted of nearly thirty people and that meetings often drew more than one hundred citizens, at least in the early years. Moreover, Michael Jackson, one of the founders of the QLG, claims that they "begged" national environmental groups to send representatives to the meetings but to no avail: "What do you do when they won't come? Tell your neighbors we can't meet because they're too busy having cocktail parties down in San Francisco?" (quoted in Sagoff 1999, 169). But these critiques miss the point: The QLG's biggest strategic innovation around participation was to shift the lines of cleavage among the "usual suspects" in the forest policy subsystem. By breaking up existing local alliances and forging new ones, leaders in the QLG managed participation in ways they might not have foreseen. The creation of the QLG broke up the local environmental group, Friends of Plumas Wilderness, and delayed the mobilization of opponents who feared being labeled as adversaries of local cooperative approaches to resolving natural resource conflicts. Participation patterns shifted, and the QLG benefited from the new lineup of allies and opponents.

The QLG was innovative in another way: They created a new venue for action outside of the typical forest policy arenas. Forestry politics at both the national and regional level in the decades leading up to the creation of the QLG was characterized by a kind of stalemate, brought on by the fact that

environmentalists and their opponents in the timber industry were targeting different policy venues. Environmentalists largely relied on the courts to
achieve their policy goals, while the timber industry fought back in Congress,
often resulting in short-term victories for each side (Burnett and Davis 2002;
Hoberg 1997). The QLG's original solution to the alleged stalemate was to
eschew the usual venues for decision making and create a new arena for decision making at the local level. The idea was to overcome the gridlock and
adversarial politics that characterized forest politics in the 1990s by abandoning the preferred venues of each side in the conflict—namely, the courts and
the legislature.

As this chapter will demonstrate, however, the QLG was only partially
successful in forging a new arena for action. As it encountered institutional
resistance to its forest management plan, the QLG looked to Congress and
eventually to the courts to realize its policy goals. The story of the group's
efforts—first to create a new venue and then to use the "same old" policy
arenas—highlights the difficulty of achieving policy stability in systems characterized by multiple policy venues, overlapping jurisdictions, liberal rules of
participation, and rapid countermobilization. This chapter first tells the story
of how and why the QLG "went local" and then examines its venue shopping
strategies at the national level.

Going Local: From Lawsuits to the Library

The conflicts over forestry in northern California in the early 1990s reflected
larger trends in U.S. forest politics described in chapter 6. Local and regional
environmental groups in the Sierra Nevada were following the lead of their
colleagues in the Pacific Northwest in using NFMA and NEPA to appeal
timber sales on the Lassen, Plumas, and Tahoe national forests. As noted in
the last chapter, local environmental group FPW was having considerable
success in using the courts to delay or halt logging in the northern Sierras.
Its success mirrored patterns elsewhere: In a study of national litigation patterns, E. S. Jones and C. P. Taylor (1995) found that environmentalists initiated the majority of NFMA and NEPA lawsuits against the forest service
and were more likely to succeed in the courts than their counterparts in the
timber industry. Malmsheimer and his colleagues (2004) found similar results
when analyzing U.S. Courts of Appeals rulings on national forest management between 1970 and 2001. Environmental interest groups made up the
vast majority of plaintiffs and appellants in the 119 analyzed cases and won
almost half the cases they appealed (48.2 percent), while commodity interests

won only 12.5 percent of their cases (Malmsheimer, Keele, and Floyd 2004, 23–24).

In many ways, the numbers speak for themselves: In the Sierra Nevada, timber harvest on the Lassen, Plumas, and Tahoe national forests had dropped from a high of 640 million board feet in 1988 to 375 million in 1992. But the lawsuits filed by FPW and other environmental groups are only part of the story. The CASPO report, released in the early 1990s, led to strict interim forest management guidelines in order to protect the California spotted owl and prevent it from being listed under the Endangered Species Act. The guidelines recommended harvesting levels of only 124 million board feet; in 1993, harvest levels did not drop to the recommended level but did decline precipitously, to 212 million board feet.

In short, the timber industry in northern California faced a rather grim political and institutional environment in the early 1990s. In addition to the immediate problem of declining local timber supplies, they were confronting longer-term changes in national forest management. A new Democratic administration under President Clinton, a new secretary of agriculture, and a Democratically controlled Congress signaled rough times ahead for the timber industry. It was clear that policy venues that had been receptive to their concerns in the past would be less so in the future. Given these circumstances, it is easy to understand why timber industry representatives in Quincy were open to the idea of sitting down with local environmentalists to try to resolve the problem locally. Timothy Duane (1997, 787) summed up the new local political situation this way: "The new logging restrictions altered the balance of power . . . forcing the timber industry and its allies to give local environmentalists a seat at the table."

The reasons why local environmental attorney Michael Jackson and environmental activist Linda Blum joined the timber industry at the table rather than continue to use the courts is less clear. As noted, the future political landscape for environmentalists looked promising on several counts and in many arenas, including the regional, state, and national levels. First, adoption of the CASPO guidelines would provide environmentalists with additional tools to protect old growth and roadless areas. Second, in 1993 Congress commissioned a scientific study of the Sierra Nevada region, later to be called SNEP (the Sierra Nevada Ecosystem Project). The scope of the study suggested that the SNEP report would steer the forest service in the direction of large-scale ecosystem management; at the very least, the report would provide environmentalists with more scientific data to legitimize their policy positions. Third, environmentalists in northern California were cultivating closer ties to regional forest service offices and personnel, to the point where Louis

Blumberg of the Wilderness Society said they "had achieved a good collaborative relationship with the forest service in California" (2001). And finally, as noted, the national political landscape in the 1990s had changed in favor of environmentalists. After twelve years of presidents Reagan and Bush, complete with record timber harvests on national forests, Bill Clinton was elected in 1992 on a decidedly greener platform. Why, under these seemingly favorable conditions, would local environmental activists agree to move the issue to a new political arena?

Part of the answer lies in the perceptions of local environmental activists and their access to resources. Despite the favorable political climate, Linda Blum did not feel as though she and other local environmentalists were winning. While they had been successful in many of their appeals, Blum did not think their legal strategy was viable in the long term: "We didn't really think we were winning. We were trying to be as strategic as possible, to do things on the limited resources we had. Ironically, at that point the foundations that were funding—and the major environmental organizations at the national level—were claiming to be leading the charge on these things. But if you turned to them for legal help when all else failed, they would tell you that they could not help" (Blum 2001).

Blum claimed that "when push came to shove" she and Jackson had to write their own legal briefs and cover all the expenses associated with the appeals. Filing each administrative appeal involved "driving deep into the forest to review every logging site and writing lengthy documents," said Blum (quoted in Sagoff 1999, 166). Without financial and legal support from regional and national environmental groups, it would be difficult to sustain the fight, one that would surely continue once the CASPO guidelines were adopted. Moreover, the CASPO guidelines were only temporary, so in two years they would probably be back in the courtrooms anyway. It is important to note that Blum, by joining the QLG and suspending her appeals, was not rejecting a legal strategy on the grounds that it was ineffective, if effectiveness is defined as delaying or halting timber sales. Rather, Blum felt that the personal costs associated with the legal strategy were too high and therefore it was not a viable long-term strategy for her.[1]

Blum and Jackson's decision to participate in a new arena indicates the complexity of the venue shopping process. Too often, venue shopping is portrayed as a relatively straightforward strategic endeavor, one guided entirely by the opportunities and constraints found in the external political environment. By this account, advocacy groups use a policy arena for as long as they continue to win in it, and they change venues as soon as the opportunities shift and they start losing. But an advocacy group's (or an individual policy actor's) behavior is shaped by more than just these external factors. Resources clearly shape venue choice. Some advocacy groups may not be able to compete in certain venues, such as national legislatures, due to a lack of material and nonmaterial resources. Moreover, as Blum's account suggests, subjective perceptions and assessments about whether a strategy is working and is sustainable also shape the venue choices of advocacy groups and individuals.

Critics of the QLG had a different explanation for why some environmentalists agreed to sit down at the table with industry. They argued that people like Jackson and Blum were pawns of a larger strategy by the timber industry. The timber industry, they argued, was creating and supporting collaborative groups like the QLG in order to recapture some of the power it had historically enjoyed at the local level, power that had slipped away when forest policy became nationalized. Put differently, supporters and critics of the QLG disagreed about whether and to what extent the QLG represented a new way of approaching natural resource conflicts or whether it was simply "old style" politics. Critics of the QLG charged that the usual suspects—namely the timber industry and its supporters—were using the QLG and other local stakeholder groups to revive a style of policymaking that environmentalists had successfully fought decades ago. For those opposed to local collaborative groups, the timber industry appeared to be changing its strategy, experimenting with new institutional arrangements that might help it win some concessions in the long term.

Decentralization Redux?

Perhaps the most significant aspect of the initial meeting of the QLG founders was not *who* was at the table, but *where* that table was located. The agreement among Coates, Jackson, and Nelson (the original QLG members) to look for a solution outside the normal channels of forest planning processes is just as important as (if not more important than) the fact that environmentalists and the timber industry were talking with one another. Indeed, regional and national environmental groups were wary of the QLG because it signified to them a return to decentralized decision making. In the past, this style of policymaking privileged local needs over national interests. Duane (1997, 791) explains why the environmental movement tends to support more centralized management schemes: "Ecosystem management remains largely in national hands because the public lands are believed to provide values that would best be realized through non-local control. Both the modern administrative state and agency management procedures have been designed to minimize the likelihood that back-room deals would determine how the nation's land and resources would be managed. State and national environmental groups have strongly supported this centralized approach, because much of their political power lies with urban constituencies who have no influence in local negotiations."

While the environmental movement enjoyed advantages at the national level, the timber industry and its supporters had more power locally (see Koontz 2002). First, the local economies in Quincy and the surrounding communities were relatively dependent on the timber industry, especially when compared to other areas in the state and the nation as a whole. Plumas County was one of only two counties in California in 1989–90 where more than 10 percent of the workforce was employed in the timber industry. Many citizens, whether or not they were directly employed in timber, understood the economic contributions of the timber industry to the community. Ron Stewart, the regional forester for the USFS at the time of the QLG's founding, noted that local citizens were generally sympathetic to the industry: "The timber industry certainly has an advantage at the local level. They are part of the local economy, so people in the community are more likely to be sensitive and understand their needs, and will be more willing to meet those needs. Groups like the Quincy Library Group get you out of the bigger argument at the national level, and that has been part of the problem because these are national forests and we must go through public input processes" (Stewart 2001). As noted elsewhere, a portion of the revenues from timber sales went directly to county school districts, creating further incentives for local citizens to support the timber industry.

Not only was support for the industry higher at the local level, but also the environmental movement was less organized and considerably weaker than they were in other policy venues and at other levels of government. While FPW was successfully filing lawsuits against timber sales, the group itself was small and rather unorganized. According to Neil Dion, the Quincy area could not support a strong activist environmental movement and even FPW fell apart after some of its members joined the QLG (2001). It made strategic sense for timber sympathizers to focus their efforts in a policy arena where their opponents were relatively weak. As Michael McCloskey, an outspoken critic of local collaborative groups, said, "[Industry] prefer[s] dealing with community representatives to having to duel with EPA [the Environmental Protection Agency] experts at the national level, or with representatives of national environmental groups" (1996).

The advantages the industry enjoyed at the local level suggest that it recognized an opportunity in the QLG and other local collaborative groups to regain some power in forest policy decision making. Whereas the timber industry would never be able to recreate the policy environment of decades ago, it might be able to recoup some lost power if it could enhance the position of local communities. The long-term goal would be to gradually change forestry rules and procedures so that local groups were granted some decision-making authority over national forest policy. Evidence to support this claim stems from the reaction of timber companies to the QLG's proposal. The QLG plan gave Sierra Pacific Industries (already the largest timber company in the state) guaranteed access to scarce timber resources. If the forest service adopted the QLG's forest management plan, other companies' share of the total timber harvest would decrease. Despite this, the timber industry as a whole did not openly oppose the QLG. As Ron Stewart said, "There was some concern in the timber industry that the QLG plan would give an unfair advantage to certain companies in the area, in what was looking like a tight timber market. And yet the timber industry itself was not willing to step up and have an internal squabble over it" (2001). The absence of internal conflict suggests that the timber industry saw promise in the QLG approach to forest management and wanted to see local stakeholder groups spread.

The timber industry (and other QLG members) may not have completely understood the effect that the QLG would have on forest policy and politics prior to its formation. In this sense, the creation of the QLG was an experiment in building a new policy arena; the policy outcome and political consequences were by no means certain.[2] More generally, the process of forming new institutions is a purposive process but not always as rational and calculated as some theorists suggest. In the end, the advantages that local collaborative groups give to particular interests probably help to explain the persistence and spread of these groups better than they explain the origins of any particular one.[3]

Deciding the Rules of the Game

The members and supporters of the QLG deny that they are pawns in a larger game, orchestrated by timber interests who want to devolve control of national forests to the local level. Members of the QLG insist that their motives were more modest: They simply wanted to empower their community, get beyond the existing stalemate in local forest politics, and find a balance between environmental and economic goals in their region. According to QLG members, they could not realize these goals within the existing system because of its winner-take-all quality. If they tried to resolve the conflict within current policy venues, they could expect more adversarial politics, seemingly endless policy stalemate, and mutual frustration.

The members of the QLG felt it was necessary to find a neutral arena outside of existing policy venues (hence, their choice of the town library as a meeting place). Any kind of organization, however, requires rules, often promotes particular norms, and rests on certain values. It is impossible, in other words, to create a neutral policy arena. As Schattschneider (1960, 30) said, "By the time a group has developed the kind of interest that leads it to organize, it may be assumed that it has also developed some kind of political bias because *organization is itself a mobilization of bias in preparation for action*" (emphasis in original). As the previous chapter demonstrated, the rules and norms concerning participation in the QLG served to exclude or minimize the role of regional and national environmental groups in the QLG discussions.

The QLG also enforced certain norms on its members. One of the more important constraints on members stemmed from an understanding, whether explicit or implicit, that individuals (particularly the environmental representatives) would stop appealing timber sales on national forests during and even after the QLG negotiations. According to Neil Dion,

> Linda Blum and others had agreed not to do certain things, like not appeal timber sales, in order to be part of the Quincy Library Group. John [Preschutti] and I did anyway—we used CASPO to oppose the Howland Flat sale and we did a great job and slammed it. John at that time was technically part of the QLG, but once they found out about the appeal, they raked him over the coals and he quit. . . . They [the QLG] did not want any interruption of timber sales, that was the deal. It was a curious idea, because they could have said that there should be no timber sales while we are waiting (Dion 2001).

Dion and Preschutti suggest that one of the unstated "rules" of the QLG was that members would forsake the administrative appeals boards and the courtrooms in the interest of promoting harmony within the group and giving it a chance to develop a new approach to forest management.

The QLG also promoted the more general values of compromise and consensus, agreeing to put aside issues that members could not agree on and to focus on the ones where they could find common ground. While this rather civil approach to resolving difficult natural resource questions is attractive, it also carries a price. Disagreement and conflict are delegitimized as forms of political expression when compromise and consensus are revered.

Moreover, the institutions that allegedly encourage adversarial politics, such as the courts, are also discredited. As noted in chapter 8, opponents of the QLG were dismissed as "conflict promoters," and environmental litigation in general was largely rejected by the QLG coalition, at least at the outset.

These norms and values initially set the QLG apart from other attempts to shape forest policy—the QLG was in fact quite proud of these differences. Another significant but less acknowledged difference was the degree to which science governed or constrained the QLG's activities. The QLG relied on scientific data and theories to craft its forest plan and promote it in Congress. However, unlike government agencies and government-sponsored technical teams, it was not required to use only peer-reviewed science. Ron Stewart was critical of the QLG on these grounds, claiming that the QLG relied very heavily on only a few key people to provide them with scientific information: "My main problem with the Quincy Library Group is that they did not seek out the Forest Service's information and used their own. . . . The Sierra Pacific Industries guy had a biology background and they relied on him and on Jackson. Until the SNEP report came out, I don't know that anybody had a good, complete basis in science. A lot of what QLG people were using was not peer reviewed, it was only observational in nature. People who did technical documents [for the government] used only peer-reviewed stuff" (Stewart 2001).

Environmental critics complained that the QLG used outdated science and refused to update its plan based on the new scientific data contained in the SNEP report and in the Sierra Nevada Forest Plan Amendment (the "framework").[4] Indeed, environmental groups had successfully challenged previous iterations of the framework by arguing that the forest service's draft EISs had failed to adequately integrate up-to-date scientific information concerning spotted owl habitat and ecosystem management. With the QLG proposal, however, it was unclear whether such action-forcing standards would be available to opponents of the plan.[5]

It was also unclear whether and to what extent the Quincy Library Group Community Stability Proposal would be subject to federal environmental laws and procedures. The QLG meetings and negotiations themselves were exempt from normal participation procedures and rules. As Ruth (2000, 76) notes, "Because [the QLG] had formed outside of federal, state, or local government, [it] was not subject to requirements of public disclosure or accountability." Environmentalists who were not part of the QLG were understandably worried, because the rules that they had used so successfully in the past might not be available in the QLG forum or in collaborative groups more generally. Their concerns grew when the QLG asked Congress to write its forest management plan into law: Opponents of the bill argued that the QLG coalition was trying to get around federal environmental laws. Representative Bruce Vento (D-MN) suggested that QLG supporters in Congress had "hijacked" the idea of local input in order to get around strict national standards for forest planning and practices: "The effort here to pass this law is to in fact superimpose this over the existing mosaic of Federal laws that guide the use of these national lands. . . . This is an effort to, in fact, circumvent the existing limits, court decisions, other factors that have provided a policy path today that in the Northwest is working, admittedly not with[out] controversy."[6] Environmentalists, for their part, worried that the QLG process would lead to more attempts at getting around NEPA and NFMA planning processes, eventually undermining the public participation requirements of these laws (see Duane 1997, 792–93).

The QLG's decision to enlist the support of Congress created a storm of protest; it was the catalyst for national environmental groups' coordinated response against the QLG forestry plan. If the QLG plan was written into law, it could establish an unwelcome precedent: Other collaborative groups might try to use Congress to get specialized legislation, leading to site-by-site land-use management schemes. Proponents of grassroots ecosystem management might welcome such a development, but many environmental organizations, particularly those organized at the national level, feared it. The following section looks at the QLG's venue shifting strategies to understand why and how they moved from their local library to the halls of Congress.

From the Library to the Legislature

The QLG's decision to exclude the forest service from their initial negotiations signified its commitment to working outside traditional channels of forest policymaking. But to move the group's ideas from paper to practice, the QLG had to return to existing policy venues; QLG members, after all, had no authority over national forest management. The QLG first solicited the support of forest service officials; when the group ran into administrative hurdles, leaders reluctantly went to Congress. Michael Jackson, cofounder of the QLG, lamented the change in strategy and venues: "We have tried to keep the issue on the ground in the local area and not affect the rest of politics," he said, "but we have been taught by environmentalists that you have to go national to win. And that is my message—you cannot win without going national. We tried to go local, but it failed" (2001).

In 1993, the leaders of the QLG presented their Community Stability Proposal to the forest supervisors of the Lassen, Plumas, and Tahoe national forests. By most accounts, the supervisors adopted a rather cautious and skeptical attitude toward the QLG and its plan. This was the first time that the supervisors of the Lassen and Tahoe national forests had heard about the QLG proposal, yet they were being asked to approve the plan on the spot (Stewart 2001). The local forest service culture meant that agency personnel took pride in their expertise and professionalism. Forest service professionals felt they "knew how to manage the forests and do it better" than the QLG or any other nonprofessionals (Peters 2001). Consequently, they did not react well when the QLG tried to tell them how to manage "their" forests.

Local agency culture is not the only factor that helps to explain the initial reaction of some local forest service officials to the QLG. The forest service was also constrained by NFMA, NEPA, and administrative laws that required the agency to go through formal public involvement procedures before making changes to forest management plans. Moreover, the forest service was in the process of developing a rangewide strategy for the California spotted owl and would have to consider how the QLG plan fit into its existing management schemes (Stewart 2001; Peters 2001). Finally, the forest service needed more revenues to cover the cost of the QLG program. Regional forester Ron Stewart cited these constraints to QLG members and then, in an effort to find a compromise, offered to consider the QLG plan as one of the alternative plans in the CASPO EIS.

The QLG was not satisfied with seeing its plan devolve into one alternative among many, and the group certainly did not want regional forest service officials to reinterpret its plan in an EIS. So, in early 1994, forty-three members of the QLG presented their proposal to USFS Chief Jack Ward Thomas and Jim Lyons, undersecretary for natural resources and environment, in Washington, D.C. At this point, the QLG was committed to finding an administrative solution, even if it meant going over the heads of local officials and appealing directly to top agency officials. But the QLG was also preparing for the possibility that Lyons and Thomas would not intervene on its behalf and that local forest service officials would thwart implementation of the QLG plan. In preparation for these potential setbacks, QLG members met with California congressional representatives and members of Congress who sat on natural resource committees. In short, the QLG was making inroads into legislative arenas in the event that it encountered roadblocks elsewhere.

In late 1994, the QLG's efforts to court top agency officials paid off. Washington, D.C.–based forest service officials agreed to designate one million dollars in "carryover" funds from their 1994 budget to QLG projects. Soon after, Secretary of Agriculture Dan Glickman announced that the agency would contribute another $4.7 million in 1996 and 1997 to implement parts of the Quincy Library Group Community Stability Proposal. In addition to granting funds to implement the plan, Jim Lyons and Secretary Glickman publicly endorsed the QLG plan and process, thereby committing others to making it work. According to Dave Peters of the regional USFS office in Quincy, Lyons's intervention put forest service line officers in a difficult situation because "they had the department trying to broker an agreement [with the QLG] at the same time that they were trying to accomplish the program of work that was set out through the normal forest service channels" (2001).

Even with the green light from Secretary Glickman and the millions of dollars in additional funding, regional forest service officials did not immediately implement the QLG plan. Again, they expressed uncertainty about its effect on spotted owl habitat and questioned whether the plan was compatible with the new CASPO guidelines, not to mention the forthcoming SNEP recommendations. The line officers were more attuned to these policy constraints than their colleagues in Washington. From the perspective of the regional foresters and forest supervisors, the QLG plan added yet another layer of planning and process onto an already complicated and dense system. Moreover, if the QLG plan threatened owl habitat or was otherwise incompatible with the latest science in the SNEP report, they would be facing more appeals and lawsuits from environmental organizations. Cabinet officials, for their part, could publicly support local stakeholder groups like the QLG while leaving the more messy business of policy integration to the line officers.

Members of the QLG soon grew impatient with the forest service and made another trip to Washington, D.C., in 1997. This time they focused exclusively on finding allies in Congress rather than renewing their efforts in the administrative arena. Republicans had gained control of both houses of Congress in 1994, so finding representatives and senators to sponsor the bill was not difficult. A bill based on the Quincy Library Group Community Stability Proposal was sponsored by Representative Wally Herger (R-CA) and cosponsored by representatives Vic Fazio (D-CA) and Robert Smith (R-OR). The QLG's sponsors and supporters tried to minimize the amount of attention to and debate around the Quincy Library Group Forest Recovery and Economic Stability Act. The bill was assigned to the House Subcommittee on Forests and Forest Health, chaired by Republican Helen Chenoweth from Idaho. Six out of ten of the legislators on the committee were from western states and were especially sympathetic to the plight of rural communities. After the bill passed unanimously in committee, it went to the floor of the House where it was debated under a modified closed rule that limited debate to one hour and restricted the number of amendments that could be added to the bill to just one. The bill passed the House with a vote of 429–1.

Despite their legislative success, several QLG members said they were initially reluctant to switch policy arenas. As John Sheehan said, "There was a horrible reluctance to go to Congress. Generally *it is nice to keep your head low in the wars*" (2001; emphasis added). Sheehan and others recognized that moving to Congress could increase attention to and criticism of their plan—it might, in other words, wake the sleeping giant that was the national environmental movement. As noted in the previous chapter, national and regional environmental groups started a serious countercampaign only after the QLG went to Congress. The QLG understood that national environmental groups were skilled lobbyists in their own right and would call on their congressional allies to oppose the bill. And lobbying by environmental groups did make a difference: The original QLG bill was amended in ways that responded to opponents' concerns. The House added a provision requiring the forest service to abide by existing environmental laws when implementing the QLG plan and to conduct an EIS of the project (Davis and King n.d.).[7] These changes were significant and suggest that the QLG's fears around "going national" were well founded. In moving to a national venue, the QLG lost some control over the substance of its Community Stability Proposal. The amendments tempered the extent to which the QLG forest plan operated independently of national policy orientations. In short, opponents to the original QLG bill were not able to stop the QLG bill from passing the House, but they did succeed in altering the content of the legislation somewhat.

The QLG bill also hit some roadblocks in the Senate. By 1998 opponents to the QLG forest plan were better organized and had convinced their longtime ally Senator Barbara Boxer (D-CA) to withdraw her support for the QLG legislation. Boxer initiated a blocking action that effectively prevented the Senate from debating the bill (Davis and King n.d.). But Senator Dianne Feinstein (D-CA) made an end run around her former ally and attached the QLG bill as a rider to the 1999 federal spending bill. When President Clinton signed the omnibus appropriations package in October, a modified forest management plan based on the original QLG proposal was enacted into law. The QLG's venue shopping strategy had worked.

Postscript: Implementation of the QLG Pilot Project

In the wake of the QLG's legislative victory, the forest service was committed to implementing the plan. Dave Peters, forest service official in the Quincy region, put it this way: "No matter what we thought about the QLG plan in the past, we must do it now. . . . This is what the people of the United

States have said through Congress, so it is our role as public servants to implement this to the best of our ability" (2001). However, in the first year of the pilot project, implementation fell short of expectations: Fuel breaks were constructed on about seven thousand acres, only 12 percent of what the legislation mandated, and logging had taken place on only two hundred acres rather than the nine thousand acres called for in the legislation (Little 2003). Then, in 1999, the forest service blocked implementation entirely, citing threats to the California spotted owl from the increased harvest levels (Leavenworth 2003).

QLG members started to blame the disappointing results on the Sierra Nevada framework, a comprehensive management plan for eleven national forests in the Sierra Nevada region, released by the forest service in January 2001. The plan's basic components include annual decreases in logging over a ten-year period to 108 million board feet (for the entire region), additional preservation of old-growth trees on four million acres, a ban on cutting trees more than thirty inches in diameter, protection of sensitive riparian ecosystems, and the thinning of thick tree strands and the burning of forest debris to "fireproof" the forests (Martin 2001). The plan was considered a victory for environmentalists, who praised it not only for the dramatic decreases in logging but also for its comprehensive ecosystem approach to forest management.

In the wake of the forest service's announcement, the QLG, Senator Feinstein, and other QLG supporters denounced the plan on the grounds that it would override provisions of the QLG pilot project. The framework, for example, would prevent "group selection" harvesting as called for in the pilot project ("The Quincy Library Group" 2001, 13). One hundred and sixty-five organizations, including the QLG, formally appealed the framework, asking President George W. Bush's new forest chief to withdraw the plan. But USFS Chief Dale Bosworth upheld the Sierra Nevada framework in November 2001. While the decision was an endorsement of the nine-year process leading up to the framework, it was not a complete victory for proponents. Bosworth made several suggestions for refining the plan, including asking California forestry officials to identify ways to "better balance the plan" with the Quincy Library Group Forest Recovery and Economic Stability Act (Brazil 2001). Environmentalists feared that these suggestions might lead to a watering down of the framework.

In early 2002, just days after the Department of Agriculture had approved the Sierra Nevada framework, environmentalists' concerns were realized when the forest service announced that it might amend the plan to allow more logging. Jack Blackwell, supervisor for California's national forests, later proposed to resume implementation of the Quincy pilot project as part of the forest service's revisions to the framework. Then, in early 2004, the forest service announced a new plan for the Sierra Nevada region. The revised plan, which was formalized later that year, more than tripled the amount of logging allowed by the Sierra Nevada framework, authorized the logging of large-diameter trees, and rolled back wildlife and forest protections under the framework.

Despite the forest service's show of support, the QLG announced in March 2003 that they were suing the agency and four federal officials on grounds that the Sierra Nevada framework violated the 1999 Herger-Feinstein Quincy Library Group Forest Recovery and Economic Stability Act among other things. In response, the Sierra Club, the Wilderness Society, and the Sierra Nevada Forest Protection Campaign filed a motion defending the Sierra Nevada framework against the QLG's lawsuit. The courts, once rejected by the QLG, resumed their place at the center of forest politics and policy.

The outcome of these court battles is still uncertain at the time of this writing. The QLG scored a victory in January 2006 when the Ninth Circuit Court of Appeals ruled in favor of a forest service logging project carried out under the aegis of the QLG legislation. But environmental litigants, having already challenged four projects in the QLG area in an effort to delay and halt the logging of 1.4 billion board feet authorized by the legislation, plan to continue their judicial efforts (Little 2006). Meanwhile, the fate of the Sierra Nevada framework is hanging in the balance as a federal court in Sacramento considers whether the forest service's changes to the Sierra Nevada framework violate existing law.

The QLG's implementation woes suggest the difficulty of achieving policy closure in a system with multiple policy venues and highly mobilized interest groups. While the QLG was winning battles in some venues, it encountered obstacles because of preexisting, regional forest planning processes. Environmental groups took advantage of these processes and policy arenas, endorsing the Sierra Nevada framework and arguing that it should take precedence over the QLG plan.

Conclusion

In the U.S. political system, opportunities for venue shopping have increased in past decades. The U.S. Congress has become a more open and decentralized institution, where legislators assert their interest in and jurisdiction over policies once firmly entrenched in specialized committees (Shepsle 1989). U.S. courts have staked a claim in many policy areas previously considered to be too "political," best left to the experts, or otherwise outside the authority of the judicial branch (Friedman 1985; Shapiro 1988; Kagan 2001). Bureaucratic agencies, for their part, have been forced to open their decision-making processes to the public, largely due to a declining faith in the objectivity, neutrality, and responsiveness of administrative experts (McCubbins, Noll, and Weingast 1987; Hoberg 1992; Kerwin 1999). And cooperation among federal, state, and local authorities, particularly in the implementation of policy, has increased the opportunities for advocacy groups to move policy issues up and down the ladder of governmental authority.

In short, the U.S. system—with its separation of powers, overlapping jurisdictions, and relatively open rules of access—provides advocacy groups with numerous opportunities to shop for an alternative policy arena when they believe they are losing to their opponents. This contrasts with the Canadian system, which, while not entirely closed, affords fewer opportunities for venue shopping. But as the QLG case shows, multiple opportunities for venue shopping may exact a price: Policy stalemate, or the constant shifting of policy as advocacy groups use different venues to mitigate or block the actions of their opponents. Venue shopping, in other words, can prolong conflicts and prevent decisive victories. In Quincy, California, this perceived stalemate is what prompted local stakeholders in the forest conflict to create a new policy arena and embrace a new process of conflict resolution. The QLG's founding identity was rooted in a rejection of litigation and the courts, and a commitment to "keep it on the ground, in the local area," as cofounder Michael Jackson put it.

As the case illustrates, the QLG did not, in the end, keep it local, nor did it avoid the courts. The QLG's decision to seek a legislative solution at the national level, and its more recent decision to sue the forest service over the Sierra Nevada framework, belied its image as a local collaborative group working outside mainstream political channels. For critics, it appeared the QLG had become just another "special interest group," pursuing the same strategies as any other Washington insider. Perhaps the multiple policy arenas in the American political system and the opportunities they provide advocacy groups are simply too tempting to resist. Why confine policy advocacy to one venue when opportunities exist elsewhere? Why be content with the pace of policy change or implementation when a change in venue might speed things up? Moreover, from the perspective of an advocacy group, it is risky to cede a policy arena to one's opponents even if a venue shift violates one's ideology or organizational commitments.

While the QLG unapologetically turned to elites at the national level, their decision to move from the library to the legislature was not taken lightly.

Members of the QLG realized that a move to a national venue could increase attention to—and more important, opposition to—their forest management plan. As Baumgartner (1989) argues, moving conflict into a national legislative arena often expands the scope of conflict. The QLG's solicitation of Congress and other national arenas, therefore, might also reflect a failure on its part to restrict conflict to venues where it perceived the best chances for success. More generally, different venues offer both costs and benefits to advocacy groups; venue shopping, therefore, is not always as uncomplicated as sometimes portrayed in the literature. Advocacy groups might reluctantly shop for a new policy venue, hoping it will benefit them but worrying that it might lead to a countermobilization by opponents.

To some extent, the QLG was right to worry about soliciting the support of national institutions. National environmental groups took more notice of the QLG's proposal when it was being debated in the halls of Congress. The warm reception to the QLG on the hill was a sign to environmental groups that the QLG was more than just a passing fad. As Meyer and Staggenborg (1996, 1645) note about social movements more generally, "When one of the opposing movements achieves little success and does not appear very threatening, it is difficult for the other side to mobilize much support. More successful movements, which present real threats, generate more support for an opposing movement." As detailed in the last chapter, the success of the QLG triggered a stronger countermobilization. Environmental opponents worried about the precedent that might be set: a local, site-specific forest management plan that appeared to be based more on political objectives than ecological ones.

The shift in venues by the QLG created another dilemma for opposing environmental groups. As one case study of the QLG points out, "The group and its legislative solution had forced virtually the entire national environmental community to air its disagreements and dissension in broad public view, driving a wedge in the larger environmental community over the efficacy of local collaboration" ("The Quincy Library Group" 2001, 15). As long as conflict over the QLG was contained, the environmental movement could "agree to disagree" about the merits of local collaborative stakeholder groups. As the conflict moved to national arenas, environmental groups felt increased pressure to take a stand on the QLG, its forest management plan, and the wisdom of collaboration itself. Changes in venue, then, create not only opportunities but also dilemmas for advocacy groups. While environmental groups might have welcomed the increased scrutiny of the QLG brought on by the shift to national venues, the shift also forced the environmental movement to confront a set of issues it would have preferred to address privately.

10

Managing Policy Conflicts

This book began as an attempt to understand why two conflicts over similar substantive issues took such different trajectories, where one expanded internationally while the other was largely confined to the local level. Since Schattschneider (1960), scholars have recognized that the degree of conflict surrounding an issue shapes its development and resolution. Where there is little or no conflict, policy tends to be made by a relatively small set of policy specialists and stakeholders. When conflict is intense, a much wider range of players claims a stake in an issue, typically opening up opportunities for participation in the decision-making process (Baumgartner 1989). Advocacy groups are presumably aware of these dynamics and thus attempt to control the scope of conflict around an issue, knowing it might be the key to realizing their policy goals.

We might presume that, despite their efforts, advocacy groups have little control over the scope of a conflict because it is potentially shaped by things like the content of an issue, the actions of policy elites, institutional rules and norms, and relatively stable power arrangements that privilege some interests over others. But the analysis here shows that advocacy groups can and do shape a conflict's scope through their strategic maneuvering, particularly in the areas of defining issues, managing actors, and shifting policy venues. Quite simply, advocacy group strategies matter. And because of their importance, the outcome of a conflict is anything but certain. One side may be favored over another due to its greater resources or biased rules, or simply because its cause is more popular. And over time, we can assume that teams with superior resources and popular causes will win more often and more easily. But a good strategy—and good strategic thinking—can often make up for other deficiencies. As Marshall Ganz (2000, 1044) puts it, "'Resourcefulness' can sometimes compensate for a lack of resources."

The case studies in this book highlight the resourcefulness of advocacy groups as they define policy issues, create and reconfigure alliances, and choose institutional venues for policymaking. One conclusion that stands out is the extent to which advocacy groups engage in sustained interaction with one another. Interest group studies and even scholarship on the policy process typically look at how interest groups interact with the state—whether it is through lobbying, elections, or litigation. Less attention is paid to how advocacy groups interact with one another. In other words, how does ongoing interaction between opposing advocacy groups shape the strategies of groups and the trajectories of policy conflicts? The cases examined here suggest that advocacy groups change their strategies not only in response to shifting political opportunities at the institutional level but also in response to the strategies of opposing groups. The dynamics of these interactions need to be explored theoretically and accounted for in our models of agenda and policy change.

The model of conflict expansion and containment outlined in chapter 1 largely accepts Schattschneider's (1960) suggestion that the majority of policy conflicts involve one group (or set of groups) who are attempting to expand conflict and a competing set of groups who are trying to restrict it. While this characterization is accurate for some policy issues and during certain phases of a conflict, for others it falls short. It assumes an enduring and static structure of competition. Schattschneider argues that the "losers" in the policy process will consistently try to expand conflict while the "winners" will attempt to contain it.[1] However, the incentives of the players necessarily change as the nature of a conflict transforms. Ongoing conflict and competition complicate the strategic choices for advocacy groups, many of whom "muddle through" by attempting to manage conflict to the best of their ability. These efforts at conflict management involve unique patterns of interaction between competing actors and groups.

The following model of conflict management describes these patterns of interaction between competing advocacy groups.[2] This model takes into account the dynamic quality of the policy process generally and the shifting strategies of political actors in particular. The key characteristic of conflict management strategies is direct engagement and competition with one's opponent. As noted by Meyer and Staggenborg (1996), direct interaction—even face-to-face confrontation—with one's opponents is increasingly common in social movement politics in the United States and elsewhere. At times, interaction between groups is indirect, such as when competing advocacy groups pursue opposing strategies (i.e., one is attempting to expand conflict, the other to contain it). In these cases, advocacy groups tend to "talk past" one another, appeal to different audiences, and petition different policy institutions. Patterns of indirect engagement are likely to change where there is ongoing and more equal political competition between advocacy groups. This competition will push advocacy groups to compete on the same rhetorical "turf," to lobby the same audience, and to pursue (or fight) policy change in the same venues as their rivals. Table 10.1 summarizes the differences between conflicts (or phases of conflicts) in which advocacy groups are pursuing competing strategies and conflicts where both groups are attempting to manage conflict. The key characteristic of the latter is that the strategies of opposing groups begin to resemble one another, typically because one side forces the other to "play its game."

The two models in table 10.1 are best viewed as parts of a dynamic whole. As suggested, in mature conflicts with relatively equal opponents, the nature of the competition is likely to evolve. In relatively new policy conflicts, competing groups tend to pursue contrasting strategies of expansion and containment. As one side (typically the "losing" side) gains in power and is strategically successful, the dynamics shift in ways consistent with the conflict management perspective. The following sections explore these shifts in the areas of issue-, actor-, and institution-based strategies.

TABLE 10.1   A Comparison of Conflict Expansion and Containment to Conflict Management

Strategic areas	Conflict expansion and containment	Conflict management
Issues	Noncontradictory argumentation. Advocacy groups use different symbols and discourse.	Engagement with opponent's arguments. Competition over popular symbols. Convergence in discourse.
Actors	One coalition attempts to increase participation while opponents try to limit it. Appeals to different audiences and allies.	Both coalitions search for allies and go public. Appeal to same audiences and competition for the same allies.
Institutions	Appeals in different venues; little direct competition.	Competition within the same venues.

Managing Issues: Converging Discourses and Symbolic Co-optation

Studies of problem definition and issue framing emphasize the fact that advocacy group leaders and issue entrepreneurs spend considerable time defining issues, assessing the causes of problems, and suggesting solutions (Baumgartner and Jones 1993; Kingdon 1995; Rochefort and Cobb 1994; Stone 1988). The conflict expansion and containment framework suggests that the general thrust of these efforts is in the direction either of raising the salience of an issue or of decreasing audience awareness and interest in a conflict. But whether the goal is to expand or contain conflict, for both parties it is best to highlight those aspects of an issue that are most favorable to one's position, what Baumgartner and Jones (1993, 110) call "noncontradictory argumentation." Because the facts associated with different components of an issue typically favor one side over another, advocacy groups will avoid crafting elaborate responses to an opponent's claims in lieu of shifting attention to another topic. In this way, they can simply change the focus of the discussion rather than directly argue with their opponents. Noncontradictory argumentation is likely to be accompanied by divergent rhetoric and symbols; if the opposing camps cannot (or refuse to) agree on what the debate is about, it is doubtful that they will share the same language and employ the same symbols. Consequently, when noncontradictory argumentation is the norm, outsiders to a debate may feel they are witnessing a "dialogue of the deaf" as neither side directly responds to the other's arguments and each side uses unique symbols and rhetoric.

In the cases examined in this book, noncontradictory argumentation was common. For example, in the Clayoquot Sound conflict, environmental advocacy groups focused attention on the ecological effects of clear-cutting while the timber industry (and to a some extent the provincial government) tried to shift attention to the economic aspects of forestry. These patterns of attention are to be expected because environmentalists clearly "win" the argument when the focus of the debate is on biodiversity, whereas timber interests tend to prevail when jobs and the economy are emphasized. In the QLG case, similar efforts were made to switch the topic of attention. Members and supporters of the QLG focused on the threat of forest fires and the benefits of stakeholder collaboration, finding widespread support for their forest management plan when these issues were highlighted. Their opponents struggled to shift attention to the issue of old-growth logging and the environmental effects of the QLG plan, but with less success.

In addition to finding examples of noncontradictory argumentation, the case studies also reveal instances where competing advocacy groups directly engaged with one another, arguing on the rhetorical turf of their opponents. The shift in strategies—from ignoring the claims of an opponent to countering them—was typically brought on by greater and more equal competition between the opposing advocacy groups, by the expansion of conflict, and by the movement of conflict to a new venue. In general, as one advocacy group's frames gain acceptance among the public and policymakers, its opponents will feel pressure to directly counter them. Initially, opponents may stick to a strategy of noncontradictory argumentation, but this strategy is less feasible as the conflict drags on and the public and policymakers expect advocacy groups to respond to the various claims being made by competing groups.

As competition for allies and supporters increases, competing advocacy groups search for claims that resonate with potential sympathizers. Successful issue frames and their attendant symbols—those that seem to resonate with key segments of the public or policymakers—will be adopted by both advocacy groups in hopes that they can win over some of the audience. In a similar fashion, the movement of policy to a new venue encourages direct rhetorical engagement with one's opponents. Given that policy venues tend to have particular norms, rules, and procedures that require a certain type of discourse or set of frames, we should witness the convergence of discourses when advocacy groups compete in the same venues.

One method of assessing who has "won" a framing contest at any point in time is to look for signs of discourse convergence. In what direction is the discourse converging? Can we find "discourse coalitions" that share the same language, rhetoric, and symbols even as they continue to have different interests in a policy? If an advocacy group has compelled its opponents to engage with it directly, and if its opponents adopt some of its symbols and rhetoric, then an advocacy group has succeeded in setting the terms of the debate. Success in setting the terms of debate, in turn, is more likely after a group has expanded the conflict to a wider audience or moved the conflict to a different venue.

In the Clayoquot Sound case, discourse convergence was especially prevalent when the conflict moved to international venues. The new setting rendered the timber industry's arguments about jobs and the B.C. economy irrelevant. Audiences in Europe and elsewhere cared little about the potential lost jobs, and this forced the timber companies and provincial officials to engage with environmental advocacy groups on their terms. Moreover, the B.C. government did not have to worry about offending timber workers back in British Columbia when they were seeking the sympathy of European politicians and American consumers. For both of these reasons, the B.C.

government and industry representatives adopted some of the discourse and symbols of their opponents.

The QLG case also provides examples of issue management, although to a lesser extent than in the case of Clayoquot Sound. Again, the impetus for a shift in strategy came about when the venues of decision making changed. When the QLG targeted Congress, opponents of the QLG started to directly counter the QLG's claims about the fire management benefits of their Community Stability Proposal. In addition, environmental opponents questioned the appropriateness of using local collaborative stakeholder groups to draw up management plans for national forests. In many ways, QLG opponents were at a disadvantage when arguing on the "turf" of the Quincy library coalition. The question of whether the QLG plan would decrease the intensity of forest fires was too technically complex to draw in a large audience. And the overwhelmingly positive image of the QLG and so-called grassroots ecosystem management made opponents look as though they were undemocratic Washington "insiders." Opponents of the QLG generally failed in their attempts to manage the issue because the terms of debate had been largely set by the QLG itself.

Discourse convergence is a mixed blessing for advocacy groups. On the one hand, advocacy groups who have forced their opponents to debate them on their rhetorical turf ("instigators") have scored a victory by setting the terms of the debate. On the other hand, their opponents ("reactors") are now directly refuting and countering their claims, potentially forcing the instigators into a defensive posture. By the same token, symbols and rhetorical appeals once "owned" by the instigators must now be fought over and perhaps shared as their opponents co-opt them.

Managing Audiences and Allies

Models of conflict expansion and containment maintain that "winning" groups generally attempt to restrict participation in a conflict because the addition of new players threatens to disrupt their monopoly on decision making. Challenging groups, on the other hand, attempt to increase outsider involvement to upset the balance of power between themselves and their opponents. These opposing pressures to expand and contain participation are evident when differences in power and access between competing advocacy groups are relatively large. Industry lobbying groups, for example, tend to have greater access to decision makers and more material resources than their environmental opponents. Typically, business groups use "insider" strategies that involve relatively few players while environmental groups rely on "outsider" strategies involving hundreds or even thousands of supporters (Kollman 1998). In extreme cases, industry forms close relationships with key members of congressional committees and subcommittees and with agency officials, forming an iron triangle that effectively excludes any outside interests.

As the relative difference in access and power between competing advocacy groups decreases, however, the strategy of dominant groups will change. Under these circumstances, dominant groups can no longer rely exclusively on their power and access to maintain current policy benefits or to forestall policy change. As an issue rises in salience and visibility with the public, policymakers face pressure to open up policy decision making and respond to the public's concerns. Dominant groups will then search for additional allies and cultivate public support, mirroring their opponents' strategies. Kollman's (1998) analysis of the lobbying strategies of interest groups confirms that even organizations who are accustomed to using inside strategies at times resort to using conflict expansion tactics. In his study, business and professional trade organizations used expansion tactics, such as talking with the press and organizing letter-writing campaigns, when an issue was highly controversial and salient with the public.[3]

In the conflict over logging in Clayoquot Sound, industry representatives and the Harcourt administration shifted from trying to contain participation to trying to gain the sympathy of the same audiences being courted by environmental groups. They also competed with environmental organizations for the support of key allies such as First Nations leaders, recognizing an opportunity to attach themselves to an important legitimizing symbol and to weaken the ties between environmental groups and native tribes. The shift in strategy was again brought on by the actions of environmental advocacy groups, who essentially drove the timber industry and the provincial government to search for allies and audiences after years of conducting their business in relative isolation from the public.

The QLG case displays a somewhat different pattern because the conflict never expanded to include broad public participation. The key strategy of the QLG was to reshuffle alliances and allegiances in the local forest policy arena. At the national level, too, the QLG succeeded in forging a broad bipartisan coalition in support of its Community Stability Proposal. This left environmental groups who opposed the QLG without the support of longtime allies in Congress such as Senator Feinstein (D-CA), and without friends in the Clinton administration, many of whom publicly endorsed the QLG even if they had personal misgivings about the project. In the end, the QLG drove a wedge in the environmental community at both the local level and at the national level. The National Audubon Society, in fact, officially broke ranks with its local chapters over the QLG, the first time in its history it had ever done so.

Competition for allies is the result of prolonged and expansive public conflict. The expansion of conflict necessarily means that the issue has attracted increased public attention. Because neither advocacy group can be entirely certain about where the sympathies of the audience lie, they must hedge their bets by attempting to win over as many segments of the public as possible. Both sides in a conflict will also search for elite allies who can intervene on their behalf and carry on the battle in particular institutional arenas. Often, competing advocacy groups will cultivate allies among different sets of elites (in different political parties, for example); but the escalating and prolonged nature of some conflicts might lead to direct competition for the same elite allies. In the QLG case, for example, both the QLG and its opponents were soliciting the support of officials in the Clinton administration and Democrats in Congress.

Managing Institutional Change

At the outset of a political conflict, it is likely that competing groups will be pursuing (or fighting) policy change in different venues. This is due in part to the fact that less dominant advocacy groups are often prevented from participating in key decision-making venues or face biases within these institutions that effectively exclude them. Challenging groups therefore have an incentive to shop for an alternative policy arena. Dominant groups, on the other hand, will continue to enjoy advantages in key venues, at least for some period of time. They tend to be familiar with the rules and procedures of existing decision-making institutions and therefore have little desire to switch to a new arena where the rules are different and the loyalties of institutional actors unknown. In short, dominant groups want to avoid venues that are less known to them and where they do not perceive much chance of success. The result is a pattern of mutual noninterference, where competing advocacy groups pursue or fight policy change in different institutional arenas.

As a conflict persists and as competition between the advocacy groups intensifies, these patterns of noninterference are likely to change. Two factors help account for this. First, over time less dominant groups could gain access to the key decision-making venue that had previously excluded them. The increased access is driven by group leaders, institutional actors within a venue, or some combination of the two. Often, institutional actors—legislators, for example—feel pressure to expand access to decision making when a conflict is highly visible and salient with the public. The result is that previously excluded groups slowly begin to compete in these venues, although perhaps not on equal footing with their opponents.

A change in strategy by dominant groups can also lead to more direct competition. If challenging groups are successful in pursuing policy change in alternative venues, then dominant groups will not forfeit these arenas to their opponents. Previously dominant groups might find that new institutions have usurped or partially usurped policymaking authority over an issue; even symbolic acts by alternative institutions can prompt dominant groups to compete in new arenas. Initially, these groups might compete rather poorly because they are not familiar with the venue, nor are they accustomed to having to defend themselves outside the cozy decision-making arrangements they enjoyed in the past. Over time, however, these advocacy groups can become just as sophisticated as their opponents. Business and industry groups, for example, eventually developed sophisticated litigation strategies to challenge environmentalists in the courts even though environmental groups initially dominated this arena.

In both of the case studies, we see patterns of noninterference transforming into patterns of direct confrontation. In the Clayoquot Sound case, FOCS initially brought the conflict to international arenas, throwing the timber industry and the provincial government off guard. Environmental groups defined the issues in the absence of counterarguments by industry and the provincial government, giving them a significant advantage. But this advantage did not endure: The Harcourt administration and the Forest Alliance (representing the timber industry) soon realized they would have to play the game in international arenas as well. The result was parallel public relations campaigns by environmental groups and the provincial government-industry alliance.

Clayoquot environmental groups, however, struck back with yet another innovative strategy: They shifted venues again, moving from international political venues to international markets. The markets strategy moved the issue beyond the reach of the provincial government, and even, to some extent, the timber industry. The key relationships in this arena were between environmental groups and consumers of timber products such as Home Depot and the *New York Times*. This shift in venue effectively bypassed the state and created a new arena for action where the rules were created by environmental groups, albeit sometimes in consultation with industry (as in the case of developing forest certification standards).

The QLG also attempted to create a new arena for action, one outside traditional administrative, judicial, and legislative venues. And as long as it confined its activity to the "library," the QLG did not face significant opposition. Local and regional environmental groups who were not part of the QLG continued to file lawsuits, preferring to work in judicial arenas that had served them well in the past. Thus, the pattern for the first few years of the QLG's existence was one of mutual noninterference. It was only when the QLG shopped for venues at the national level that it came head to head with environmental advocacy groups. The increasing policy success of the QLG meant that opponents could no longer adopt a "wait and see" stance. The competition later became even more direct: The QLG and environmental organizations (the Sierra Club, Wilderness Society, and Sierra Nevada Forest Protection Campaign) were on opposite sides of a lawsuit concerning the 2001 Sierra Nevada framework as recently as 2003. The outcome of the lawsuit—and thus the fate of the Sierra Nevada framework—is still uncertain.

Direct competition in the same institutional venues occurs because one side has forced another to shift its attention to a new arena. Meyer and Staggenborg (1996), in their study of social movements and countermovements, note that this direct engagement can lead competing movements to adopt similar organizational forms: "When movement organizations respond to opportunities in specific arenas, they adopt structures to help them operate in those venues" (Meyer and Staggenborg 1996, 1649). An advocacy group that is forced to compete in a new venue might have to shift its organizational structure, perhaps by becoming more professional in order to use judicial arenas. This kind of organizational change was apparent in the QLG, which became more closed and hierarchical as it began to compete in national venues. These changes are most evident in recent years: In November 2001 the QLG voted to discontinue all public meetings so as not to "waste more time and energy on repeated meetings." In announcing its decision the QLG emphasized, "This does *not* mean that QLG ceases operations. It means only that QLG has decided to focus its efforts on processes that have a better chance of actually causing implementation of the Pilot Project" (Quincy Library Group 2001). While unstated, the "processes" referred to include litigation. The QLG's organizational structure has changed to resemble the professional environmental groups it once condemned.

In the case of Clayoquot Sound, similar dynamics were at work. In this case, the timber industry trade organizations and loggers' unions adopted some of the same strategies environmental groups use when forced to compete in public arenas. Industry-sponsored "Share" groups (representing timber workers) staged protests and direct actions, mimicking the tactics of the forest advocacy groups. Organizationally, these groups had to adapt to these new tactics and arenas. The Forest Alliance, a trade organization for timber companies, had to change its organizational structure to launch international public relations campaigns, becoming more heterogeneous in its strategies and tactics.

The conflict management framework outlined here recognizes that in mature conflicts with relatively equal opponents, direct engagement and competition between advocacy groups is common. Direct engagement between competing groups, in turn, leads to a close "coupling" of strategies and tactics, driven largely by an ascendant advocacy group that is forcing its opponents to react to its strategies. As researchers, we must pay attention to whether and to what extent such coupling takes place, and what influence it has on advocacy groups and the policy process more generally. Does direct competition force advocacy groups to be more innovative in their strategies and tactics? Who benefits more from direct engagement? Meyer and Staggenborg (1996, 1652) suggest that groups who adopt a reactive posture are at a disadvantage: "The threats created by opposing movements . . . are a mixed blessing. While they increase issue attention and provide tactical opportunities, they also limit the content of those opportunities. When a countermovement mobilizes successfully, the initiating movement may find itself trapped into reactive tactics aimed at defending the status quo rather than free to pursue proactive efforts to win new advantages. . . . In the face of powerful counter mobilization, a movement may expend all of its resources reacting to its opponents' initiatives."

This study has examined the interplay of opposing groups, looking at how the claims, alliances, and venue shopping strategies of advocacy groups evolve in response to the strategies of opponents as well as to shifts in the external political environment. By examining cases over time, these strategic changes become apparent and are traceable to small shifts in political opportunities and to the actions of competing groups. However, additional research is necessary to tease out the dynamics involved in protracted conflicts with highly mobilized, competing advocacy groups. Comparative studies that look at a variety of policy arenas in different countries can help us understand whether and to what extent these dynamics are affected by the nature of the policy subsystem and by the institutional structures in which they unfold.

It is fair to say that the game of politics may be getting more complicated, thus putting a premium on good strategic thinking. The advocacy groups involved in forestry policy in both Canada and the United States face a complex environment where authority over natural resources is fragmented, where countermobilization is rapid and sophisticated, and where political opportunities (and promises) shift as new administrations take charge. And all of this unfolds in the context of existing institutions, past policies, and the vagaries of external markets. More generally, with thousands of organized advocacy groups, multiple policy arenas, and frequently shifting political terrain, strategizing itself is an uncertain enterprise. As Lowery and Gray (2004, 171) put it, "The environment in which organized interests operate is a very complex one," rife with competition, uncertainty, and strategic conundrums. The flexible, adaptive, and innovative players—the ones who are able to "bend with the wind," those who are willing to target new institutions and try new tactics, even if they are unproven or outside the usual tactical repertoire—are likely to be the most successful in these complex political environments.

Appendix

Sample Interview Questions

Sample Questions for Clayoquot Sound Environmental Activists

1. Can you provide me with some background of your organization? When was it founded, what strategies do you employ, and what are your most important campaigns?
2. When did your organization get involved in the Clayoquot Sound campaign? In what capacity? Why did you get involved with it?
3. What were the biggest challenges in the early part of the campaign (pre-1993)? What about the latter part of the campaign?
4. Has your strategy changed over the years? If so, how?
5. What has been your most important strategy or tactic in the campaign to preserve Clayoquot Sound? Please explain.
6. What has been your media strategy? Are you satisfied with the coverage given to Clayoquot Sound and B.C. forest issues more generally?
7. Have you worked with other advocacy groups or policy actors? Who did you work most closely with and why? What was the nature of your collaboration?
8. Did you have any disagreements with your allies? Over what issues? How did you resolve these differences?
9. Please explain your relationship to First Nations.
10. Did the election of the NDP government in 1991 change things? How?

11. Do you consider any politicians in the B.C. government to be your allies?

12. Did you target the federal government? Why or why not? Do you consider anyone in the federal government to be an ally?

13. Did you use the courts to change policy? Why or why not?

14. What audiences have been most receptive to your message? Please explain.

15. Did your organization take part in the provincial-led task forces? What was your overall experience with these?

16. Have you worked with U.S. or international NGOs? What effect did their involvement have on the campaign?

17. Did you have any concerns about "going global"? What were they and why?

18. What was the role of your organization in the international markets campaign? In your opinion, how important was this component of the campaign?

19. Has the global attention to Clayoquot Sound changed things at the provincial level? How?

20. What, in your opinion, accounts for the success of the Clayoquot Sound campaign?

21. Who, in your opinion, should have ultimate authority over resource decisions in British Columbia?

22. Some of your critics have argued that these issues are for British Columbia and Canada to decide, not the international community. How would you respond to these criticisms?

Sample Questions for QLG Members

1. Please describe your involvement with the QLG. When did you get involved and why?

2. (To environmental members.) It appears that in 1992, environmentalists were "winning." If this is true, why did you agree to compromise with your former opponents?

3. What kept the QLG together? What issues united you? How central was the fire issue to the group? What issues were controversial and how did you resolve these?

4. Please describe the nature of the early QLG meetings.

5. Who was included in the meetings? Was anyone excluded? Why?

6. How did you handle suggestions from outsiders, or new QLG members?

7. Do you have any allies? What is the nature of your alliances? Who are your most important allies?

8. What role did the USFS play in the early years, and did their role change over the years?

9. Describe your relationship with local and regional environmental groups. Did any of them oppose the QLG plan?

10. How would you characterize your relationship with national environmental organizations?

11. At what point did you sense opposition to the QLG? How did you handle your opponents and their criticisms?

12. When did you approach USFS officials in Washington, D.C.? Why?

13. When did you decide to approach Congress? Why? Did you have any reservations about going to Congress? If so, why?

14. What were the consequences of going to Congress?

15. Did you have a media strategy? What was it?

16. How would you describe your strategy overall?

17. Why do you think the QLG was successful? What factors were most important?

18. Who should have decision-making authority over the national forests in your area? Please explain.

19. Critics argue that these are national forests and should not be managed by locals. How would you respond to this?

20. In retrospect, is there anything you would change about your strategy?

Notes

Introduction

1. An advocacy group is an organization that has mobilized to achieve collective goals, such as the realization of group rights or the protection of common pool resources. Advocacy groups pursue political change through conventional means such as lobbying, litigation, elections, and public education, although they might also sponsor or join marches, protests, rallies, and boycotts (see Minkoff 1995). Interest groups are usually defined more broadly as "voluntary associations independent of the political system that attempt to influence the government" (Andrews and Edwards 2004).

2. Much of the classic interest group literature is concerned with understanding how "interests" in society overcome collective action problems to form organizations and how interest groups, once organized, maintain themselves. The pluralist debate grew out of the classic interest group literature and asks whether and to what extent interest group politics is elitist in nature versus democratic. This literature has a rich history, but the questions it asks are not central to the study here. Rather, I draw heavily on the agenda-setting and policy-change literature, which looks at how issues get on governmental and public agendas. This literature naturally leads to questions of strategy because political actors push for issues to get on agendas as well as try to prevent certain problems from gaining attention. One of the most important models of agenda and policy change in recent years is Baumgartner and Jones's "punctuated equilibrium" model, which argues that long periods of policy stability are punctuated by bursts of policy change (Baumgartner and Jones 1993).

3. At a workshop in Aarhus, Denmark, in July 2005, more than a dozen international scholars explicitly focused on the need for and possibilities of comparative agenda-setting studies.

4. For sample interview questions, see the appendix.

5. The archives are now housed at the Clayoquot Biosphere Trust in Tofino, British Columbia.

6. This archive consists of multiple filing cabinets full of primary materials relating to the conflict. The enormous volume of documents prevented me from reviewing all of them. I relied instead on a sample of documents prepared by Professor Warren Magnuson and graduate student Karena Shaw at the University of Victoria. (The documents were prepared for a workshop at the University of Victoria, "The Politics of

Clayoquot Sound," May 8–12, 1997.) I supplemented these documents with additional materials from the archive when I needed more detail about a particular event or phase of the conflict. In total, I reviewed close to a thousand pages of documents.

7. See www.qlg.org/.

Chapter 1. The Expansion and Containment of Policy Conflict

1. I occasionally refer to the QLG "coalition," which includes not only members of the QLG but their key public supporters in Congress, the forest service, academic circles, and the like.

2. Interest group scholars have replaced the image of rigid "iron triangles," where policy is decided by a small group of stakeholders, with images of "issue networks" and "advocacy coalitions" to describe a much broader set of actors who shape policy in any particular issue area (Heclo 1978; Sabatier and Jenkins-Smith 1993). Despite the widely accepted notion that policymaking today is much more pluralistic than in the past, recent research shows that many issues being debated in Congress attract only a small set of lobbyists, most notably those representing business interests (Baumgartner and Leech 2001).

3. The public agenda is the list of problems or issues that a good portion of the mass public is paying attention to or considers to be the most important problems facing the country. The government agenda, defined by Kingdon (1995, 3), is "the list of subjects or problems to which governmental officials, and people outside of government closely associated with those officials, are paying some serious attention at any given time."

4. Cobb and Elder (1972, 104–8) note that the audience to a conflict consists of various "publics" whose relationship to the conflict differs. They propose four general types of publics that range from specific groups who take an immediate interest in conflicts within a particular issue area (identification and attention groups) to mass publics who are less immediately affected by an issue but whose interest in and knowledge about an issue can be relatively high (in the case of attentive publics) or relatively low (as in the case of the general public).

5. It is best to envision a continuum when considering whether a conflict is expanded or contained. There are no hard-and-fast rules for determining whether a conflict is expanded or contained; rather, we can talk about the relative degree of expansion or containment of an issue compared to other policy conflicts, or compared to the same issue at a different point in time.

6. It is an oversimplification to suggest that all issues break down into conflict between those who want policy change and those who prefer the status quo. In some cases, all parties to a conflict might be advocating policy change of some sort, but they disagree about the extent or nature of those changes. Nevertheless, for many issues we can identify groups who are interested in change and those who are interested in either less change or no change.

7. The literature on framing is extensive, much of it found in communications and social movement studies. For a representative sample of theoretical materials,

case studies, and critiques, see Gamson (1989), Gamson and Modigliani (1989), Gamson (1992), Gamson and Wolfsfeld (1993), Entman (1993), Iyengar (1996), Snow and Benford (1997), Benford (1997), Steinberg (1997).

8. Whether issue redefinitions prove fleeting or lasting should be explored further in the study of the politics of problem definition.

9. On the importance of causal stories in policy debates, see Stone (1988, especially chapter 8). If too many problems are linked together, the public might perceive this amalgamation of problems as too complex and intractable to solve. In such cases, issue linkage can have a negative effect on issue salience and mobilization because the public may think that any solution would be ineffective, prohibitively expensive, or require too great of a policy change.

10. Institutions are conceptualized here broadly as the "rules of the game," ranging from formal constitutional mandates that specify the relationship between federal and state (or provincial) governments, to bureaucratic norms that affect the role of public participation in agency decision making, to public policies themselves (on this latter definition of institutions see Pierson 1993).

11. This is assuming that there are no external shocks to the policy subsystem. A change in party control of the legislative or executive branch, for example, could change the calculations of policy actors. A committee or agency that was once sympathetic to an advocacy group's policy position could, almost overnight, express some hostility to existing policy or at least a willingness to modify current policy.

12. *U.S. v. Students Challenging Regulatory Agency Procedures* 412 U.S. 669 (1973). In the early 1990s, the Supreme Court retreated from this position, requiring environmental litigants to prove particular harm and demonstrate specific injury before being allowed in court. See McSpadden (2000).

Chapter 2. Forest Policy in British Columbia and the Conflict over Clayoquot Sound

1. Direct and indirect employment in the forest industry ranged from 93,800 jobs in 1990 to 99,100 jobs in 1996, and down to 90,600 jobs in 1999. These figures include employment in the Ministry of Forests as well as in the private sector (Council of Forest Industries 2000).

2. The federal government has some jurisdiction over three issues that affect the forest: fisheries, First Nations, and international trade (Cashore and others 2001, 21). The federal Canadian Fisheries Act prohibits the deposit of substances that degrade or alter fish habitat in a way that would harm fish; this might include sediment from logging operations. Moreover, the federal government is responsible for addressing First Nation land claims and thus might be involved in forest policy if these lands are designated forestry lands. Finally, the federal government's authority over international trade means it is involved in disputes with the United States over softwood lumber exports.

3. Additional tenure arrangements include timber sale licenses, woodlot licenses, pulpwood agreements, and timber licences. The two main forms are the tree farm licenses and timber supply areas (see Cashore and others 2001, chapter 4 appendix).

4. The tenure system essentially grants quasi–property rights to timber companies. In the Clayoquot Sound conflict, MacMillan Bloedel and Interfor asserted these rights in the B.C. courts when protesters threatened to slow down or halt logging in the tree farm license areas. The courts repeatedly found in favor of the companies, granting injunctions that prohibited protesters from deliberately interfering with the companies' logging operations. In a 1993 B.C. Supreme Court decision favoring MacMillan Bloedel, Justice Bouck emphasized MacMillan Bloedel's legal rights to the timber and concluded that protesters were denying them these rights by blocking logging roads into the tree farm license areas. See *MacMillan Bloedel Limited v. Sheila Simpson* et al. 1993.

5. For an analysis of the NDP's ten years in power and its subsequent loss to the conservative Liberal Party, see Carroll and Ratner (2005).

6. Two multinational corporations, MacMillan Bloedel and Interfor, were the main timber companies involved in the deforestation of Clayoquot Sound from the 1970s to the 1990s; they held the majority of logging rights in the area.

7. One activist suggested (somewhat tongue in cheek) that if MacMillan Bloedel had confined logging to the rear of the island, outside the view of Tofino residents, the issue might never have caught on. Personal interview with Paul George, founder of Western Canada Wilderness Committee (WCWC), February 4, 2000.

8. Meares Island, Vargas Island, and Flores Island are the main islands composing Clayoquot Sound. The town of Tofino is located on the mainland toward the south end of the sound. Its water is supplied in part from watersheds on adjacent Meares Island, mainly from the Sharp Creek reserve.

9. An independent consulting firm, at the request of the B.C. government, conducted the comparative study in 1996 (Kamieniecki 2000). A more recent study by Professor Benjamin Cashore of Yale University also points to the stringency of B.C. forest laws compared to other jurisdictions, but environmentalists charge that the government has misinterpreted the report, "spinning it" in a far more favorable light than the study warrants (see Matthaus n.d.).

Chapter 3. Constructing the Global

1. Environmental groups in the United States used the decline of northern spotted owl population as a vehicle for getting the forest service to set aside large tracts of old-growth forest in the Pacific Northwest as spotted owl habitat. In the future, environmental groups might attach forest preservation to the issue of climate change, given that trees are now recognized as important carbon "sinks," meaning that they store significant amounts of carbon dioxide. As Andy Kerr, a well-known forest campaigner, said, "Sometimes the way to solve problems is by going bigger, not smaller. . . . The problems of global warming, unsustainable farming and forest destruction can become solvable if you put them all together" (quoted in Barnard 2001, B1).

2. As the Europeans settled Canada, the federal government typically entered into negotiations with First Nations. The most important exception to this rule was in British Columbia, where treaties with First Nations were far less common. In fact,

the provincial government refused to acknowledge aboriginal title to any land in British Columbia up until the late 1980s. In 1988, Premier Vander Zalm created the Ministry of Native Affairs and ended the nonrecognition of native land claims (see Hoberg and Morawski 1997, 394; Howlett 2001, 120–39).

3. The first Meares Island blockades, involving both native and non-native environmentalists, occurred just weeks after the Supreme Court of Canada ruled in favor of native rights to nontreaty areas in *Guerin, et al. v. Her Majesty the Queen* (see Tennant 1996). Michael Howlett notes that native groups in Canada started targeting judicial venues in the 1970s and 1980s after facing obstacles in political venues. First Nations were largely successful, forcing "politicians and administrators to include the province's Aboriginal peoples in any consideration of a wide range of land use practices and policies, including forestry" (Howlett 2001, 120).

4. The results of the poll were summarized in the *Vancouver Sun* (see Baldrey 1993).

5. Many First Nations representatives denied a close connection with either the environmentalists' or the government's position. But their objections found less of an audience, suggesting that power is displayed in the mere ability to assert a linkage between issues and policy positions. The substance and frequency of issue linkages, in other words, is tied into the power of the various players. Both government and environmentalists were privileged in this respect, whereas those in the native community who were denying such links were less successful in their efforts.

6. For more information about the politics behind CORE and other task forces, see Hoberg (1996).

7. Paul George (2000) of WCWC noted that it was probably better that Clayoquot Sound was treated separately, because the decision was highlighted as a result. In addition, environmental activists held the government to its claims of openness when they felt their voices were going unheard.

8. Perhaps officials within the B.C. government recognized this as a possible outcome and hence wanted to exclude Clayoquot Sound from the CORE process.

9. The use of visual images is especially important when social movements and advocacy groups court the news media, which are accustomed to using visuals to create spectacle and drama (see Gamson and Wolfsfeld 1993).

10. The tour was sponsored by Greenpeace United Kingdom.

11. While the maps may have helped to identify the issue initially, Harcourt's proenvironmental decision was influenced by the conflict in Clayoquot Sound. He was trying to appease environmentalists who were still upset about the 1993 land-use decision on Clayoquot.

12. When the government announced its decision in 1993 to allow logging in two-thirds of Clayoquot, they were similarly criticized by environmentalists and some conservation biologists for only considering Clayoquot Sound rather than the entire Vancouver Island region (see Bohn 1993c).

13. See, for example, Clayoquot Rainforest Coalition, "MacMillan Bloedel's Criminal Record" (advertisement). Harcourt ran on the NDP's "green" image, but his ability to set his administration apart from his rather antienvironmental predecessor

was challenged when some of his own party members renounced the April 1993 compromise decision.

14. See, for example, a pamphlet produced by the Forest Alliance of British Columbia (n.d.), "What Greenpeace Isn't Telling Europeans."

15. The practice of venue shopping in the Clayoquot Sound case will be covered in chapter 5.

Chapter 4. From Local to Global

1. Advocacy coalitions include a wide range of actors, including activists; government officials at the local, state, and national level; journalists; academics; and other researchers.

2. According to Edella Schlager (1999, 245) the initial version of the Advocacy Coalition Framework did not pay much attention to collective action problems, but "instead assumed that individuals who held shared beliefs would act collectively to realize those beliefs." Subsequent work has attended to these issues, but "substantial refinements remain to be made."

3. Mike Mullin noted that only one decision in the group's twenty-year history was decided by the directors without a vote of the general membership (Mullin 1999). This decision had to do with a meeting with Rainforest Action Network (a group based in San Francisco) where groups had to decide whether or not to sign a declaration concerning the issue of native sovereignty.

4. Doern and Conway (1994) trace the growth of Canadian environmental organizations in the latter part of the twentieth century; they report three hundred recognized environmental groups in 1975 and about two thousand in 1990. Almost a thousand of these were located in western Canada.

5. Ecotrust Canada did not get involved in the campaign until 1994 so it is not listed in table 4.1. NRDC is a U.S.-based organization.

6. It is almost impossible to know how many activists switched their focus from other forest campaigns in British Columbia to the Clayoquot Sound campaign. My interviews cannot reveal the extent to which this occurred; what is clear is that the conflict over Clayoquot Sound mobilized both active and previously inactive individuals given that the 1993 protests were the largest of their kind in Canadian history.

7. Eleven Toronto activists were arrested at the Toronto Stock Exchange in late August for protesting the trading of MacMillan Bloedel and Interfor stocks. Another notable event that signified the nationalization of the issue was when a caravan of activists traveled from St. John's, Newfoundland, to Clayoquot Sound in September 1993.

8. As noted, the Clayoquot activists also targeted European politicians, but to a lesser extent. For example, Langer and Lenz were invited to make a presentation to the European Union parliament, which then debated whether to pass a resolution banning B.C. forest products. (It subsequently failed.)

9. Tamara Stark of Greenpeace Canada said that Valerie Langer contacted Karen Mahon (also of Greenpeace) in 1992, asking if they would be interested in getting involved in the campaign.

10. Greenpeace has at least 2.5 million members worldwide and maintains offices in forty-one countries. It also has a small fleet of ships, a helicopter, direct action teams (groups of individuals who perform civil disobedience, e.g., hang banners, block whaling ships, etc.), and access to satellite media technology.

11. It would be inaccurate, however, to suggest that strategic benefits were the only thing driving their decision on whether to join the conflict. Certainly, these INGOs had a substantive interest in preserving Clayoquot Sound and B.C. forests more generally. The old-growth forests in British Columbia are of particular concern and value to these groups because British Columbia is one of the few places that has large, contiguous tracts of intact forest.

12. Many of these groups went on to campaign for the preservation of the Great Bear Rainforest in northern British Columbia. In April 2001, the B.C. government, First Nations, logging companies, and environmentalists announced they had reached an agreement to protect more than half a million hectares and defer logging in more than a million hectares in the Great Bear Rainforest. In February 2006 the B.C. government agreed to protect five million acres in the Great Bear Rainforest and to develop ecosystem-based management on an additional ten million acres.

13. Early in the conflict even Canadian environmental groups were labeled as outsiders by many of the logging groups in and around Clayoquot. According to Ian Gill of Ecotrust Canada, which is based in Vancouver, "We are viewed as outsiders among the pro-industry crowd because they don't like anybody coming in and telling them what to do. You can be from Port Alberni or Parksville [small cities outside Clayoquot Sound] and you are still an outsider" (2000).

14. Interestingly, this document was shared with an official in the Ministry of Forests, suggesting that the timber companies and the B.C. government cooperated in the Clayoquot countercampaign.

15. The timber industry directly courted the media by visiting the offices of the *Vancouver Sun* several times in 1993. Shortly thereafter, the paper reorganized the forestry and environmental beats so that more emphasis was placed on urban environmental issues. Mark Hume, a reporter for the *Sun*, said he was discouraged from covering forestry issues on Vancouver Island. Managing editor Scott Honeyman defended the shift in focus this way: "My feeling was that we were not dealing with urban environmental problems in our own backyard at all. Instead, we were covering sexy block-a-road protests and some of them were just becoming photo opportunities" (Bula 1993, C2).

16. An analysis of advocacy groups in the debate over outer continental shelf energy leasing by Jenkins-Smith and his colleagues indicates that material groups (advocacy groups representing private interests) are less constrained in their expression of beliefs and policy positions than purposive groups (Jenkins-Smith, St. Clair, and Woods 1991).

Chapter 5. Venue Shopping in an International Context

1. Support for the idea that the Canadian public would side with environmentalists rather than the timber industry comes from public opinion surveys that show

Canadians scoring very high on measures of environmental concern and efficacy. In the late 1980s, Canadians chose the environment as the most important issue facing Canada (Paehlke 2000). In the early 1990s, public opinion surveys indicated that upward of 85 percent of British Columbians were concerned about the rates of timber harvest and supported measures to end clear-cutting (Kamieniecki 2000).

2. The CORE report on the Clayoquot Sound Land Use Decision noted that there was "widespread public concern" over the stock purchase and recommended that the government appoint a "Conflict of Interest Commissioner" to look into the matter (Owen 1993, 7).

3. The federal government has since passed national endangered species legislation, the 2002 Species at Risk Act. Environmentalists criticized proposed species protection bills for leaving listing decisions up to the discretion of Canada's legislative cabinet and for failing to include a citizen's suit provision that would allow individuals and groups to litigate if the government failed to adequately enforce the law ("Critics take aim at Canada's endangered species act" 2001). They also characterized the Species at Risk Act as a "paper tiger" due to its reliance on voluntary measures and its discretionary language, among other things (Barlee 2002, 7).

4. In 1993 Greenpeace lost its case in the B.C. Supreme Court, and in 1996 Greenpeace and FOCS lost their appeal in the Supreme Court of Canada. Similar injunctions were declared invalid in Manitoba, Saskatchewan, and Ontario, as well as in the United States, England, and Australia (Greenpeace Canada 1993; see also Greenpeace Canada 1994; Friends of Clayoquot Sound 1996–1997).

5. However, this could be changing. The new forest policies in British Columbia may provide environmental groups with the kind of leverage they need to use the courts more effectively. In 1997, lawyers for the Sierra Legal Defence Fund appeared before the Forest Appeals Commission to challenge Interfor's appeal of a fine it had received for violating the Forest Practices Code (Langer 1997). Some scholars point more generally to an increasing "judicialization" of environmental policy in Canada (see Knopff and Glenn 1996).

6. FOCS later accused MacMillan Bloedel of paying employees to attend the rally, although they did not present any clear evidence to support the charge.

7. In 1993, 71 percent of Canada's forest products exports went to the United States, 9 percent to the European Union, and 12 percent to Japan.

8. The annual rate of cut in Clayoquot Sound dropped from a high of almost one million cubic meters in 1988 to 24,000 cubic meters in 2000. The rate of cut, however, increased in 2002 to 145,000 cubic meters. See figure 2.1.

Chapter 6. U.S. Forest Policy and the Birth of the Quincy Library Group

1. George Perkins Marsh was one of the first and most eloquent conservationists. His 1864 book, *Man and Nature: The Earth as Modified by Human Action*, challenged the prevailing idea that resources were unlimited. He also hypothesized a link between the downfall of civilizations and deforestation. For a brief history of the early conservationists, see Pisani (1997).

2. In some states, including Nevada, Alaska, Utah, Oregon, and Idaho, the federal government owns more than half of all the land in the state.

3. By the early 1940s timber harvest on national forests had climbed to 3 billion board feet, and by 1952 harvest levels were almost 4.5 billion board feet (Burnett and Davis 2002). By 1970, the national forests were supplying a third of the nation's timber (Beesley 1996).

4. The controversy over clear-cutting in the Bitterroot Valley in Montana in the early 1960s led to congressional hearings on forest service policy and produced the critical Bolle Report (Bolle 1997).

5. For details about the appeals process, see U.S. Office of Technology Assessment (1992, especially chapter 5) and also Gericke and Sullivan (1994).

6. Interestingly, FPW's plan allowed four times as much timber harvest as the forest service's own proposals in the early 1990s; the reductions were due in part to the potential listing of the California spotted owl as an endangered species.

Chapter 7. Retreating to the Local

1. Environmental representatives in the QLG were quite concerned about the survival of the California spotted owl and would not allow others in the group to ignore the issue.

2. Best (1989) calls this the "contextual constructionist" perspective, where the research focus is on the claims-making activities of policy actors. For an example of this methodology in the context of another case, see Linder (1995).

3. The Sequoia forest fire was only one of several notable fires in various parts of California in the early 1990s and came on the heels of the high-profile Yellowstone fires of 1988. Other notable fires during this time included the 1991 "tunnel" fire outside Berkeley that burned sixteen hundred acres, destroyed twenty-nine hundred structures, and took twenty-five lives; the 1992 "Fountain" fire in northern California that consumed sixty-four thousand acres of wildlands; and the 1993 "Southern California Firestorm," which also burned sixty-four thousand acres. In other parts of the country, fires also raged. In Colorado, for example, fourteen firefighters died in the 1994 Storm King Mountain fire.

4. In recent decades, there has been an influx of preservation-minded individuals into rural areas, and rural economies have been shifting away from resource extraction. See Robb and Riebsame (1997, especially chapter 4).

5. Environmental groups were particularly critical of the way this trade-off was framed, but they also benefited from the dramatic images and stark contrasts, which are key components of issue expansion (Plein 1997; see also Dietrich 1992). Moreover, the simplicity of the message no doubt expanded the conflict (see generally Cobb and Elder 1972, and specifically Davis 1995).

6. Interestingly, the 1997 QLG bill (when introduced in the House) made no reference to endangered species other than the spotted owl, suggesting (at least to some critics) that the QLG was not interested in preservation per se.

7. Quoted in *Congressional Record* 143 (July 9, 1997): H 4933.

8. Quoted in *Congressional Record* 143 (July 9, 1997): H 4928.

9. Quoted in *Congressional Record* 143 (July 9, 1997): H 4932.

10. Some representatives initially opposed the QLG bill but eventually voted for the legislation after it was amended. The QLG passed the House of Representatives 429–1 on July 9, 1997.

11. Quoted in *Congressional Record* 143 (July 9, 1997): H 4929–30.

12. Quoted in *Congressional Record* 143 (July 9, 1997): H 4941.

13. Similar photographs of Montana's Bitterroot National Forest became a point of controversy between environmentalists and the USFS years later. Two photos—one taken in 1909, another in 1997—were used in a General Accounting Office report to illustrate how today's forests have become dangerously overstocked as a result of decades of fire suppression. The 1909 photo, showing an open forest, allegedly represents what western forests looked like before they were altered. The photographs supported Clinton's plan to reduce fire risk through logging and burning. However, at least one environmental activist argued that the 1909 photo was taken after significant logging had taken place. He claims that the original forests were more diverse and dense than the photo suggests, and not as much logging is needed to restore them to their original (and more fire-resistant) state (Easthouse 2000).

14. Quoted in *Congressional Record* 143 (July 9, 1997): H 4925.

15. Quoted in *Congressional Record* 143 (July 9, 1997): H 4933.

16. Quoted in *Congressional Record* 143 (July 9, 1997): H 4941.

17. Quoted in *Congressional Record* 143 (July 9, 1997): H 4942.

18. Quoted in *Congressional Record* 143 (July 9, 1997): H 4933.

19. The QLG proposal was also popular because it is often difficult for Congress to find policy closure in the face of increasing interest group permeability and fragmentation in Congress. Consequently, legislators look for coalitions who present them with "predigested policies": "Since the organizations involved in coalitions work hard to iron out any differences they might have so as to present Congress with a united front, they reduce the level of conflict that legislators see and thus make it more likely that Congress will act favorably on these 'predigested policies'" (Scholzman and Tierney 1986, 307; see also Bosso 1987, chapter 10).

20. Of course, the civility movement is not without its critics, some of whom question whether there was a golden age of discourse in America, where contestants in political conflicts gracefully debated the merits and demerits of policy proposals without commenting on the character of their opponents. Others suggest that naming and blaming contests are the result of an impassioned (rather than cynical) politics and can serve important civic purposes. As Tony Kushner (1998, 5–6) put it, "Civic, not civil, discourse is what matters, and civic discourse mandates the assigning of blame."

21. Quoted in *Congressional Record* 143 (July 11, 1997): H 5170.

22. Quoted in *Congressional Record* 143 (July 17, 1997): S 7711.

23. Interestingly, a 1996 report stated that the fire frequency in the Sierras was not necessarily much greater, nor were the fires more severe, than in the past (Wildlands Resources Center 1996). Louis Blumberg, with the benefit of hindsight, told me that he still believes forest fires are a problem, but he thinks the fire threat was

"overplayed." In his opinion, severe weather will result in big forest losses, regardless of the type of fuel reduction programs put in place (2001).

24. For an in-depth (and rather technical) critique of the QLG fuels management plan, see Ingalsbee (n.d.).

25. Quoted in *Congressional Record* 143 (July 9, 1997): H 4927.

26. Many environmental groups continue to accuse Congress and the timber industry of using the fire issue as an excuse to increase logging. Some forest service employees claim that fear of forest fires is undercutting forest preservation policies. Andy Stahl, a member of Forest Service Employees for Environmental Ethics, argues that protimber members of Congress are seeking out sympathetic agency staff in the Fire and Aviation Division of the USFS to validate their fuels reduction (and timber extraction) plans. Stahl argues that Fire and Aviation Division staff members "are notorious for their quick and ready access to pro-timber members of Congress" (Stahl 2000, 29).

27. The QLG bill was amended in the House to make it clear that the study area would be subject to federal environmental laws.

28. Quoted in *Congressional Record* 143 (July 9, 1997): H 4927.

29. A somewhat different tactic for broadening the significance of the QLG plan emerged later when Californians for Alternatives to Toxics tried to link the QLG plan to the controversial issue of pesticides. The group argued that the QLG fuels program (which they called a "timber harvesting scheme") might require heavy doses of herbicides to clear forest understory. Over the past decades, opposition to the forest service's policy of aerial spraying (to control the accumulation of brush) had grown. In the 1970s and 1980s, citizens' groups filed lawsuits challenging the forest service's EISs, statements that said the herbicides would have insignificant effects on human health. While the USFS won many of these lawsuits, public controversy over and interest in the aerial spraying program continued into the 1990s (see Ruth 2000). If QLG opponents could link the QLG plan to this already controversial policy, they might be able to expand the issue further. However, their efforts were not visibly successful.

30. The question of whether, or to what extent, science can resolve policy conflicts is of course a rich topic and has been the subject of many scholarly inquiries. Some argue that the public, having witnessed the politicization of science in modern-day interest group politics, does not revere or trust scientific knowledge. As Sheila Jasanoff (1996, 67) notes, "The gap between what experts do and what makes sense to people accounts for a massive public rejection of technical rationality in modern societies." In other words, we cannot hope that science will resolve public debates over the efficacy of various policy solutions.

31. Quoted in *Congressional Record* 143 (July 9, 1997): H 4928.

Chapter 8. Allies, Opponents, and Audiences

1. Quoted in *Congressional Record* 143 (July 9, 1997): H 4940.

2. It should be noted that other members and observers of the QLG felt that it was open to "outsiders." For example, Terry Terhaar (from the Pacific Rivers Council) said that she "never saw a single door closed." However, she did admit that the deal

had already been made, and that she "couldn't disrupt that deal. But I could influence all of the details between the broad planks" (quoted in Marston 1997c).

3. The timber company MacMillan Bloedel used a similar tactic in the Clayoquot Sound case. According to Greenpeace, the company falsely suggested that MacMillan Bloedel and Greenpeace were coming to an agreement over Clayoquot Sound after the two had met in a series of closed meetings initiated by the First Nations. Greenpeace denied that any agreement existed, charging MacMillan Bloedel with "trying to convince their customers, the media and other environmental groups that the conflict has been solved through the current discussions," and noting that "our campaign is the only tool we have and we cannot continue to let [MacMillan Bloedel] undermine it" (Berman and Anderson 1994).

4. Of course, there is nothing inherently problematic in the notion that some members of the QLG increasingly identified with the group and lost their identities as representatives of separate interests. But it became a problem when the QLG was characterized by its supporters in Congress as representative of diverse interests, and as a microcosm of the larger universe of interests in the forestry policy debate. I suggest here that the QLG, while it might have started out as representative, eventually developed its own identity such that it could be seen as another interest group lobbying for its particular interests or policy preferences.

5. Quoted in *Congressional Record* 143 (July 9, 1997): H 4928.

6. Quoted in *Congressional Record* 143 (July 9, 1997): H 4941.

7. Quoted in *Congressional Record* 143 (July 9, 1997): H 4929.

8. It should be noted that Dion had worked with the Wilderness Society in the past, when he was a member of FPW and even after it disbanded. In other words, the alliance between local, regional, and national groups on this issue was not manufactured for the benefit of appearance but had some history behind it.

9. From 2001 to 2005, the QLG received more media attention, largely due to its opposition to the Sierra Nevada framework. Twenty-four news stories (including editorials) appeared in the *San Francisco Chronicle* and *Sacramento Bee*, most of which chronicled the fate of the Sierra Nevada framework under the George W. Bush administration. In many of these articles, reporters acknowledged environmental opposition to the QLG, which was difficult to ignore given that environmentalists supported the Sierra Nevada framework while the QLG largely opposed it because it conflicted with the QLG pilot project.

10. The original QLG plan included a "working circle" concept that required timber taken from the Lassen, Plumas, and Tahoe national forests to be processed in local mills. Sierra Pacific Industries later asked Congress to remove this provision so they could send the timber to their other mills located throughout the state (see Duane 1997, 788).

Chapter 9. Lawsuits, Libraries, and Legislatures

1. This distinction is important in part because accounts of the QLG often suggest that everyone who came to the table was equally dismayed by adversarial

legalism. As such, they claim that the QLG was a rejection of this form of politics, when at least for some participants it appears to be as much about resignation and a lack of resources.

2. The QLG is considered here to be an advocacy group; however, the group also created a new institution or policy arena by trying to assert some authority over forest policy decision making.

3. For a general discussion and critique of theories of institutional origins, see Hall and Taylor (1996).

4. For the details of the Sierra Nevada framework, see U.S. Department of Agriculture (2001).

5. George Hoberg's (1998, 25) comparison of spotted owl protection in the United States and Canada highlights the importance of having action-forcing standards: "When evidence is clear, the U.S. institutional framework allows environmentalists to harness science effectively. . . . Institutional rules in the U.S. enabled environmentalists to force science upon reluctant administrative agencies."

6. Quoted in *Congressional Record* 143 (July 9, 1997): H 4926.

7. Some opponents of the bill still worried about potential loopholes in the legislation. Debbie Sease of the Sierra Club testified before a Senate hearing that the QLG bill circumvented important procedural safeguards by shortening the amount of time for completing an EIS on the project and for failing to guarantee that the project could be changed based on the EIS (U.S. Congress, Senate, "Hearing on S. 1028," 1997).

Chapter 10. Managing Policy Conflicts

1. Sometimes it is difficult to identify in any definitive sense the "winners" and "losers" in a dynamic policy conflict. We might be able to talk about relative winners and losers, but even this is a moving target.

2. I use the term "conflict management" differently than Cobb and Elder (1972), who refer to the conflict management role of government.

3. Kollman notes (1998, 37) that these tactics are unlikely to expand conflict on a national scale. However, his data suggest that advocacy groups who are accustomed to using inside channels cannot always rely on these to realize their goals. Occasionally, if their opponents successfully raise the salience and visibility of the issue, they must respond by imitating some of the opponents' tactics.

References

Amy, Douglas J. 1987. *The Politics of Environmental Mediation*. New York: Columbia University Press.

Andrews, Kenneth T., and Bob Edwards. 2004. "Advocacy Organizations in the U.S. Political Process." *Annual Review of Sociology* 30: 479–506.

Apsey, Michael. 1983. Notes for speech to the Association of British Columbia Professional Foresters Annual Meeting, Kamloops, B.C., February 17. Clayoquot Sound Archives.

Armstrong, Patrick. 1992. "Canada, Brazil: No Comparison." *Vancouver Sun*, May 22, A17.

Baldrey, Keith. 1993. "Public Backs Logging Plan." *Vancouver Sun*, November 3, A3.

Barlee, Gwen. 2002. Presentation to the Senate Standing Committee on Energy, the Environmental and Natural Resources on Bill C-5, the Species at Risk Act. November 21. Available at www.wildernesscommittee.org/campaigns/species/sara/senate_pres.pdf (accessed December 12, 2005).

Barnard, Jeff. 2001. "Focus Shifts in Battle for Forests." *Seattle Post-Intelligencer*, March 3, B1.

Barnett, Tom. n.d. "Some Thoughts on Clayoquot Sound." Clayoquot Sound Archives.

Baumgartner, Frank R. 1989. *Conflict and Rhetoric in French Policymaking*. Pittsburgh, PA: University of Pittsburgh Press.

Baumgartner, Frank R., and Bryan D. Jones. 1993. *Agendas and Instability in American Politics*. Chicago: University of Chicago Press.

Baumgartner, Frank R., Bryan D. Jones, and Michael C. MacLeod. 2000. "The Evolution of Legislative Jurisdictions." *The Journal of Politics* 62 (2): 321–49.

Baumgartner, Frank R., and Beth L. Leech. 2001. "Interest Niches and Policy Bandwagons: Patterns of Interest Group Involvement in National Politics." *The Journal of Politics* 63 (4): 1191–213.

Beesley, David. 1996. "Reconstructing the Landscape: An Environmental History, 1820–1960." In *Sierra Nevada Ecosystem Project: Final Report to Congress*, vol. II, ed. University of California, SNEP Science Team and Special Consultants. Davis: University of California, Centers for Water and Wildland Resources.

Benford, Robert. 1997. "An Insider's Critique of the Social Movement Perspective." *Sociological Inquiry* (November): 409–30.

Berman, Tzeporah, and Patrick Anderson. 1994. Memo to Nelson Keitlah, Chief Francis Frank, and Clifford Atleo. October 17. Clayoquot Sound Archives.

Berman, Tzeporah, Gordon Brent Ingram, Maurice Gibbons, Ronald Hatch, Loys Maingon. 1994. *Clayoquot and Dissent*. Vancouver, B.C.: Ronsdale Press.

Bernstein, Steven, and Benjamin Cashore. 2000. "Globalization, Four Paths of Internationalization and Domestic Policy Change: The Case of EcoForestry in British Columbia, Canada." *Canadian Journal of Political Science* (March): 67–99.

Best, Joel, ed. 1989. *Images of Issues: Typifying Contemporary Social Problems*. New York: Aldine de Gruyter.

Birkland, Thomas. 1997. *After Disaster: Agenda Setting, Public Policy, and Focusing Events*. Washington, DC: Georgetown University Press.

Bischel, David A. 1998. "Passage of the Quincy Library Group Bill Is Good for California's Forests and Rural Communities Alike." Press statement, October 21. Available at http://foresthealth.org/oct21.htm (accessed February 1, 2001).

Blomquist, William, and Edella Schlager. 2005. "Political Pitfalls of Integrated Watershed Management." *Society and Natural Resources* 18 (2): 101–17.

Blum, Linda. 2001. Telephone interview. February 6.

Blumberg, Louis. 2001. Telephone interview. February 20.

Bohn, Glenn. 1992. "Award-Winning Activist Brings Environmental Gospel to Washington." *Vancouver Sun*, May 2, A5.

———. 1993a. "Harcourt Accuses Environmental Minister of 'Blackmail'." *Vancouver Sun*, January 12, B2.

———. 1993b. "Minister Vows to Get Tough with B.C. Logging Companies." *Vancouver Sun*, November 1, B1.

———. 1993c. "Preserving Our Forests: How Much Is Enough?" *Vancouver Sun*, April 17, B1.

———. 1994. "B.C. Clearcuts Featured in a Book Unveiled Today." *Vancouver Sun*, February 8, B3.

Bolle, Arnold W. 1997. "The Bitterroot Revisited: A University [Re]View of the Forest Service." In *American Forests: Nature, Culture, and Politics*, ed. Char Millar. Lawrence: University Press of Kansas.

Bossin, Bob. 2000. "The Lessons of Clayoquot." *Ideas* (radio broadcast). Host: Paul Kennedy. Canadian Broadcast Corporation.

Bosso, Christopher. 1987. *Pesticides and Politics: The Life-Cycle of a Public Issue*. Pittsburgh, PA: University of Pittsburgh Press.

Bowman, Ann O'M. 2002. "American Federalism on the Horizon." *Publius* 32 (2): 3–22.

Brazil, Eric. 2001. "Opponents Blast Plan for Sierra; Timber, Cattle, Recreation Groups Attack Forest Service Proposal." *San Francisco Chronicle*, April 21, A2.

British Columbia Government Communications Office. 1993. "Clayoquot Communications Update." Memo. April 28. Clayoquot Sound Archives.

British Columbia Ministry of Environment. 1996. "B.C.'s Land-Use Practices to Be Focus at International Summit." Press release. Vancouver, B.C. October 17.

British Columbia Ministry of Forests. 1982. "Summary of Response to Ministry of Forests Public Involvement Policy and Practice." May 13.

———. n.d. "Forest Management Certification." Available at www.for.gov.bc.ca/het/certification (accessed May 25, 2005).

Browne, William P. 1990. "Organized Interests and Their Issue Niches: A Search for Pluralism in a Policy Domain." *Journal of Politics* 52 (2): 477–509.

Bryner, Gary. 1999. "Balancing Preservation and Logging: Public Lands Policy in British Columbia and the Western United States." *Policy Studies Journal* 27 (2): 307–27.

Bula, Frances. 1993. "No Clearcut Answers: Media and the Environmental Movement Divided on Benefits of Selective Reporting." *Vancouver Sun*, May 22, C2.

Burnett, Miles, and Charles Davis. 2002. "Getting Out the Cut: Politics and National Forest Timber Harvests, 1960–1995." *Administration and Society* 34 (2): 202–28.

Burrows, Mae. 2001. "Multistakeholder Processes: Activist Containment versus Grassroots Mobilization." In *Sustaining the Forests of the Pacific Coast,* eds. Debra J. Salazar and Donald K. Alper. Seattle: University of Washington Press.

Busenberg, George. 2004. "Wildfire Management in the United States: The Evolution of a Policy Failure." *Review of Policy Research* 21 (2004): 145–56.

Callahan, Deborah. 1997. "Local Control: The Pitfalls and Promises for Environmental Protection." Speech delivered at the League of Conservation Voters Greenvote Forum. April 24.

Campbell, Michelle L., and Vernon G. Thomas. 2002. "Constitutional Impacts on Conservation: Effects of Federalism on Biodiversity Protection." *Environmental Policy and Law* 35 (5): 223–32.

Carroll, William K., and R. S. Ratner. 2005. "The NDP Regime in British Columbia, 1991–2001: A Post-Mortem." *The Canadian Review of Sociology and Anthropology* 42 (2): 167–96.

Cashore, Benjamin, George Hoberg, Michael Howlett, Jeremy Rayner, and Jeremy Wilson. 2001. *In Search of Sustainability: British Columbia Forest Policy in the 1990s.* Vancouver: University of British Columbia Press.

Cawley, R. McGreggor, and John Freemuth. 1997. "A Critique of the Multiple Use Framework in Public Lands Decisionmaking." In *Western Public Lands and Environmental Politics*, ed. Charles Davis. Boulder, CO: Westview Press.

Charleson, Karen. 1993. "Parks: Another Insult to Natives." *Vancouver Sun*, January 15, A19.

Christensen, Jon. 1996. "Everyone Helps a California Forest—Except the Forest Service." *High Country News*, May 13. Available at www.hcn.org/1996/may13/dir/Feature_Everyone_h.html (accessed February 7, 1999).

Clary, David A. 1986. *Timber and the Forest Service.* Lawrence: University Press of Kansas.

Clayoquot Rainforest Coalition. n.d. "MacMillan Bloedel's Criminal Record." Advertisement. Clayoquot Sound Archives.

Clayoquot Sound Sustainable Development Strategy. 1992. "Clayoquot Strategy News." Newsletter (May). Clayoquot Sound Archives.

Clifford, Frank. 1997. "House OKs Increase in Logging to Cut Fire Risk." *Los Angeles Times*, July 10, 3.

Coady, Linda. 1993. Presentation on the Communications Aspects of Clayoquot. May 7. Clayoquot Sound Archives.

Coates, Bill. n.d. "Finding Common Ground: Restoring a Small-Town Economy and National Forests to Health." Available at www.qlg.org/pub/miscdoc/coates. htm (accessed February 5, 2001).

Cobb, Roger W., and Charles D. Elder. 1972. *Participation in American Politics: The Dynamics of Agenda-Building*. Baltimore, MD: Johns Hopkins University Press.

Cobb, Roger W., and Marc Howard Ross, eds. 1997. *Cultural Strategies of Agenda Denial*. Lawrence: University Press of Kansas.

Cockburn, Alexander. 1997. "Bill and Dianne Go to Tahoe; Under the Guise of Saving a Forest, the 'Quincy' Plan Would Pave the Wilds with Clear-Cuts." Editorial. *Los Angeles Times*, July 17, B9.

Conservation International, Earth Island Institute, National Audubon Society, National Parks and Conservation Association, Rainforest Action Network, Sierra Club, Wilderness Society, Western Ancient Forest Campaign. 1993. "Will Canada Do Nothing to Save Clayoquot Sound—One of the Last Great Temperate Rainforests in the World?" Advertisement. Clayoquot Sound Archives.

Cooper, Mary H. 1998. "National Forests: Should Recreation Take Priority over Logging?" *CQ Researcher* 8 (39): 905–28.

Council of Forest Industries. 2000. *2000 Factbook*. Available at www.cofi.org/reports/factbooks.htm (accessed May 6, 2005).

"Critics Take Aim at Canada's Endangered Species Act." 2000. CNN on-line. Available at www.cnn.co.uk/2000/NATURE/08/21/caribou.em/index.html (accessed May 26, 2001).

Davis, Charles, and M. Dawn King. n.d. "The Quincy Library Group and Collaborative Planning within U.S. National Forests." Available at www.qlg.org/pub/Perspectives/daviskingcasestudy.htm (accessed November 3, 2000).

Davis, Steven. 1995. "The Role of Communication and Symbolism in Interest Group Competition: The Case of the Siskiyou National Forest, 1983–1992." *Political Communication* 12: 27–42.

Dietrich, William. 1992. *The Final Forest: The Battle of the Last Great Trees of the Pacific Northwest*. New York: Penguin Press.

Dion, Neil. 2001. Personal interview. March 17.

Doern, Bruce G., and Thomas Conway. 1994. *The Greening of Canada*. Toronto: University of Toronto Press.

Donovan, Mark C. 2001. *Taking Aim: Target Populations and the Wars on Drugs and AIDS*. Washington, DC: Georgetown University Press.

Dowie, Mark. 1995. *Losing Ground: American Environmentalism at the Close of the Twentieth Century*. Cambridge, MA: MIT Press.

Downs, Anthony. 1972. "Up and Down with Ecology: The Issue Attention Cycle." *The Public Interest* 28: 38–50.

Duane, Timothy P. 1997. "Community Participation in Ecosystem Management." *Ecology Law Quarterly* 24: 771–800.

Easthouse, Keith. 2000. "Drawing Fire." *Forest Magazine*. November/December: 35–40.

Ecotrust, Pacific GIS, and Conservation International. 1995. *The Rainforests of Home: An Atlas of People and Places. Part 1: Natural Forests and Native Languages of the Coastal Temperate Rainforest.* Portland, OR.

Ecotrust Canada. 1997. *Seeing the Ocean Through the Trees: A Conservation-Based Development Strategy for Clayoquot Sound.* Victoria, B.C.: Ecotrust Canada.

Edelman, Murray. 1988. *Constructing the Political Spectacle.* Chicago: University of Chicago Press.

———. 1993. "Contestable Categories and Public Opinion." *Political Communication* 10: 231–42.

Edelson, David, Louis Blumberg, and Frannie Hoover Waid. 1994. Memo to Michael Jackson, Mike Yost, Linda Blum, and Harry Reeves. Natural Resources Defense Council. May 27. Clayoquot Sound Archives.

Entman, Robert M. 1993. "Framing: Toward Clarification of a Fractured Paradigm." *Journal of Communication* 43: 51–58.

Evans, Steve. 1993. Memo to Michael Jackson and the Quincy Library Group. Friends of the River. August 29.

Fiorino, Daniel J. 1995. *Making Environmental Policy.* Berkeley: University of California Press.

Forest Alliance of British Columbia. 1994. *U.K. Tour Report.* Clayoquot Sound Archives.

———. n.d. "What Greenpeace Isn't Telling Europeans." Pamphlet. Clayoquot Sound Archives.

ForestEthics. 2006. "The Great Bear Rainforest Agreement: A Backgrounder." Available at www.forestethics.org/article.php?id=1327 (accessed July 3, 2006).

Forest Stewardship Council. n.d. "FSC-BC Preliminary Standards." Available at www.fsc-bc.org/Preliminary_Standards.htm (accessed May 25, 2005).

Foy, Joe. 2000. Personal interview. February 4.

Friedman, Lawrence. 1985. *Total Justice.* New York: Russell Sage Foundation.

Friends of Clayoquot Sound. 1996–1997. Newsletter (Fall/Winter).

———. n.d. "Markets Campaigns." Available at www.focs.ca/logging/markets campaigns.asp (accessed December 18, 2005).

Gamson, William A. 1975. *The Strategy of Social Protest.* Homewood, IL: Dorsey Press.

———. 1989. "News as Framing." *American Behavioral Scientist.* November/December: 157–61.

———. 1992. *Talking Politics.* New York: Cambridge University Press.

Gamson, William A., and Andre Modigliani. 1989. "Media Discourse and Public Opinion on Nuclear Power: A Constructionist Approach." *American Journal of Sociology* 95: 1–37.

Gamson, William A., and Gadi Wolfsfeld. 1993. "Movements and Media as Interacting Systems." *Annals* 528 (July): 114–25.

Ganz, Marshall. 2000. "Resources and Resourcefulness: Strategic Capacity in the Unionization of California Agriculture." *American Journal of Sociology* 105 (4): 1003–162.

George, Paul. 2000. Personal interview. February 4.

Gericke, Kevin L., and Jay Sullivan. 1994. "Public Participation and Appeals of Forest Service Plans—An Empirical Examination." *Society and Natural Resources* 7: 125–35.

Gill, Ian. 1995. "Maps of B.C. 'Treasures' Unfairly Expensive." *Vancouver Sun*, November 21, A15.

———. 2000. Personal interview. February 4.

Glasbergen, Pieter, ed. 1998. *Co-operative Environmental Governance: Public-Private Agreements as a Policy Strategy*. Dordrecht, The Netherlands: Kluwer Academic Publishers.

Greenpeace Canada. 1993. "Greenpeace Canada Granted Leave to Challenge Mac-Millan Bloedel Injunction." Press release, November 25. Clayoquot Sound Archives.

———. 1994. "Brief Legal History of Clayoquot Sound." Internal memo, January 6. Clayoquot Sound Archives.

Gusfield, Joseph R. 1981. *The Culture of Public Problems: Drinking, Driving, and the Symbolic Order*. Chicago: University of Chicago Press.

Haas, Ernst B. 1980. "Why Collaborate? Issue-Linkage and International Regimes." *World Politics* 32: 357–405.

Hacker, Jacob S. 1997. *The Road to Nowhere: The Genesis of President Clinton's Plan for Health Care Security*. Princeton, NJ: Princeton University Press.

Hajer, Maarten A. 1995. *The Politics of Environmental Discourse: Ecological Modernization and the Policy Process*. New York: Oxford University Press.

Hall, Peter A., and Rosemary C. R. Taylor. 1996. "Political Science and the Three New Institutionalisms." *Political Studies* 44: 936–57.

Hamilton, Gordon. 1993. "A Global War with Cold War Techniques." *Vancouver Sun*, June 30, A1.

Harcourt, Michael. 1993. Draft of letter to Vice President Al Gore. January 22. Clayoquot Sound Archives.

Harrison, Kathryn. 1996a. "Environmental Protection in British Columbia: Post-material Values, Organized Interests, and Party Politics." In *Politics, Policy, and Government in British Columbia*, ed. R. K. Carty. Vancouver: University of British Columbia Press.

———. 1996b. *Passing the Buck: Federalism and Canadian Environmental Policy*. Vancouver: University of British Columbia Press.

Heclo, Hugh. 1978. "Issue Networks and the Executive Establishment." In *The New American Political System*, ed. Anthony King. Washington, DC: American Enterprise Institute for Public Policy Research.

Hildyard, Nicholas. 1993. "Foxes in Charge of the Chickens." In *Global Ecology: A New Arena of Political Conflict*, ed. Wolfgang Sachs. Atlantic Highlands, NJ: Zed Books, Ltd.

Hilgartner, Stephan, and Charles L. Bosk. 1988. "The Rise and Fall of Social Problems." *American Journal of Sociology* 94: 53–78.

Hoberg, George. 1992. *Pluralism by Design: Environmental Policy and the American Regulatory State.* New York: Praeger.

———. 1996. "The Politics of Sustainability: Forest Policy in British Columbia." In *Politics, Policy, and Government in British Columbia*, ed. R. K. Carty. Vancouver: University of British Columbia Press.

———. 1997. "From Localism to Legalism: The Transformation of Federal Forest Policy." In *Western Public Lands and Environmental Politics*, ed. Charles Davis. Boulder, CO: Westview Press.

———. 1998. "Distinguishing Learning from Other Sources of Policy Change: The Case of Forestry in the Pacific Northwest." Paper presented at the Annual Meeting of the American Political Science Association, Boston, MA, September 3–6.

Hoberg, George, and Edward Morawski. 1997. "Policy Change Through Sector Intersection: Aboriginal and Forest Policy in Clayoquot Sound." *Canadian Public Administration* 40 (3): 387–414.

Hojnacki, Marie. 1997. "Interest Groups' Decisions to Join Alliances or Work Alone." *American Journal of Political Science* 41 (1): 61–87.

Holmer, Steve. 1998. "Quincy Library Group Bill Alert." E-mail to forest activists. April 29.

Howlett, Michael. 2001. "The Courts, Aboriginal Rights, and BC Forest Policy." In *In Search of Sustainability: British Columbia Forest Policy in the 1990s*, ed. Benjamin Cashore, George Hoberg, Michael Howlett, Jeremy Rayner, and Jeremy Wilson. Vancouver: University of British Columbia Press.

Howlett, Michael, and Keith Brownsey. 1996. "From Timber to Tourism: The Political Economy of British Columbia." In *Politics, Policy, and Government in British Columbia*, ed. R. K. Carty. Vancouver: University of British Columbia Press.

Howlett, Michael, and M. Ramesh. 2002. "The Policy Effects of Internationalization: A Subsystem Adjustment Analysis of Policy Change." *Journal of Comparative Policy Analysis* 4 (1): 31–50.

Ingalsbee, Timothy. n.d. "S: 1028: Outdated Policies That Will Increase Fire Risk, Endanger Firefighters, and Harm Forest Ecosystems." Available at www.americanlands.org/forestweb/qlgpaper.txt (accessed May 16, 2000).

Iyengar, Shanto. 1991. *Is Anyone Responsible? How Television Frames Political Issues.* Chicago: University of Chicago Press.

———. 1996. "Framing Responsibility for Political Issues." *Annals* 59 (July): 60.

Jackson, Michael. 2001. Personal interview. March 18.

Jasanoff, Shelia. 1996. "The Dilemma of Environmental Democracy." *Issues in Science and Technology* 13 (1): 63–70.

Jenkins-Smith, Hank C., Gilbert K. St. Clair, and Brian Woods. 1991. "Explaining Change in Policy Subsystems: Analysis of Coalition Stability and Defection over Time." *American Journal of Political Science* 35 (4): 851–80.

John Muir Project of Earth Island Institute. 1997. "Help Stop S:1028, the Quincy Logging Bill!" E-mail to forest activists. October 3. Clayoquot Sound Archives.

Jones, E. S., and C. P. Taylor. 1995. "Litigating Agency Change: The Impact of the Courts and Administrative Appeals Process on the Forest Service." *Policy Studies Journal* 23 (Summer): 310–36.

Kagan, Robert A. 2001. *Adversarial Legalism: The American Way of Law*. Cambridge, MA: Harvard University Press.

Kamieniecki, Sheldon. 2000. "Testing Alternative Theories of Agenda Setting: Forest Policy Change in British Columbia, Canada." *Policy Studies Journal* 28 (1): 176–89.

Keck, Margaret E., and Kathryn Sikkink. 1998. *Activists Beyond Borders: Advocacy Networks in International Politics*. Ithaca, NY: Cornell University Press.

Kennedy, Robert F. Jr. 1993. "Logging Clayoquot Will Strip Province of Its Natural Beauty: Quiet Wilderness Areas in the United States Have Been Ruined by Failed Forestry Practices." *Vancouver Sun*, February 20, B4.

Kenya Consumers' Organization. 1993. Letter to Premier Harcourt. February 2. Clayoquot Sound Archives.

Kersh, Rogan, and James A. Morone. 2005. "Obesity, Courts, and the New Politics of Public Health." *Journal of Health Politics, Policy, and Law* 30 (5): 839–68.

Kerwin, C. 1999. *Rulemaking: How Government Agencies Write Law and Make Policy*. 2nd ed. Washington, DC: Congressional Quarterly Press.

Kingdon, John. 1995. *Agendas, Alternatives, and Public Policies*. 2nd ed. New York: HarperCollins.

Klandermans, Bert. 1984. "Mobilization and Participation: Social-Psychological Expansions of Resource Mobilization Theory." *American Sociological Review* 49: 583–600.

Knopff, Rainer, and J. E. Glenn. 1996. "Courts, Tribunals, and the Environment in Canada." In *Federalism and the Environment: Environmental Policymaking in Australia, Canada, and the United States*, ed. Kenneth M. Holland, F. L. Morton, and Brian Galligan. Westport, CT: Greenwood Press.

Kollman, Ken. 1998. *Outside Lobbying: Public Opinion and Interest Group Strategies*. Princeton, NJ: Princeton University Press.

Koontz, Tomas. 2002. *Federalism in the Forest: National versus State Natural Resource Policy*. Washington, DC: Georgetown University Press.

Krajnc, Anita. 2002. "Conservation Biologists, Civic Science, and the Preservation of B.C. Forests." *Journal of Canadian Studies* 37: 219–38.

Kristianson, Gerry. 1996. "Lobbying and Private Interests in British Columbia Politics." In *Politics, Policy, and Government in British Columbia*, ed. R. K. Carty. Vancouver: University of British Columbia Press.

Kushner, Tony. 1998. "Matthew's Passion." *The Nation*, November 9, 4–6.

Ladd, Anthony E., Thomas C. Hood, and Kent D. Van Liere. 1983. "Ideological Themes in the Antinuclear Movement: Consensus and Diversity." *Sociological Inquiry* (53): 252–72.

Langer, Valerie. 1997. "Interfor: Guilty as Charged!" Friends of Clayoquot Sound newsletter. Spring.

———. 2000a. "Building a Campaign." Presentation made at the Northwest Wilderness Conference, Seattle, WA, March 31–April 2.

———. 2000b. Personal interview. March 31.

Langer, Valerie, Maryjka Mychajilowycz, Sergio Paone, Matthew Price, and Jill Thompson. 1998. "Implementing the Scientific Panel: Three Years and Counting." Tofino, B.C.: Friends of Clayoquot Sound. Clayoquot Sound Archives.

Lautens, Trevor. 1994. "I'm Ready to Fight for Trees." *Vancouver Sun*, March 19, A23.

Lawrence, Regina. 2000. *The Politics of Force: Media and the Construction of Policy Brutality*. Berkeley: University of California Press.

Leavenworth, Stuart. 2003. "Forest Policy May Be Changed: The Possible Increase in Logging Alarms Environmentalists, but Some Back Plan." *Sacramento Bee*, February 4, A3.

Lee, Robert Mason. 1993a. "Anti-Logging Rock Group Met by Hundreds Chanting." *Vancouver Sun*, July 15, A1–A2.

———. 1993b. "Worldwide Campaign against Logging Hits Forest Firm." *Vancouver Sun*, November 12, A1.

———. 1994. "15,000 Forest Workers Drown Out Premier." *Vancouver Sun*, March 22, A1.

Leman, Christopher. 1981. "The Canadian Forest Ranger: Bureaucratic Centralism and Private Power in Three Provincial Natural Resources Agencies." Paper presented at the Annual Meeting of the Canadian Political Science Association, Halifax, Nova Scotia, May 27–29.

Lertzman, Ken, Jeremy Rayner, and Jeremy Wilson. 1996. "Learning and Change in the British Columbia Forest Policy Sector: A Consideration of Sabatier's Advocacy Coalition Framework." *Canadian Journal of Political Science* 29: 111–33.

Linder, Stephan H. 1995. "Contending Discourses in the Electric and Magnetic Fields Controversy: The Social Construction of EMF Risk as a Public Problem." *Policy Sciences* 28: 209–30.

Lipsky, Michael. 1968. "Protest as a Political Resource." *American Political Science Review* 62: 1144–58.

Litfin, Karen. 2000. "Advocacy Coalitions Along the Domestic-Foreign Frontier: Globalization and Canadian Climate Change Policy." *Policy Studies Journal* 28 (1): 236–52.

Little, Jane Braxton. 1997. "House OKs Plan to Cut Danger of Forest Fires." *Sacramento Bee*, July 10, A6.

———. 1999. "Quincy Library Group Bars Outsiders." *High Country News*, April 26. Available at www.hcn.org/servlets/hcn.Article?article_id=4957 (accessed May 25, 2005).

———. 2003. "Quincy Library Group." Red Lodge Clearinghouse. Available at www.redlodgeclearinghouse.org/stories/quincy.html (accessed May 21, 2005).

———. 2006. "Forest Service Wins Key Battle Over Project." *Sacramento Bee*, January 24, B1.

Lohmann, Larry. 1993. "Resisting Green Globalism." In *Global Ecology: A New Arena of Political Conflict*, ed. Wolfgang Sachs. Atlantic Highlands, NJ: Zed Books, Ltd.

Lowe, Philip, and David Morrison. 1984. "Bad News or Good News: Environmental Politics and the Mass Media." *Sociological Review* 32: 75–90.

Lowenberger, Fred. 1993. Copy of letter written to the *New York Times*. January 27. Clayoquot Sound Archives.

Lowery, David, and Virginia Gray. 2004. "A Neopluralist Perspective on Research on Organized Interests." *Political Research Quarterly* 57 (1): 163–75.

MacMillan Bloedel. 1994. "Some Opinions on British Columbia's Forests are a Little Out of Date." Advertisement. Clayoquot Sound Archives.

MacMillan Bloedel Limited v. Sheila Simpson et al. 1993.

MacMillan Bloedel Public Affairs Office. 1994. "Greenpeace, Clayoquot Sound, and MacMillan Bloedel." Briefing notes for MacMillan Bloedel customers. Clayoquot Sound Archives.

MacQueen, Ken. 1992. "Prince Philip Views Forest Dispute Site." *The Record*, March 10, A9.

Malmsheimer, Robert W., Denise Keele, and Donald W. Floyd. 2004. "National Forest Litigation in the U.S. Court of Appeals." *Journal of Forestry* 102 (2): 20–25.

Marston, Ed. 1997a. "My Experience with the Quincy Group Wasn't Positive." *High Country News* 29 (18). September 29. Available at http://www.hcn.org/1997/sep29/dir/sidebar_my_experie.html (accessed February 17, 1999).

———. 1997b. "The Timber Wars Evolve into a Divisive Attempt at Peace." *High Country News* 29 (18). September 29. Available at http://www.hcn.org/servlets/hcn.Article?article_id=3656 (accessed July 2, 2006).

———. 1997c. "I Was Always Welcomed There." *High Country News* 29 (18). September 29. Available at http://www.hcn.org/1997/sep29/dir/sidebar_I_was_alwa.html (accessed February 17, 1999).

Martin, Glen. 1999. "The Future of Logging; Federal Officials to Announce Plans for Lassen, Plumas and Tahoe Forests." *San Francisco Chronicle*, August 18, A15.

———. 2001. "U.S. Shifts Policy on Sierra—Trees, Wildlife Protected." *San Francisco Chronicle*, January 13, A1.

Matthaus, Lisa. n.d. "You Can't See the Facts for the Trees." Available at www.sierraclub.ca/bc/media/commentary/08_19_04.shtml (accessed May 7, 2005).

May, Peter J. 1991. "Reconsidering Policy Design: Policies and Publics." *Journal of Public Policy* 11 (2): 187–206.

———. 1992. "Policy Learning and Failure." *Journal of Public Policy* 12 (4): 331–54.

Mazza, Patrick. 1997. "Cooptation or Constructive Engagement: Quincy Library Group's Effort to Bring Together Loggers and Environmentalists Under Fire." *Cascadia Planet*, August 9. Available at www.tnews.com/text/quincy.library.html (accessed February 27, 2001).

McAdam, Doug. 1982. *Political Process and the Development of Black Insurgency, 1930–1970*. Chicago: University of Chicago Press.

McCarthy, John D., and Mayer N. Zald. 2002. "The Enduring Vitality of the Resource Mobilization Theory of Social Movements." In *Handbook of Sociological Theory*, ed. Jonathan H. Turner. New York: Kluwer Academic/Plenum Publishers.

McCloskey, Michael. 1996. "The Skeptic: Collaboration Has Its Limits." *High Country News* 28. Available at www.hcn.org/1996/may13/dir/Opinion_The_skepti. html (accessed February 17, 1999).

McCubbins, M., R. Noll, and B. Weingast. 1987. "Administrative Procedures as Instruments of Political Control." *Journal of Law, Economics, and Organization* 3 (2): 243–77.

McNish, Jacquie. 1993. "When Stars Speak Out." *Globe and Mail*, November 6, A1.

McSpadden, Lettie. 2000. "Environmental Policy in the Courts." In *Environmental Policy*, ed. Norman J. Vig and Michael E. Kraft, 4th ed. Washington, DC: Congressional Quarterly Press.

Merelman, Richard M. 1966. "Learning and Legitimacy." *American Political Science Review* 60 (3): 548–61.

Meyer, David S., and Suzanne Staggenborg. 1996. "Movements, Countermovements, and the Structure of Political Opportunities." *American Journal of Sociology* 101 (6): 1628–60.

Minkoff, Debra C. 1995. *Organizing for Equality: The Evolution of Women's and Racial Ethnic Organizations in America, 1955–1985*. New Brunswick, NJ: Rutgers University Press.

Morton, F. L. 1996. "The Constitutional Division of Powers with Respect to the Environment in Canada." In *Federalism and the Environment: Environmental Policymaking in Australia, Canada, and the United States*, ed. Kenneth M. Holland, F. L. Morton, and Brian Galligan. Westport, CT: Greenwood Press.

Mullin, Mike. 1999. Personal interview. July 13.

Mychajilowycz, Maryjka. 1999. Personal interview. July 13.

Natural Resources Canada. 1994–1995. *A Balancing Act: The State of Canada's Forests*. Ottawa, Ontario.

———. 1995–1996. *Sustaining Forests at Home and Abroad: The State of Canada's Forests*. Ottawa, Ontario.

———. 1997–1998. *The People's Forests: The State of Canada's Forests*. Ottawa, Ontario.

———. 1998–1999. *Innovation: The State of Canada's Forests*. Ottawa, Ontario.

———. 1999–2000. *Forests in the New Millennium: The State of Canada's Forests*. Ottawa, Ontario.

Noel, Erin, John Buckley, Laurel Ames, Linda Conklin, Glenda Edwards, and Craig Thomas. 1994. "A Grassroots Look at the Quincy Library Group." Letter to the QLG from California environmental organizations. April. Available at www. qlg.org/pub/archive/archive94/grassroots.htm (accessed February 2, 2001).

Noss, Reed F., and Allen Y. Cooperrider. 1994. *Saving Nature's Legacy: Protecting and Restoring Biodiversity*. Washington, DC: Island Press.

Nuu-chah-nulth First Nations. 1993. Advertisement. Clayoquot Sound Archives.

Nuu-chah-nulth Tribal Council. 1990. "Land Question: Land and Sea Resources." Brochure. Clayoquot Sound Archives.

Olson, Mancur. 1965. *The Logic of Collective Action: Public Goods and the Theory of Groups*. Cambridge, MA: Harvard University Press.

Orfield, Gary. 2004. "No Child Left Behind: A Federal-, State-, and District-Level Look at the First Year." *HGSE News*. Available at http://gseweb.harvard.edu/news/features/orfield02092004.html (accessed April 30, 2005).

O'Toole, Randal. 1998. "Purity Weakens Greens." *Denver Post*, January 4, G-01.

Owen, Stephen. 1993. Public Report and Recommendations Re: Issues Arising from the Government's Clayoquot Sound Land Use Decision. Victoria, B.C.: Commission on Resources and Environment. April 22. Clayoquot Sound Archives.

Paehlke, Robert. 2000. "Environmentalism in One Country: Canadian Environmental Policy in an Era of Globalization." *Policy Studies Journal* 28 (1): 160–75.

Paone, Sergio. 1999. Personal interview. July 13.

Peters, Dave. 2001. Personal interview. March 19.

Pierson, Paul. 1993. "When Effect Becomes Cause: Policy Feedback and Political Change." *World Politics* 45: 595–628.

———. 2000. "Not Just What, but *When*: Timing and Sequence in Political Processes." *Studies in American Political Development* 14 (Spring): 72–92.

Pisani, Donald. 1997. "Forests and Conservation, 1865–1890." In *American Forests: Nature, Culture, and Politics*, ed. Char Miller. Lawrence: University Press of Kansas.

Piven, Frances Fox, and Richard A. Cloward. 1979. *Poor People's Movements: Why They Succeed, How They Fail*. New York: Vintage Books.

Plein, L. Christopher. 1997. "Strategies of Agenda Denial: Issue Definition and the Case of bST." In *Cultural Strategies of Agenda Denial: Avoidance, Attack, and Redefinition*, ed. Roger W. Cobb and Marc Howard Ross. Lawrence: University Press of Kansas.

Pollack, Philip, Stuart A. Lilie, and M. Elliot Vittes. 1993. "Hard Issues, Core Values and Vertical Constraint: The Case of Nuclear Power." *British Journal of Political Science* 23: 29–50.

Portz, John. 1994. "Plant Closings, Community Definitions, and the Local Response." In *The Politics of Problem Definition: Shaping the Policy Agenda*, ed. David A. Rochefort and Roger W. Cobb. Lawrence: University Press of Kansas.

Posner, Paul L. 1998. *The Politics of Unfunded Mandates: Whither Federalism?* Washington, DC: Georgetown University Press.

Preschutti, John. 2001. Personal interview. March 17.

Princen, Thomas, and Matthias Finger. 1994. *Environmental NGOs in World Politics*. London: Routledge.

Pross, A. Paul. 1993. "Canadian Pressure Groups: Talking Chameleons." In *Pressure Groups*, ed. Jeremy J. Richardson. Oxford: Oxford University Press.

"The Quincy Compromise." 1998. Editorial. *San Francisco Chronicle*, May 4, A22.

"The Quincy Library Group." 2001. Case Study. Presented at the Workshop on Collaborative Resource Management in the Interior West, Red Lodge, MT, October 18–22.

Quincy Library Group. 1993. "Library Group Meeting—4/29/93." Available at www.qlg.org/pub/archive/archive93/spi.htm (accessed February 5, 2001).

———. 1998. Letter to K. Cannaughton.

———. 2001. "Library Group Votes to Discontinue Regular Public Meetings." Announcement. Available at www.qlg.org/pub/act/discontinue.htm (accessed June 6, 2005).

Recchia, Steven Paul. 1998. "Resource Mobilization and Canadian Environmental Groups." Paper presented at the 1998 Annual Meeting of the Western Political Science Association, Los Angeles, CA, March 19–21.

Riker, William H. 1986. *The Art of Political Manipulation*. New Haven, CT: Yale University Press.

Robb, James J., and William E. Riebsame, eds. 1997. *Atlas of the New West: Portrait of a Changing Region*. Boulder: University of Colorado Center for the American West.

Rochefort, David A., and Roger W Cobb. 1994. *The Politics of Problem Definition*. Lawrence: University Press of Kansas.

Roe, E. 1994. *Narrative Policy Analysis: Theory and Practice*. Durham, NC: Duke University Press.

Rothman, Hal K. 1997. "A Regular Ding-Dong Fight: The Dynamics of Park Service–Forest Service Controversy During the 1920s and 1930s." In *American Forests: Nature, Culture, and Politics*, ed. Char Millar. Lawrence: University Press of Kansas.

Ruth, Larry. 2000. "Conservation on the Cusp: The Reformation of National Forest Policy in the Sierra Nevada." *UCLA Journal of Environmental Law & Policy* 18 (Summer): 1–97.

Sabatier, Paul A., and Hank C. Jenkins-Smith. 1993. *Policy Change and Learning: An Advocacy Coalition Approach*. Boulder, CO: Westview Press.

———. 1999. "The Advocacy Coalition Framework: An Assessment." In *Theories of the Policy Process*, ed. Paul A. Sabatier. Boulder, CO: Westview Press.

Sagoff, Mark. 1999. "The View from Quincy Library: Civic Engagement in Environmental Problem-Solving." In *Civil Society, Democracy and Civic Renewal*, ed. Robert K. Fullinwider. Lanham, MD: Rowman & Littlefield.

Schattschneider, E. E. 1960. *The Semisovereign People: A Realist's View of Democracy in America*. New York: Holt, Rinehart, and Winston.

Schlager, Edella. 1999. "A Comparison of Frameworks, Theories, and Models of Policy Processes." In *Theories of the Policy Process*, ed. Paul A. Sabatier. Boulder, CO: Westview Press.

Scholzman, Kay Lehman, and John T. Tierney. 1986. *Organized Interests and American Democracy*. New York: Harper and Row.

Schon, D. A., and M. Rein. 1994. *Frame Reflection: Toward the Resolution of Intractable Policy Controversies*. New York: Basic Books.

Schrepfer, Susan R. 1997. "Establishing Administrative 'Standing': The Sierra Club and the Forest Service, 1897–1956." In *American Forests: Nature, Culture, and Politics*, ed. Char Millar. Lawrence: University Press of Kansas.

Shaiko, Ronald. 1999. *Voices and Echoes for the Environment: Public Interest Representation in the 1990s and Beyond.* New York: Columbia University Press.

Shapiro, Martin M. 1988. *Who Guards the Guardians? Judicial Control of Administration.* Athens: University of Georgia Press.

Share the Clayoquot Society. 1989. "423 Residents of the West Coast Communities of Ucluelet and Tofino Met at the First Public Meeting of 'Share the Clayoquot Society' in Ucluelet." Press Release. November 22. Clayoquot Sound Archives.

Sheehan, John. 2001. Personal interview. March 20.

Sheppard, Robert. 1994. "Premier Harcourt's European Vacation." *Globe and Mail*, February 8, A19.

Shepsle, K. 1989. "The Changing Textbook Congress." In *Can the Government Govern?* ed. J. Chubb and P. Peterson. Washington, DC: The Brookings Institution.

Shiva, Vandana. 1993. "The Greening of the Global Reach." In *Global Ecology: A New Arena of Political Conflict*, ed. Wolfgang Sachs. Atlantic Highlands, NJ: Zed Books, Ltd.

"Sierra Logging Bill Needs Major Revisions." 1997. Editorial. *San Francisco Chronicle*, October 21, A22.

Siziba, Costa. 1993. Letter to Premier Harcourt. Clayoquot Sound Archives.

Smith, Gordon. 1996. "Small Group Threw Water on Sale of Burnt Trees." *San Diego Union-Tribune*, May 4, A3.

Smith, Joseph. 2005. "Congress Opens the Courthouse Doors: Statutory Changes to Judicial Review Under the Clean Air Act." *Political Research Quarterly* 58 (March): 139–49.

Snow, David A., and Robert D. Benford. 1997. "Master Frames and Cycles of Protest." In *Social Movements: Perspectives and Issues*, ed. Steven M. Buechler and F. Kurt Cylke Jr. Mountain View, CA: Mayfield Publishing Company.

Sonner, Scott. 1997. "Forest Consensus near Passage." *Journal of Commerce*, October 29, 8A.

Stahl, Andy. 2000. "Playing Politics with Fire." *Forest Magazine* (November/December): 29.

Stanbury, W. T., and Ilan B. Vertinsky. 1997. "Boycotts in Conflicts over Forestry Issues: The Case of Clayoquot Sound." *Commonwealth Forestry Review* 76 (1): 18–24.

Stark, Tamara. 2000. Personal interview. February 4.

Steinberg, Marc W. 1997. "Tilting the Frame: Considerations on Collective Action Framing from a Discursive Turn." *Theory and Society* 27: 845–72.

Stewart, Ron. 2001. Telephone interview. March 27.

Stone, Deborah. 1988. *Policy Paradox and Political Reason.* Glenview, IL: Scott, Foresman, and Company.

Tarry, Scott E. 2001. "Issue Definition, Conflict Expansion, and Tort Reform: Lessons from the American General Aviation Industry." *Policy Studies Journal* 29 (4): 571–87.

Tennant, Paul. 1996. "Aboriginal Peoples and Aboriginal Title in British Columbia Politics." In *Politics, Policy, and Government in British Columbia*, ed. R. K. Carty. Vancouver: University of British Columbia Press.

"Timber Wars in Congress." 1998. Editorial. *San Francisco Chronicle*, April 26 (Sunday edition), A22.

U.S. Congress. House. 1997. Subcommittee on Forests and Forest Health of the Committee on Resources. "Hearing on H.R. 858." 105th Cong., 1st sess. Washington, DC: Government Printing Office.

U.S. Congress. Senate. 1997. Subcommittee on Forests and Public Land Management of the Committee on Energy and Natural Resources. "Hearing on S. 1028 The Quincy Library Group Forest Recovery and Economic Stability Act of 1997." July 24. Text from *Federal Information System Corporation Federal News Services.* Available from *Congressional Universe* (online service). Bethesda, MD: Congressional Information Service.

U.S. Department of Agriculture. 2001. *Sierra Nevada Forest Plan Amendment Final Environmental Impact Statement, Record of Decision.* Washington, DC: Government Printing Office (January).

U.S. Office of Technology Assessment. 1992. *Forest Service Planning: Accommodating Uses, Producing Outputs, and Sustaining Ecosystems.* Washington, DC: Government Printing Office (February).

U.S. v. Students Challenging Regulatory Agency Procedures, 412 U.S. 669 (1973).

Vanderford, Marsha. 1989. "Vilification and Social Movements: A Case Study of Pro-Life and Pro-Choice Rhetoric." *Quarterly Journal of Speech* 75: 166–82.

VanNijnatten, Debora L. 1999. "Participation and Environmental Policy in Canada and the United States: Trends over Time." *Policy Studies Journal* 27 (2): 267–87.

Weber, Edward P. 2000. "A New Vanguard for the Environment: Grass-Roots Ecosystem Management as a New Environmental Movement." *Society & Natural Resources* 13: 237–59.

Wildlands Resources Center. 1996. *Sierra Nevada Ecosystem Project Final Report to Congress: Assessments and Scientific Basis for Management Options.* Report No. 37. Davis: University of California.

Wilson, C. 2000. "Policy Regimes and Policy Change." *Journal of Public Policy* 20 (3): 247–74.

Wilson, Jeremy. 1990. "Wilderness Politics in British Columbia: The Business Dominated State and the Containment of Environmentalism." In *Policy Communities and Public Policy in Canada: A Structural Approach*, ed. William D. Coleman and Grace Skogstad. Mississauga, Ontario: Copp Clark Pitman.

———. 1998. *Talk and Log: Wilderness Politics in British Columbia, 1965–1996.* Vancouver: University of British Columbia Press.

Wondolleck, Julia M., and Steven L. Yaffee. 2000. *Making Collaboration Work: Lessons from Innovation in Natural Resource Management.* Washington, DC: Island Press.

Woolley, John T., and Michael Vincent McGinnis. 1999. "The Politics of Watershed Policymaking." *Policy Studies Journal* 27 (3): 578–94.

Wu, Ken. 2000. Personal interview. June 1.

———. 2006. E-mail correspondence. February 10.

Yassa, Sami, Louis Blumberg, and Frannie Hoover Waid. 1994. Letter to Michael Jackson and the QLG. March 31. Available at www.qlg.org/pub/archive/archive94/TWSSCNRDC033194.htm (accessed February 2, 2001).

Yearley, Steven. 1996. *Sociology, Environmentalism, and Globalization.* London: Sage Publications.

Yee, Albert S. 1996. "The Causal Effect of Ideas on Policies." *International Organization* 50 (1): 69–108.

Zafonte, Matthew, and Paul Sabatier. 2004. "Short-Term versus Long-Term Coalitions in the Policy Process: Automotive Pollution Control, 1963–1989." *Policy Studies Journal* 32 (1): 75–107.

Zald, Mayer N. 1996. "Culture, Ideology, and Strategic Framing." In *Comparative Perspectives on Social Movements: Political Opportunities, Mobilizing Structures, and Cultural Frames,* ed. Doug McAdam, John D. McCarthy, and Mayer N. Zald. Cambridge: Cambridge University Press.

Index

Note: Page numbers followed by t refer to tables, page numbers followed by f refer to figures, and page numbers followed by n plus a number refer to notes.